Windows® 95 For Dummies®

COMPUTER BOOK SERIES FROM IDG

Cheat Sheet

W9-ARK-232

Helpful Hints

- ✔ Don't turn off your computer without giving Windows 95 fair warning. First, click on the Start button and then choose Sh<u>u</u>t Down from the menu. When Windows 95 asks if you're sure you want to shut down, click on Yes. When Windows 95 says it's okay to turn off your computer, go ahead and turn it off.

- ✔ Don't know what a certain button does in a program? Rest your mouse pointer over the button for a few seconds; a helpful box often pops up to explain the button's purpose.

- ✔ If you're baffled, try pressing F1, that "function key" in the upper-left corner of your keyboard. A "help" window appears, bringing hints on your current program.

- ✔ To quickly organize the windows on the desktop, click on the taskbar's clock with your *right* mouse button. When a menu appears, click on one of the tile options, and all your open windows will be neatly tiled across your screen.

- ✔ To keep icons organized in neat rows across your desktop or in windows, click on the icon's background. When the menu pops up, choose <u>A</u>uto Arrange from the Arrange <u>I</u>cons menu.

Click on these words to see helpful menus

Click here to shrink the window

Click here for a helpful menu

Click here to enlarge the window

Click here to close the window

Click here to move up the page

Click here to move down the page

Click on the arrows to move up or down a single line

Point here, hold down the mouse button, and move the mouse to change the window's size

Helpful Hints Dept. - Notepad

File Edit Search Help

Push the mouse across your desk, and the mouse's arrow will move across your screen.

Push the mouse's left button with your finger to "click" the mouse. Push the button twice in rapid succession to "double-click."

By pointing to different parts of the window and either "clicking" or "double-clicking," you can perform different chores.

. . . For Dummies: #1 Computer Book Series for Beginners

COMPUTER BOOK SERIES FROM IDG

Windows® 95 For Dummies®

Cheat Sheet

Handling Files within a Program

To Do This . . .	Do This . . .
Start a new file	Press Alt, F, N.
Open an existing file	Press Alt, F, O.
Save a file	Press Alt, F, S.
Save a file under a new name	Press Alt, F, A.
Print a file	Press Alt, F, P.

Organizing a Pile of Windows

To Do This . . .	Do This . . .
See a list of all windows	Look at the names open on the taskbar.
Move from one window to another window	Press Alt+Tab+Tab or click on the window's name on the taskbar.
Tile the windows across the screen	Click on the taskbar's clock with the *right* mouse button and then click on Tile Horizontally or Tile Vertically.
Cascade the windows across the screen	Click on the taskbar's clock with the *right* mouse button and then click on Cascade.
Shrink a window into an icon	Click on the window, press Alt+spacebar, and press N.
Make a window fill the screen	Click on the window, press Alt+spacebar, and press X.

DOS Window Stuff

To Do This . . .	Do This . . .
Toggle DOS program from a full-screen display to a window-sized display	Press Alt+Enter.
Change a DOS program from an icon to a full screen	Click on the program's icon on the taskbar.
Close a DOS window	Use that program's normal exit command and then click on the X in the window's upper-right corner.

Explorer and My Computer Programs

To Do This . . .	Do This . . .
Copy a file to another location on the *same* disk drive	Hold down Ctrl and drag it there.
Copy a file to a *different* disk drive	Drag it there.
Move a file to another location on the *same* disk drive	Drag it there.
Move a file to a *different* disk drive	Hold down Alt and drag it there.
Remember how to copy or move files	Hold down the *right* mouse button while dragging and then choose Copy or Move from the menu.
Select several files	Hold down Ctrl and click on the filenames.
Look at a different directory	Double-click on that directory's icon.

Cut and Paste Stuff

To Do This . . .	Press These Keys . . .
Copy highlighted stuff to the Clipboard	Ctrl+C or Ctrl+Insert.
Cut highlighted stuff to the Clipboard	Ctrl+X or Shift+Delete.
Paste stuff from the Clipboard to the current window	Ctrl+V or Shift+Insert.
Copy an entire screen to the Clipboard	PrintScreen (Shift+PrintScreen on some keyboards).
Copy the current window to the Clipboard	Alt+PrintScreen.

IDG BOOKS WORLDWIDE

. . . For Dummies: #1 Computer Book Series for Beginners

by Andy Rathbone

IDG Books Worldwide, Inc.
An International Data Group Company

Foster City, CA ♦ Chicago, IL ♦ Indianapolis, IN ♦ Braintree, MA ♦ Dallas, TX

Windows® 95 For Dummies®

Published by
IDG Books Worldwide, Inc.
An International Data Group Company
919 E. Hillsdale Blvd.
Suite 400
Foster City, CA 94404

Library of Congress Catalog Card No.: 94-74297

ISBN: 1-56884-240-6

Printed in the United States of America

10 9 8 7 6

1B/SV/QY/ZV

Distributed in the United States by IDG Books Worldwide, Inc.

Distributed by Macmillan Canada for Canada; by Computer and Technical Books for the Caribbean Basin; by Contemporanea de Ediciones for Venezuela; by Distribuidora Cuspide for Argentina; by CITEC for Brazil; by Ediciones ZETA S.C.R. Ltda. for Peru; by Editorial Limusa SA for Mexico; by Transworld Publishers Limited in the United Kingdom and Europe; by Al-Maiman Publishers & Distributors for Saudi Arabia; by Simron Pty. Ltd. for South Africa; by IDG Communications (HK) Ltd. for Hong Kong; by Toppan Company Ltd. for Japan; by Addison Wesley Publishing Company for Korea; by Longman Singapore Publishers Ltd. for Singapore, Malaysia, Thailand, and Indonesia; by Unalis Corporation for Taiwan; by WS Computer Publishing Company, Inc. for the Philippines; by WoodsLane Pty. Ltd. for Australia; by WoodsLane Enterprises Ltd. for New Zealand.

For general information on IDG Books Worldwide's books in the U.S., please call our Consumer Customer Service department at 800-762-2974. For reseller information, including discounts and premium sales, please call our Reseller Customer Service department at 800-434-3422.

For information on where to purchase IDG Books Worldwide's books outside the U.S., contact IDG Books Worldwide at 415-655-3021 or fax 415-655-3295.

For information on translations, contact Marc Jeffrey Mikulich, Director, Foreign & Subsidiary Rights, at IDG Books Worldwide, 415-655-3018 or fax 415-655-3295.

For sales inquiries and special prices for bulk quantities, write to the address above or call IDG Books Worldwide at 415-655-3200.

For information on using IDG Books Worldwide's books in the classroom, or ordering examination copies, contact Jim Kelly at 800-434-2086.

For authorization to photocopy items for corporate, personal, or educational use, please contact Copyright Clearance Center, 222 Rosewood Drive, Danvers, MA 01923, or fax 508-750-4470.

About the Author

Andy Rathbone started geeking around with computers in 1985 when he bought a boxy CP/M Kaypro 2X with lime-green letters. Like other budding nerds, he soon began playing with null-modem adaptors, dialing up computer bulletin boards, and working part-time at Radio Shack.

In between playing computer games, he served as editor of the *Daily Aztec* newspaper at San Diego State University. After graduating with a comparative literature degree, he went to work for a bizarre underground coffee-table magazine that sort of disappeared.

Andy began combining his two interests, words and computers, by selling articles to a local computer magazine. During the next few years, Andy started ghostwriting computer books for more famous computer authors, as well as writing several hundred articles about computers for technoid publications like *Supercomputing Review, CompuServe Magazine, ID Systems, DataPro,* and *Shareware.*

In 1992, Andy and *DOS For Dummies* author/legend Dan Gookin teamed up to write *PCs For Dummies,* which was runner-up in the Computer Press Association's 1993 awards. Andy subsequently wrote the first edition of *Windows For Dummies* plus *OS/2 For Dummies, Upgrading & Fixing PCs For Dummies, Multimedia & CD-ROMs For Dummies,* and *MORE Windows For Dummies.*

Andy is currently contributing regularly to *CompuServe Magazine,* a magazine mailed monthly to CompuServe members. (Feel free to drop him a line at 75300,1565.)

Andy lives with his most-excellent wife, Tina, and their cat in San Diego, California. When not writing, he fiddles with his MIDI synthesizer and tries to keep the cat off both keyboards.

Welcome to the world of IDG Books Worldwide.

IDG Books Worldwide, Inc., is a subsidiary of International Data Group, the world's largest publisher of computer-related information and the leading global provider of information services on information technology. IDG was founded more than 25 years ago and now employs more than 7,500 people worldwide. IDG publishes more than 235 computer publications in 67 countries (see listing below). More than 60 million people read one or more IDG publications each month.

Launched in 1990, IDG Books Worldwide is today the #1 publisher of best-selling computer books in the United States. We are proud to have received 8 awards from the Computer Press Association in recognition of editorial excellence, and our best-selling ...*For Dummies*™ series has more than 17 million copies in print with translations in 25 languages. IDG Books Worldwide, through a recent joint venture with IDG's Hi-Tech Beijing, became the first U.S. publisher to publish a computer book in the People's Republic of China. In record time, IDG Books Worldwide has become the first choice for millions of readers around the world who want to learn how to better manage their businesses.

Our mission is simple: Every one of our books is designed to bring extra value and skill-building instructions to the reader. Our books are written by experts who understand and care about our readers. The knowledge base of our editorial staff comes from years of experience in publishing, education, and journalism — experience which we use to produce books for the '90s. In short, we care about books, so we attract the best people. We devote special attention to details such as audience, interior design, use of icons, and illustrations. And because we use an efficient process of authoring, editing, and desktop publishing our books electronically, we can spend more time ensuring superior content and spend less time on the technicalities of making books.

You can count on our commitment to deliver high-quality books at competitive prices on topics consumers want to read about. At IDG Books Worldwide, we value quality, and we have been delivering quality for more than 25 years. You'll find no better book on a subject than an IDG book.

John J. Kilcullen

John Kilcullen
President and CEO
IDG Books Worldwide, Inc.

IDG Books Worldwide, Inc., is a subsidiary of International Data Group, the world's largest publisher of computer-related information and the leading global provider of information services on information technology. International Data Group publishes over 235 computer publications in 67 countries. More than sixty million people read one or more International Data Group publications each month. The officers are Patrick J. McGovern, Founder and Board Chairman; Kelly Conlin, President; Jim Casella, Chief Operating Officer. International Data Group's publications include: **ARGENTINA'S** Computerworld Argentina, Infoworld Argentina; **AUSTRALIA'S** Computerworld Australia, Computer Living, Australian PC World, Australian Macworld, Network World, Mobile Business Australia, Publish!, Reseller, IDG Sources; **AUSTRIA'S** Computerwelt Oesterreich, PC Test; **BELGIUM'S** Data News (CW); **BOLIVIA'S** Computerworld; **BRAZIL'S** Computerworld, Connections, Game Power, Mundo Unix, PC World, Publish, Super Game; **BULGARIA'S** Computerworld Bulgaria, PC & Mac World Bulgaria, Network World Bulgaria; **CANADA'S** CIO Canada, Computerworld Canada, InfoCanada, Network World Canada, Reseller; **CHILE'S** Computerworld Chile, Informatica; **COLOMBIA'S** Computerworld Colombia, PC World; **COSTA RICA'S** PC World; **CZECH REPUBLIC'S** Computerworld, Elektronika, PC World; **DENMARK'S** Communications World, Computerworld Danmark, Computerworld Focus, Macintosh Produktkatalog, Macworld Danmark, PC World Danmark, PC Produktguide, Tech World, Windows World; **ECUADOR'S** PC World Ecuador; **EGYPT'S** Computerworld (CW) Middle East, PC World Middle East; **FINLAND'S** MikroPC, Tietoviikko, Tietoverkko; **FRANCE'S** Distributique, GOLDEN MAC, InfoPC, Le Guide du Monde Informatique, Le Monde Informatique, Telecoms & Reseaux; **GERMANY'S** Computerwoche, Computerwoche Focus, Computerwoche Extra, Electronic Entertainment, Gamepro, Information Management, Macwelt, Netzwelt, PC Welt, Publish, Publish; **GREECE'S** Publish & Macworld; **HONG KONG'S** Computerworld Hong Kong, PC World Hong Kong; **HUNGARY'S** Computerworld SZT, PC World; **INDIA'S** Computers & Communications; **INDONESIA'S** Info Komputer; **IRELAND'S** ComputerScope; **ISRAEL'S** Beyond Windows, Computerworld Israel, Multimedia, PC World Israel; **ITALY'S** Computerworld Italia, Lotus Magazine, Macworld Italia, Networking Italia, PC Shopping Italy, PC World Italia; **JAPAN'S** Computerworld Today, Information Systems World, Macworld Japan, Nikkei Personal Computing, SunWorld Japan, Windows World; **KENYA'S** East African Computer News; **KOREA'S** Computerworld Korea, Macworld Korea, PC World Korea; **LATIN AMERICA'S** GamePro; **MALAYSIA'S** Computerworld Malaysia, PC World Malaysia; **MEXICO'S** Compu Edicion, Compu Manufactura, Computacion/Punto de Venta, Computerworld Mexico, MacWorld, Mundo Unix, PC World, Windows; **THE NETHERLANDS'** Computer! Totaal, Computable (CW), LAN Magazine, Lotus Magazine, MacWorld; **NEW ZEALAND'S** Computer Buyer, Computerworld New Zealand, Network World, New Zealand PC World; **NIGERIA'S** PC World Africa; **NORWAY'S** Computerworld Norge, Lotusworld Norge, Macworld Norge, Maxi Data, Networld, PC World Ekspress, PC World Nettverk, PC World Norge, PC World's Produktguide, Publish& Multimedia World, Student Data, Unix World, Windowsworld; **PAKISTAN'S** PC World Pakistan; **PANAMA'S** PC World Panama; **PERU'S** Computerworld Peru, PC World; **PEOPLE'S REPUBLIC OF CHINA'S** China Computerworld, China Infoworld, China PC Info Magazine, Computer Fan, PC World China, Electronics International, Electronics Today/Multimedia World, Electronic Product World, China Network World, Software World Magazine, Telecom Product World; **PHILIPPINES'** Computerworld Philippines, PC Digest (PCW); **POLAND'S** Computerworld Poland, Computerworld Special Report, Networld, PC World/Komputer, Sunworld; **PORTUGAL'S** Cerebro/PC World, Correio Informatico/Computerworld, MacIn; **ROMANIA'S** Computerworld, PC World, Telecom Romania; **RUSSIA'S** Computerworld-Moscow, Mir - PK (PCW), Sety (Networks); **SINGAPORE'S** Computerworld Southeast Asia, PC World Singapore; **SLOVENIA'S** Monitor Magazine; **SOUTH AFRICA'S** Computer Mail (CIO),Computing S.A.,Network World S.A., Software World; **SPAIN'S** Advanced Systems, Amiga World, Computerworld Espana, Communicaciones World, Macworld Espana, NeXTWORLD, Super Juegos Magazine (GamePro), PC World Espana, Publish; **SWEDEN'S** Attack, ComputerSweden, Corporate Computing, Macworld, Mikrodatorn, Natverk & Kommunikation, PC World, CAP & Design, Datalngenjoren, Maxi Data,Windows World; **SWITZERLAND'S** Computerworld Schweiz, Macworld Schweiz, PC Tip; **TAIWAN'S** Computerworld Taiwan, PC World Taiwan; **THAILAND'S** Thai Computerworld; **TURKEY'S** Computerworld Monitor, Macworld Turkiye, PC World Turkiye; **UKRAINE'S** Computerworld, Computers+Software Magazine; **UNITED KINGDOM'S** Computing /Computerworld, Connexion/Network World, Lotus Magazine, Macworld, Open Computing/Sunworld; **UNITED STATES'** Advanced Systems, AmigaWorld, Cable in the Classroom, CD Review, CIO, Computerworld, Computerworld Client/Server Journal, Digital Video, DOS World, Electronic Entertainment Magazine (E2), Federal Computer Week, Game Hits, GamePro, IDG Books Worldwide, Infoworld, Laser Event, Macworld, Maximize, Multimedia World, Network World, PC Letter, PC World, Publish, SWATPro, Video Event; **URUGUAY'S** PC World Uruguay; **VENEZUELA'S** Computerworld Venezuela, PC World; **VIETNAM'S** PC World Vietnam.
05/17/95

Dedication

To my wife, parents, sister, and cat.

Acknowledgments

Thanks to Dan Gookin and his wife Sandy, Matt Wagner, Wally Wang, Sandy Blackthorn, Kristin Cocks, Bob Garza, Terrie and David Solomon, the Kleskes, the Tragesers, and the Dooleys.

(The publisher would like to give special thanks to Patrick J. McGovern, without whom this book would not have been possible.)

Credits

**Senior Vice President
and Publisher**
Milissa L. Koloski

Associate Publisher
Diane Graves Steele

Acquisitions Editor
Megg Bonar

Brand Manager
Judith A. Taylor

Editorial Managers
Kristin A. Cocks
Mary C. Corder

Editorial Executive Assistant
Richard Graves

Editorial Assistants
Stacey Holden Prince
Kevin Spencer

Acquisitions Assistant
Suki Gear

Production Director
Beth Jenkins

**Supervisor of
Project Coordination**
Cindy L. Phipps

Supervisor of Page Layout
Kathie Schnorr

Pre-Press Coordinator
Steve Peake

Associate Pre-Press Coordinator
Tony Augsburger

Media/Archive Coordinator
Paul Belcastro

Project Editors
Kristin A. Cocks
Jennifer Wallis

Editors
Tamara S. Castleman
Diana R. Conover
Diane L. Giangrossi
Michael Kelly
Colleen Rainsberger
Michael Simsic

Technical Reviewers
Jim McCarter
Kevin Spencer

Project Coordinator
Valery Bourke

Production Staff
Gina Scott
Carla C. Radzikinas
Patricia R. Reynolds
Melissa D. Buddendeck
Dwight Ramsey
Robert Springer
Theresa Sánchez-Baker
Cameron Booker
Elizabeth Cárdenas-Nelson
Dominique DeFelice
Maridee Ennis
Drew R. Moore
Laura Puranen
Anna Rohrer

Proofreader
Phil Worthington

Indexer
Sharon Hilgenberg

Cover Design
Kavish + Kavish

Contents at a Glance

Cartoons at a Glance

By Rich Tennant

Table of Contents

Introduction

• •

Welcome to *Windows 95 For Dummies!* This book is almost identical to *Windows For Dummies,* but it's been completely revamped to describe Windows 95, the latest version of Microsoft Windows.

The basic premise of the book boils down to this: Some people want to be Windows wizards. They love interacting with dialog boxes. In their free moments, they randomly press keys on their keyboards, hoping to stumble onto a hidden, undocumented feature. They memorize long strings of computer commands while they're organizing their socks-and-underwear drawer.

And you? Well, you're no dummy, that's for sure. In fact, you're light-years ahead of most computer nerds. You can make conversation with a neighbor without mumbling about "stacked RAM drives," for example. But, when it comes to Windows and computers, the fascination just isn't there. You just want to get your work done, go home, fill the cat's water dish, and relax for a while. You have no intention of changing, and there's nothing wrong with that.

That's why this book will come in handy. It won't try to turn you into a Windows wizard, but you'll pick up a few chunks of useful computing information while reading it. You won't become a Windows 95 wizard, but you'll know enough to get by quickly, cleanly, and with a minimum of pain so you can move on to the more pleasant things in life.

About This Book

Don't try to read this book at one sitting; there's no need to. Instead, treat this book like a dictionary or an encyclopedia. Turn to the page with the information you need and say, "Ah, so that's what they're talking about." Then put down the book and move on.

Don't bother trying to remember all the Windows 95 buzzwords, like "Select the menu item from the drop-down list box." Leave that stuff for the computer geeks. In fact, if anything technical comes up in a chapter, a road sign warns you well in advance. That way you can either slow down to read it or speed on around it.

You won't find any fancy computer jargon in this book. Instead, you'll find subjects like these, discussed in plain old English:

- ✔ Preparing your computer to run Windows 95
- ✔ Running favorite DOS and Windows programs under Windows 95
- ✔ Performing chores in Windows 95 that you used to do in Windows 3.1
- ✔ Finding the file you saved yesterday
- ✔ Starting programs by clicking on an icon
- ✔ Figuring out the Windows 95 replacements for Program Manager and File Manager

There's nothing to memorize and nothing to learn. Just turn to the right page, read the brief explanation, and get back to work. Unlike other books, this one enables you to bypass any technical hoopla and yet still get your work done.

How to Use This Book

Something in Windows 95 will eventually leave you scratching your head. No other program brings so many buttons, bars, or babble to the screen. When something in Windows 95 has you stumped, use this book as a reference. Look for the troublesome topic in this book's table of contents or index. The table of contents lists chapter and section titles and page numbers. The index lists topics and page numbers. Page through the table of contents or index to the spot that deals with that particular bit of computer obscurity, read only what you have to, close the book, and apply what you've read.

There's no learning involved. There's no remembering, either, unless you want to remember something so you don't have to grab the book the next time the same situation comes up.

If you're feeling spunky and want to learn something, read a little further. You'll find a few completely voluntary extra details or some cross-references to check out. There's no pressure, though. You won't be forced to learn anything that you don't want to or that you simply don't have time for.

If you have to type something into the computer, you'll see easy-to-follow text like this:

```
C:\> TYPE THESE LETTERS
```

In the preceding example, you type **TYPE THESE LETTERS** after the `C:\>` and then press the keyboard's Enter key. Typing words into a computer can be confusing, so a description of what you're supposed to type usually follows. That way, you can type the words exactly as they're supposed to be typed. You won't, for example, accidentally type **"TYPE THESE LETTERS"** — complete with quotation marks — as many users do after seeing text like *At the DOS prompt, type "TYPE THESE LETTERS"* in other computer manuals.

Whenever I describe a message or information that you'll see on-screen, I present it as follows:

```
This is a message on-screen.
```

This book doesn't wimp out by saying, "For further information, consult your manual." No need to pull on your wading boots. This book covers everything you need to know to use Windows 95. The only thing you won't find is general information about using DOS or other software packages. Yep — even though Windows 95 doesn't use DOS, it comes with a copy of DOS for running DOS programs. The best crowbar for DOS is this book's grandfather, *DOS For Dummies,* published by IDG Books Worldwide. Other *...For Dummies* books mercifully explain other popular software packages, as well.

Note that if you do need to know something about DOS to use Windows 95, that part of DOS is covered here in enough detail for you to get the job done. You'll also find help for some of the more popular Windows programs.

Please Don't Read This!

Computers thrive on technical stuff. Luckily, you're warned in advance when you're heading for something even vaguely obtuse. Chances are it's just more minute details concerning something you've already read about. Feel free to skip any section labeled Technical Stuff. Those niblets of information aren't what this book's about. But, if you're feeling particularly ornery, keep reading and you may learn something. (Just don't let anybody see you do it.)

And What about You?

Well, chances are that you have a computer. You have Windows 95, or are thinking about picking up a copy. You know what *you* want to do with your computer. The problem is with making the *computer* do what you want it to do.

You've gotten by one way or another, hopefully with the help of a computer guru — either a friend at the office or somebody down the street. Unfortunately, though, that computer guru isn't always around. This book can be a substitute for the computer guru during your times of need. Keep a fresh bag of Cheetos in your desk drawer, however, just in case you need a quick bribe.

How This Book Is Organized

The information in this book has been well sifted. This book contains seven parts, and each part is divided into chapters related to the part's theme. Each chapter is divided into short sections to help you navigate the stormy seas of Windows 95. Sometimes you may find what you're looking for in a small, boxed tip. Other times you may need to cruise through an entire section or chapter. It's up to you and the particular task at hand.

Here are the categories (the envelope, please):

Part I: Bare-Bones Windows 95 Stuff (Start Here)

This book starts out with the basics. You find out how to turn on your computer, and you examine all your computer's parts and what Windows 95 does to them. This part walks you through the steps for installing Windows 95 and explains all the Windows 95 stuff that everybody thinks you already know. It explains the new features in Windows 95, separating the wheat from the chaff while leaving out any thick, technical oatmeal. You'll discover whether your computer has enough oomph to run Windows 95. And you end this part (with great relief) by turning off your computer.

Part II: Making Windows 95 Do Something

The biggest problem with using Windows 95 isn't opening programs or moving windows around on-screen. It's making Windows 95 do something *useful*. Here, you find ways to overcome the frustratingly playful tendencies of Windows 95 and force it to shovel the walkway or blow leaves off the driveway.

Part III: Using Windows 95 Applications (and Running DOS, Should the Mood Strike)

Windows 95 comes with a whole bunch of free programs. In this part, you find practical information about your new word processor, automatic phone dialer, electronic Rolodex, and bunches of other goodies.

But there's more. See, for years, Windows was simply fancy clothing over an ugly DOS belly — curly hairs and all. If you ever left Windows, you'd fall into the ugly DOS navel underneath. Windows 95 doesn't need DOS anymore, thank goodness; Windows 95 is finally robust enough to run by itself. That's not to say that DOS has disappeared, however. Windows 95 keeps a copy of DOS around for any DOS programs you might have in the closet. This part offers tips to keep you from falling into the DOS navel — especially if you still cling to a few DOS programs under Windows.

Part IV: Been There, Done That: Quick References for Moving to Windows 95

More than 60 million copies of Windows 3.1 are floating around out there. That means that more than 60 million Windows 3.1 users will be muttering, "How do I make Windows 95 work like the *old* version?" This part of the book offers quick tips, work-arounds, and quick-reference charts to help translate your work from the Windows 3.1 language to the new Windows 95 dialect.

Part V: Help!

Are your windows stuck? Broken? Do you need new screens? Although glass doesn't shatter when Windows 95 crashes, it can still hurt. In this part, you find some soothing salves for the most painful and irritating maladies.

Part VI: The Part of Tens

Everybody loves lists (unless they're published by the IRS). This part contains lists of Windows-related trivia — ten aggravating things about Windows 95 (and how to fix them), ten DOS commands you shouldn't run under Windows, ten weird Windows 95 icons and what they mean, ten expensive things that make Windows 95 easier, ten mystifying acronyms, and other solutions to tense problems.

Icons Used in This Book

Already seen Windows 95? Then you've probably noticed its *icons,* which are little pictures for starting various programs. The icons in this book fit right in. They're even a little easier to figure out:

Watch out! This signpost warns you that pointless technical information is coming around the bend. Swerve away from this icon, and you'll be safe from the nerdy technical drivel.

This icon alerts you about juicy information that makes computing easier. For example, keep a damp sponge on hand in case your Saint Bernard decides to sniff your keyboard.

Don't forget to remember these important points. (Or at least dog-ear the pages so you can look them up again a few days later.)

The computer won't explode while you're performing the delicate operations associated with this icon. Still, wearing gloves and proceeding with caution is a good idea when this icon is near.

Already familiar with Windows 3.1? This icon marks information that can ease the transition from Windows 3.1 to Windows 95.

Where to Go from Here

Now you're ready for action. Give the pages a quick flip and maybe scan through a few sections that you know you'll need later. Oh, and this is *your* book — your weapon against the computer criminals who've inflicted this whole complicated computer concept on you. So personalize your sword: Circle the paragraphs you find useful, highlight key concepts, cover up the technical drivel with sticky notes, and draw smiley faces in the margins. The more you mark up the book, the easier it will be for you to find all the good stuff again.

Part I

Bare-Bones
Windows 95 Stuff
(Start Here)

The 5th Wave   **By Rich Tennant**

In this part . . .

*W*indows 95 is an exciting, modern way to use the computer. That means it's as confusing as a new car's dashboard. Even the most wizened old computer buffs stumble in this strange new land of boxes, bars, and bizarre oddities like *Virtual Device Drivers*.

Never used a computer before but bought Windows 95 because it's "easy to use"? Well, Windows 95 can be intuitive, but that doesn't mean it's as easy to figure out as a bowling ball.

In fact, most people are dragged into Windows without a choice. Your new computer probably came with a version of Windows already installed. Or maybe you had installed Windows 95 at the office, where everyone has to learn it except for Scott, who plays racquetball with the boss. Or perhaps your favorite program, like PageMaker, requires a version of Windows, so you've had to learn to live with the darn thing.

And you can adjust to Windows 95, just like you eventually learned to live comfortably with that funky college roommate who kept leaving hair clogs in the shower.

Whatever your situation, this part keeps things safe and sane, with the water flowing smoothly. If you're new to computers, the first chapter answers the question you've been afraid to ask around the lunch room: "Just what is this Windows thing, anyway?"

Chapter 1

What Is Windows 95?

. . . .

In This Chapter

▶ Understanding what Windows 95 is and what it does

▶ Finding out whether you still need DOS

▶ Deciding why you should bother to use Windows 95

▶ Finding out whether your computer will work with Windows 95

. . . .

*O*ne way or another, you've probably already heard about Windows. Windows posters line the walls of computer stores. All the flashy computer magazines are shouting "Windows" loudly enough to disturb sleeping animals. And you've probably heard at least one person tell you that Windows is a computer paradise, filled with beautiful graphics and relaxing menus.

But be prepared: Windows is no panacea, no matter how you want to pronounce that word. Windows may be a paradise compared with DOS, but even Hawaii has cockroaches. And they're huge! (At least the one I saw in a fancy Kona restaurant a few years ago was. It was so huge that my wife thought it was fake — part of the jungle decor and all. Then it started to clean its antennae. The waitress picked it up and let it go outside. Didn't like to kill animals, she said.)

You probably won't find a cockroach in your Windows box, but be prepared for a few other surprises. . . .

This chapter fills you in on the basics of the latest version of Windows, called Windows 95. The chapter explains what Windows 95 is and what it can do. You also examine how Windows 95 and DOS work together, letting you run programs from either camp.

What Are Windows and Windows 95?

Windows is just another computer program, like the zillions of others lining the store shelves. But it's not a program in the normal sense — something that enables you to write letters or play Spatula Invaders. Rather, Windows changes the way you work with your computer.

For years, computer programs have made computers cling to the typewriter look. Just as on a typewriter, people type letters and numbers into the computer. The computer listens and then places letters and numbers onto the screen. This time-tested system works well. But it takes a long time to learn, and it's as boring as an oral hygiene pamphlet.

It's boring because computer geeks designed computers for other computer geeks many moons ago. They thought that computers would be forever isolated in narrow hallways where somber young people with clipboards and white lab coats jotted down notes while the big reels whirled. Nobody expected normal people to use computers — especially not in their offices, their dens, or, heaven help us, their kitchens.

- ✔ Windows software dumps the typewriter analogy and updates the *look* of computers. Windows replaces the words and numbers with pictures and buttons. It's splashy and modern, like an expensive new coffeemaker.

- ✔ Because Windows software looks and acts differently from traditional computer programs, learning it can take a few days. After all, you probably couldn't make perfect coffee the first day, either.

- ✔ Windows 95 is the latest version of Windows software. It's the version that updates Windows 3.1, just like Windows 3.1 replaced Windows 3.0, which replaced, well, you get the idea.

What Does Windows Do?

Like the mother with the whistle in the lunch court, Windows controls all the parts of your computer. You turn on your computer, start Windows, and start running Windows programs. Each program runs in its own little *window* on-screen. Yet Windows keeps things safe, even if the programs start throwing food at each other.

While it's keeping order, Windows makes computing a little easier. Windows purges an ugly computing custom called the *DOS command line.* The command line lives next to a confusing little symbol, *the DOS prompt,* which looks something like this:

```
C:\>
```

With DOS, people boss around their computers by typing a command at the prompt. To start the WhipIt program, for example, they type the program's name and then press Enter, like this:

```
C:\> WHIPIT
```

That is, they type **whipit** at the prompt and then press Enter. The computer dutifully loads the WhipIt program and brings it to the screen. DOS is tense, shoulder-tightening stuff. You must memorize the names of all your programs because DOS doesn't offer any clues — not even a quick spelling tip. (For more information on DOS, see the section "What Is DOS, and Do I Still Need It?")

Windows, in contrast, replaces that dreary DOS prompt with little pictures. To start your WhipIt program in Windows, for example, you look for the picture representing your WhipIt program. It may look something like this:

By selecting the picture of the whip, Windows users can start the WhipIt program even if they can't spell. Figures 1-1 and 1-2 compare the way Windows 95 and DOS look.

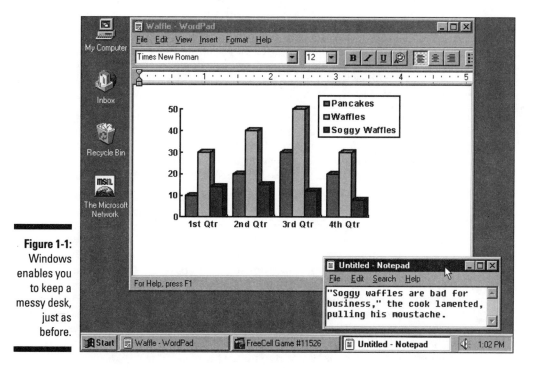

Figure 1-1: Windows enables you to keep a messy desk, just as before.

```
C:\>
```

Figure 1-2:
The DOS
screen
shows only
the prompt.

Windows fills the screen with lots of fun little boxes and pictures; DOS is for no-nonsense minimalists who never put bumper stickers on their cars.

- ✔ Some people say that colorful pictures make Windows easier to use; others say that Windows is a little too arty. To write a letter in Windows, for example, do you select the picture of the notepad, the quill, or the clipboard? And what do you do with the icon of the little man juggling?

- ✔ A computer environment that uses little pictures and symbols is called a *graphical user interface*, or *GUI*. (It's pronounced *gooey*, believe it or not.) Pictures require more computing horsepower than letters and numbers, so Windows 95 requires a relatively powerful computer. (You'll find a list of its requirements in Chapter 2.)

- ✔ Windows gets its name from all the cute little windows on-screen. Each window shows some information: a picture, perhaps, or a program you're running. You can put several windows on-screen at the same time and jump from window to window, visiting different programs. (Actually, the windows look like little squares, but who would buy a program called Squares?)

- ✔ When the word *Windows* starts with a capital letter, it refers to the Windows program. When the word *windows* starts with a lowercase letter, it refers to windows you see on-screen. When the word Windows ends with the number *95,* it refers to the latest version of the Windows software, Windows 95.

Because Windows uses graphics, it's much easier to use than to describe. To tell someone how to move through a document in a DOS-based program, you simply say, "Press the PgDn key." In Windows, you say, "Click in the vertical scroll bar beneath the scroll box." Those directions sound awfully weird, but after you've done it, you'll say, "Oh, is that all? Golly!" (Plus, you can still press the PgDn key in Windows. You don't have to "click in the vertical scroll bar beneath the scroll box" if you don't want to.)

What Is DOS, and Do I Still Need It?

MS-DOS is as boring as the words it stands for: Microsoft Disk Operating System. An age-old method of working with computers, DOS handles the chores required to make the computer do its traditional computer stuff: shuffle information to and from various parts of your computer and put it on your screen for you to labor over.

When you turn on a computer that uses DOS, DOS wakes up, takes control, and starts making things happen. It handles all the dreadful, background computing mechanics so you can concentrate on what's happening on-screen.

DOS protects you from that internal computer stuff, but DOS is kind of technical itself. That's why Microsoft invented Windows. For years, Windows would ride on top of DOS, insulating you from your computer's technical side. When you told Windows to do something, it would turn around and tell DOS to do something. Until recently, Windows was just a translator, converting languages and collecting cash for its services.

The newest version of Windows, Windows 95, no longer needs DOS. It's pretty much outgrown it, although Windows 95 comes with a version of DOS in case you need to run an old DOS program.

After all, Microsoft wrote both DOS and Windows, so it's no big deal for them to toss in an old DOS version for long-time computer users who still have piles of old DOS software.

- ✔ With Windows 95, Windows and DOS are no longer two separate programs. Instead, Windows 95 has absorbed the code that made DOS work. That way, Windows 95 can run DOS programs in a window on-screen, or a DOS program can grab the entire screen — whichever looks best. Either way, you don't have to buy a separate copy of DOS anymore; Windows 95 can run your DOS programs as if they were Windows programs.

- ✔ Windows 95 can even bring up a C:\> thing in a window for people who want to use the "DOS command line." Instead of using a mouse to start programs, these people type the name of the program at the command line and press Enter.

- ✔ DOS is too disgusting to be discussed in detail this early. If you're into it, turn to Chapter 14.

DOS rhymes with boss. Don't pronounce it as *dose* unless you're pretending you're a novice at the software store to see whether the salesperson will try to rip you off.

Boring technical glop

Computer nerds spend their idle hours arguing whether Windows 95 is a full-fledged operating system or a shell.

An *operating system* controls a computer's innards at a bare-bones, blood-pumping level. DOS is an operating system because it handles all the raw, messy mechanics of computing. When you tell DOS to copy something to a floppy disk, DOS wakes up the floppy drives and tells the computer to find the appropriate information and move it, one morsel at a time, to the floppy disk. All you do is type the COPY command; DOS jumps in there and does the rest.

A *shell,* on the other hand, rides on top of DOS, making DOS easier to use. (Sure, the DOS COPY command is easy enough, but *try* remembering other commands, like MODE LPT1:=COM2:.) Shells always have DOS in the background, just as Windows used to. Now, Microsoft says Windows 95 has replaced DOS — it has absorbed the DOS code. Other people say Windows 95 still relies on parts of DOS, so it's not a full-fledged operating system. The debate rages. Luckily, computer nerds tend to mumble, so you don't have to listen.

Why Should I Bother Using Windows?

DOS is time tested and traditional, but, like IRS forms, it's a bunch of cryptic words and numbers. It's a mean, spiteful computer program. You have to know what strange words to type at the DOS prompt before your computer will even listen to you.

Windows, in contrast, puts all its cards on the table. You don't have to memorize any program names; you just look for the right pictures. Just as the international symbols over rest rooms help when you drink too much espresso in Paris, pictures can make computing easier.

Windows outdoes DOS in another way. All DOS programs work differently from each other. For example, your word processor and your database require different commands for printing. If you work with four different programs, you have to memorize four different print commands.

Microsoft bossed around all the companies that write software for Windows, so all Windows programs work pretty much the same way. No matter who wrote the program, you use the same three keystrokes in any Windows program to print your work. Imagine relying on just one yellow sticky note rather than having dozens of sticky notes circling your monitor!

In DOS, only one program can be on-screen at a time. Because Windows programs run in little windows, you can run as many programs as you can fit on-screen. This feature makes it easier to, say, grab an address from one window and stick it into a letter you're writing in another window. (Finding that other window is another problem. Chapter 8 can help you locate lost windows.)

Finally, you'll probably have to start using Windows sooner or later. Windows has become so fashionable that most software companies are abandoning their DOS programs and writing Windows versions instead. It was bound to happen. Make room in the garage to dump those DOS programs next to the 8-tracks.

- ✔ Today, people are buying a lot more Windows programs than DOS programs. That's why Windows 95 has pretty much replaced DOS. Windows is where the money's at.

- ✔ The box doesn't say so, but Windows 95 comes with a free word processor, an address book, a calendar, a drawing program, and a few other goodies. These freebies, which can handle the computing needs of many people, are described in Part III of this book. (These freebies are another reason why people are switching from DOS to Windows.)

- ✔ The store shelves are packed with programs that say "For Windows" on the box. Those programs don't include Microsoft Windows, however. They're designed to run from *within* Microsoft Windows. You have to buy Windows separately and install it on your computer first.

- ✔ Programs and computer parts that say *Designed for Windows 95* on their box have been tested to work with Windows 95 and take advantage of the new features in Windows 95.

Should I Bother Using Windows 95?

Windows 3.1 users are elbowing each other nervously by the watercooler and whispering the Big Question: Why bother buying Windows 95, going through the hassle of installing it, and learning all its new programs? Windows 95 offers improvements over Windows 3.1.

First, Windows 95 is a little easier for beginners to figure out. There's a lot less pointing and clicking involved when finding files and starting programs. For example, Windows 95 keeps track of the past 15 files or programs you've used and stores their names in a special spot. Want to load the file again? Just click on the file's name from the pop-up list. No wading through menus or opening programs. White-gloved Windows 95 opens the car door and lets you start moving immediately.

You'll see lots more little buttons with pictures on them — *icons* — used in Windows 95 programs. Don't know what the icon with the little policeman picture is supposed to do? Then just rest your mouse pointer over the icon; after a few seconds, a window often pops up on-screen, explaining the icon's reason to be. The most helpful messages appear when you rest the pointer over the unlabelled buttons that hang out along the tops of programs, like word processors and spreadsheets — in their toolbar areas.

Windows 95 finally allows longer filenames. After 15 years of frustration, IBM-PC users can call their files something more descriptive than RPT_45.TXT. In fact, it offers you 255 characters to describe your computer creations.

Ready to upgrade your computer? Windows 95 can give you a hand with its upgraded "Plug and Play" concept. A new Windows 95 "Wizard" keeps better track of the parts inside your computer and can alert you when internal brawls start. Better yet, it stops many brawls from even starting by making sure that two computer parts aren't assigned the same areas of your computer's memory.

- ✔ Windows 95 automates many computing chores. To install a program, for example, just push the floppy (or compact disc) into the drive and click the Add/Remove Programs button. Windows will search all your drives for the installation program and run it automatically. Windows 95 can automatically search for any new hardware you've installed as well, recognizing quite a few of the most popular upgrades.

- ✔ Tired of your twiddling your thumbs while Windows formats a floppy? Windows 95 can handle floppy chores in the background so you can continue playing your card game. (And boy, the new card came, FreeCell, is an incredibly delicious time-waster.)

- ✔ Dare I say the word, *Macintosh?* Windows looks more and more like the age-old Mac every year. That means Windows 95 will make Macintosh users feel more at home than ever.

Bracing Yourself for Windows 95

DOS, for all its faults, at least *looks* simple because the programs run one at a time. They take their time on the center stage and then exit politely, letting another program hit the spotlight.

With Windows, however, everything happens at the same time. Its many different parts run around like hamsters with an open cage door. Programs cover each other up on-screen. They overlap corners, hiding each other's important parts. Occasionally, they simply disappear.

Be prepared for a bit of frustration when things don't behave properly. You'll be tempted to stand up, bellow, and toss a nearby stapler across the room. After that, calmly pick up this book, find the trouble spot listed in the index, and turn to the page with the answer.

(And don't forget to pick up the stapler. Jerry Schuster from Anaheim reports that his stapler jammed in the janitor's vacuum cleaner, and the guy stopped emptying the trash cans in the whole department.)

- ✔ Windows software may be accommodating, but that can cause problems, too. For example, Windows 95 often offers more than three different ways for you to perform the same computing task. Don't bother memorizing each command. Just choose one method that works for you and stick with it. For example, Andrew and Deirdre Kleske use scissors to cut their freshly delivered pizza into slices. It stupefies most of their house guests, but it gets the job done.

- ✔ Windows 95 runs best on a powerful computer with the key word *386DX, 486, Pentium,* or *testosterone* somewhere in the description. Look for lots of *RAM* (random-access memory), too, as well as a huge hard disk. You'll find the finicky computer requirements for Windows 95 in Chapter 2.

Chapter 2

Ignore This Chapter on Computer Parts (Because You'll Probably Come Back to It Later)

• •

In This Chapter

▶ Learning the names for the gizmos and gadgets on the computer

▶ Understanding what all those things do

▶ Finding out what stuff you need in order to use Windows

▶ Making a list of what computer equipment you have

• •

*T*his chapter introduces computer gizmos and gadgets. Go ahead and ignore it. Who cares what all your PC gadgetry is called? Unless your PC's beeping at you like a car alarm, don't bother messing with it. Just dog-ear the top of this page, say, "So, that's where all that stuff is explained," and keep going.

In Windows, you just press the buttons. Windows scoots over to the right part of your computer and kick-starts the action. In case Windows stubs a toe, this chapter holds the Band-Aids. And, as always, the foul-smelling technical chunks are clearly marked; just hold your nose while stepping over them gingerly.

The Computer

The computer is that beige box with all the cables. It probably answers to one of three names: IBM (called *True Blue* when people try to dump their old one in the classifieds), an *IBM compatible* or *clone,* or a plain old PC.

Most people just call their computers *PCs* because that's what IBM called its first *personal computer* back in 1981. In fact, IBM's first PC started this whole personal computing craze, although some people lay the blame on video games.

The concept of a small computer that could be pecked on in an office or den caught on well with the average Joe, and IBM made gobs of money. So much money, in fact, that other companies immediately ripped off IBM's design. They *cloned,* or copied, IBM's handiwork to make a computer that worked just like it. These clone computers are *compatible* with IBM's own PC; they can use the same software as IBM's PC without spitting up.

Clones generally have an obscure brand name and a lower price on their invoice, but they work just as well (or better) than IBM's own line of computers. In fact, more people own clones than personal computers from IBM's own line. (Just look at IBM's latest quarterly earnings statements for proof.)

✔ People used to say that *IBM-compatible* computers were made by big corporations, such as COMPAQ and Toshiba. A *clone,* on the other hand, was thrown together by a kid in a back room. The distinction has waned through the years. If it's not IBM's computer, it's a clone.

✔ Windows runs equally well on IBM-compatible computers and on IBM's own computers; the key word is *IBM.* Computers from other planets, like as the Macintosh, can't run Windows, but their owners don't care. They just stifle their giggles when you try to figure out how to create a Windows *program group.*

✔ Some muscular people heft their desktop PCs onto one side and put them in a special stand. Other computers are designed to work sideways. These upright PCs are called *tower PCs.* The tilt doesn't affect their performance, but it makes them look really cool — especially when they use Windows' Black Leather Jacket color scheme. (The hairy-armed crowd can check out Chapter 10 for leather jacket tips.)

✔ As other companies built *compatible* computers, they strayed a bit from IBM's design. Tandy, for example, added sound. A few years ago, IBM itself strayed from its classic design by launching a new *PS series* of computers. Some of these design quirks can befuddle Windows — especially when you first install it. After you tell Windows what brand of computer it's dealing with, however, any hard feelings are soothed. All this stuff is covered in Chapter 3.

✔ Laptop and notebook computers can run Windows with no problems. Airplane-bound laptoppers should check out this chapter's mouse section for a mouse substitute.

When laptopping on an airplane, drop a few smoked almonds on your neighboring passenger's thigh. If he doesn't wake up, you can use his kneecap as a makeshift mousepad for a few double-clicks.

Microprocessor

The computer's *brain* is a small chip of silicon buried deep inside the computer's case. Resembling a Girl Scout's Thin Mint with square corners, this flat little wafer is the *microprocessor,* but nerds tend to call it a *central processing unit,* or *CPU.* (You may have seen flashy microprocessor TV commercials that say, "Intel Inside." Intel is a leading CPU developer.)

The computer's microprocessor determines how fast and powerful the computer can toss information around. Refer to Table 2-1 for a look at the power of your particular computer.

Table 2-1	**Microprocessor Power Ratings**			
Computer Name	**Fancy Name**	**Micro-processor**	**Vintage**	**Power**
PC	Personal Computer	8088	1981	A mere babe. This one was not strong enough to run Windows.
XT	eXtended Technology	8088	1983	A toddler. The XT used the same microprocessor as as the PC, but it came with a 10 MB hard drive (Windows won't baby-sit).
AT	Advanced Technology	80286	1984	A hyper teenager. This one was the start of the newer, more powerful class of chips that ends with the number *86.* Windows tolerates this chip.

(continued)

Table 2-1 *(continued)*

Computer Name	Fancy Name	Micro-processor	Vintage	Power
386-class	386SX, 386DX	80386SX, 80386 DX	1986	The start of something big, these are the grandfather of today's "386-class" power-houses. The 386SX is too old to run Windows 95, but the 386DX can still creak along — just barely.
386-class	486SX, 486DX, 486DX2, 486DX4	80486SX, 80486DX, 80486DX2, 80486DX4	1989	The fading workhorse, these chips run Windows 95 without problem.
386-class	Pentium	Pentium	1993	These power-houses make Windows 95 squeal ecstatically. They're the current favorite.

✔ A microprocessor is the current evolution of the gadget that powered those little 1970s pocket calculators. It performs all the computer's background calculations, from juggling spreadsheets to putting a picture of "Calvin and Hobbes" on-screen.

✔ Microprocessors are described by two numbers: the chip's class (8088, 286, 386, and so on) and the chip's processing speed, measured in *megahertz,* or *MHz.* The bigger the numbers, the faster Windows performs. For example, a 50 MHz 486 microprocessor is faster than a 33 MHz 486 microprocessor.

✔ I apologize for all the numbers in the preceding paragraph.

Windows works best with the 386 and higher classes of microprocessors, which include 486 chips and the lofty Pentium. It's slow on a 286, and it doesn't let you run your favorite DOS programs in little windows on-screen. Don't bother trying to run Windows on an XT or an age-old original IBM PC. It chokes.

TECHNICAL STUFF

General obfuscation about 386DX and 386SX code words

Today, the 386-class microprocessors are the most fashionable CPUs. They're the most powerful, and they can take advantage of the special memory features of Windows. The first 386 chip really scared people, and so did its price tag. Corporations snapped them up; everyone else saved their allowance.

Intel, the chip's creator, wanted to capture the thin-wallet crowd, so Intel's engineers hunkered down in the coffee room and released a less powerful (and less expensive) 386 chip called the *386SX*.

To avoid confusion between the 386 and its new little brother, Intel renamed its first 386 chip as a *386DX*. Technically speaking (and that's why this information is fenced into a little box), 386DX and 386SX chips can handle the same computing tasks: They can divvy up the computer's memory among greedy programs and enable them all to run wild at the same time.

But the programs run a little more slowly with a 386SX chip. Both the SX and DX versions of the 386 can take advantage of Windows' special 386 Enhanced mode.

Windows is even faster with a 486 chip, and the *SX* and *DX* stuff applies to 486 chips, as well. But those chips are another story with their own technical gobbledygook. (And, strangely enough, 486 chips and Pentiums are still referred to as "386-class" chips.)

Disks and Disk Drives

The computer's disk drive, that thin slot in its front side, is like the drawer at the bank's drive-up teller window. That disk drive enables you to send and retrieve information from the computer.

You can push anything that's flat into a disk drive, but the computer recognizes only one thing: *floppy disks*. Things get a little weird here, so hang on tight. See, by some bizarre bit of mechanical wizardry, computers store information as a stream of magnetic impulses.

A disk drive spits those little magnetic impulses onto the floppy disk for safe storage. The drive can slurp them back up, too. You just push the disk into the disk drive and tell Windows whether to slurp or spit. That's known as *copy to* or *copy from* in computer parlance.

Disks come in two main sizes: a sturdy $3^1/_2$-inch disk, and a rather flimsy $5^1/_4$-inch disk. Both are called floppy disks, but only one of them flops around when you dangle it by one corner.

Math coprocessors and 486 stuff that only scientists care about

Microprocessors perform mathematical calculations all day. They absorb numbers, scratch their heads, and spit out the right answer. Everything a computer does requires calculations, from figuring out California's latest sales tax to moving a dot across the screen three inches.

Strangely enough, computer graphics require the largest number of calculations. The microprocessor can get bogged down by all those calculations — especially when scientists do important science stuff, like simulating a drop of milk splashing into a bowl.

To speed things up, scientists and other hardcore computer folk place a second computer chip called a *math coprocessor* inside their computers. Although the regular microprocessor handles the calculations required for everyday computing, the math coprocessor jumps in to handle the extra hard-core, number-crunching stuff. Windows works slightly faster with a math co-

processor — especially if you're working with gargantuan spreadsheets (or milk drops).

The 486DX is the first chip to include a built-in math coprocessor. None of the other chips, including the 486DX's little brother, the 486SX, has one. (With those other chips, you need to buy a separate math coprocessor and have Dave at the computer store stick it on your computer's motherboard.) Finally, the latest 486DX2 varieties use new technology to make them a little faster.

Oh, and because of some legal oddities, buying a single 486DX chip is cheaper than buying a 486SX chip and adding a separate math coprocessor.

And here's one last little technical oddity: Math coprocessor chips end with the number 7. A math coprocessor for an 8088 is an 8087. A math coprocessor-processor for a 286 is a 287. A math coprocessor for a — well, you get the idea.

✔ The 3 ½-inch disk drives automatically grab the disk when you push it in far enough. You hear it *clunk,* and the disk sinks down into the drive. If it doesn't, you're putting it in the wrong way. (The disk's silver edge goes in first, with the little round silver thing in the middle facing down.) To retrieve the disk, push the button protruding from around the drive's slot and then grab the disk when the drive kicks it out.

✔ The 5 ¼-inch disks require an extra step. Push the disk into the drive until it doesn't go in any farther and then flip down the drive's little lever. (The disk's oval-shaped hole edge goes in first; the disk's smooth side faces up, with the rough-edged side facing down.) To retrieve the disk, flip the little lever back up and grab the disk as the drive kicks it out.

✔ A disk you can carry around the house is a *floppy disk.* A hidden disk that lurks deep in the bowels of the computer is a *hard disk* or *hard drive.*

✔ Hard disks are thick little Frisbees inside the computer that can hold hundreds of times more information than floppy disks. They're also much quicker at reading and writing information. (They're a great deal quieter, too, thank goodness.) Windows insists on a hard drive because it's such a huge program. The programs that run under Windows can be pretty huge, too.

✔ Because floppy disks are portable, using them is the easiest way to move information from one computer to another. You install Windows or any other program onto the computer by using floppy disks (or compact discs, which are described later in this section). You take the floppy disks out of the box and place them into the disk drive, one at a time, when a message on the computer screen tells you to. The computer copies the information from the floppy disk onto its hard drive.

✔ Computer stores sell blank floppy disks so that you can copy your work onto them and put them in a safe place. Unless your new box of blank disks has the word *preformatted,* you can't use them straight out of the box. They must be *formatted* first. This merry little chore is covered in Chapter 12.

✔ Computers love to *copy* things. When you're copying a file from one disk to another, you aren't *moving* the file. You're just placing a copy of that file onto that other disk.

✔ Floppy disks come in many flavors, each holding different amounts of information. Different disks are designed for different sizes and types of disk drives. The disk's box describes what sort of disks are inside, but the bare disks rarely offer a clue as to their capacity. Table 2-2 provides a handy identification chart for that disk you found behind the bookcase.

Table 2-2		True-to-Life Disk Facts		
Size	*Name*	*Storage Capacity*	*Label Jargon*	*Looks Like This*
5 ¼-inch	Low-density	360K, or about 240 pages of double-spaced text	DS/DD 40 tpi	Square, bendable, and usually black; has a large hole in the center that's lined with a little plastic reinforcing ring.
5 ¼-inch	High-density	1.2MB, or about 800 pages of text	HD DS/HD 96 tpi	Most common. Square, bendable, and usually black; has a large hole in the center without a little plastic reinforcing ring, but that's not always a good indicator.
3 ½-inch	Low-density	720K, or about 500 pages of text	DS/DD DD 135 tpi	Square and rigid; has a little arrow in one corner. The arrow points away from a single, small square hole in another corner.

(continued)

Table 2-2 (continued)

Size	Name	Storage Capacity	Label Jargon	Looks Like This
3½-inch	High-density	1.44MB, or about 900 pages of text	DS/HD HD	Most common. Square and rigid; has a little arrow in one corner and two small square holes in corners opposite from the arrow. The letters HD are often stamped on the disk.
3½-inch	Extended density	2.8MB, or about 1,800 pages of text	DS/ED ED	Square and rigid; very new and still quite shy. Chances are that you'll never have to recognize it by looking for little ED letters stamped on the disk.

What disk drives does Windows like?

On the box, Windows recommends that you have a hard drive with at least 6MB of free space, but it's keeping its fingers crossed behind its back. Windows can easily eat up 15MB of space. Windows programs can eat up even more space. Nobody will laugh if you use a 200MB hard disk and reserve at least half of that for Windows and your Windows programs.

Also, Windows requires a 5 ¼-inch, high-capacity floppy disk drive or a 3 ½-inch disk drive.

Finally, be aware that the terms *capacity* and *density* are often used interchangeably. The important part is the first part — *high* or *low*.

Be forewarned, however, that Windows comes with *high-density* disks. If your 3 ½-inch disk drive isn't *high-capacity*, you won't be able to use the Windows disks straight out of the box. Instead, you'll have to mail a coupon to Microsoft asking for the low-density, 720K disks that are designed for your antiquated drives. Getting the disks can take from two weeks to a month, which can stifle the excitement of bringing home a new piece of software.

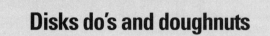

Disks do's and doughnuts

✔ Do label your disks so you know what's on them.

✔ Do at least make a valiant effort to peel off a disk's old label before sticking on a new one. (After awhile, those stacks of old labels make the disk too fat to fit into the drive.)

✔ Do feel free to write on the label after it has been placed on the disk. But use a felt-tipped pen if you're writing on a 5 ¼-inch disk; ball-point pens can damage the fragile disk inside.

✔ Do not touch the exposed part of the 5 ¼-inch disks.

✔ Do not write on the disk's sleeve rather than the label. Disks always end up in each other's sleeves, leading to mistaken identities and faux pas.

✔ Do not fold a floppy disk in half.

✔ Do copy important files from your hard disk to floppy disks on a regular basis. (This routine is called *backing up* in computer lingo. You can buy special backup packages to make this chore a little easier. Not much, but a little.)

✔ Do not try to use high-density disks in a low-capacity drive. They don't work.

✔ Do use low-density disks in a high-capacity drive, but only if you have to. They weren't designed for high-capacity drives, and they can cause problems.

✔ Do not listen to silver-tongued people who say you can *notch* a low-density disk to turn it into a high-density disk. It just doesn't work consistently and reliably.

✔ Do not leave disks lying in the sun.

✔ Do not place disks next to magnets. Don't place them next to magnets disguised as paper clip holders, either, or next to other common magnetized desktop items, such as older telephones.

What does write-protected mean?

Write protection is supposed to be a helpful safety feature, but most people discover it through an abrupt bit of computer rudeness: Windows 95 stops them short with the threatening message shown in Figure 2-1 while they are trying to copy a file to a floppy disk.

Figure 2-1:
Windows 95 sends an error message if a disk is write-protected.

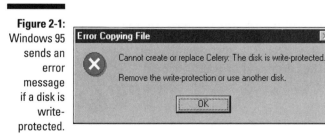

Error Copying File

Cannot create or replace Celery: The disk is write-protected.

Remove the write-protection or use another disk.

OK

A *write-protected disk* has simply been tweaked so that nobody can copy to it or delete the files it contains. Write protection is a simple procedure, surprisingly enough, requiring no government registration. You can write-protect and unwrite-protect disks in the privacy of your own home.

✔ To write-protect a 5 ¼-inch disk, fold a little black write-protect sticker over that big square notch on the disk's side. That cheap little sticker protects your disk's priceless contents from any changes or accidental deletions. You can *copy* information from the disk, but you can't *write* any information to it. You can't *delete* any information from it, either. (Those cheap little write-protect stickers come inside your expensive box of disks. In case you can't find yours, a little piece of masking tape does the trick.)

✔ To remove the write protection on a 5 ¼-inch disk, simply peel off that little tab. Rub any leftover stickum off the disk and wipe your fingers on your pants.

✔ To write-protect a 3 ½-inch disk, look for a tiny black sliding tab in a square hole in its corner. Slide the tab with a pencil or your thumbnail so that the hole is uncovered. The disk is now write-protected.

✔ To remove the write protection on a 3 ½-inch disk, slide the little black plastic thingy so that the hole is covered up.

✔ Yes, it's confusing. The notch must be *covered* for you to write-protect a 5 ¼-inch disk. The square hole must be *uncovered* for you to write-protect a 3 ½-inch disk.

✔ If you encounter the write-protect error shown in Figure 2-1, then wait until the drive stops making noise. Remove the disk, unwrite-protect the disk, and put it back in the drive. Then repeat what you were doing before you were so rudely interrupted.

The Mouse and That Double-Click Stuff

The *mouse* is that rounded plastic thing that looks like a bar of electronic soap. Marketing people thought that the word *mouse* sounded like fun, so the name stuck. Actually, think of your mouse as your electronic finger because you'll be using it in Windows to point at stuff on-screen.

A mouse has a little roller, or mouse ball, embedded in its belly. (Where were the animal-rights people?) When you move the mouse across your desk, the ball rubs against electronic sensor gizmos. The gizmos record the mouse's movements and send the information down the mouse's tail, which connects to the back of the computer.

As you move the mouse, you see an *arrow,* or *pointer,* move simultaneously across the computer screen. Here's where your electronic finger comes in: When the arrow points at a picture of a button on-screen, you press, or *click,* the left button on the mouse. The Windows button is selected, just as if you'd pressed it with your finger. It's a cool bit of 3-D computer graphics that makes you want to click buttons again and again.

- You control just about everything in Windows by pointing at it with the mouse and pressing and releasing the mouse button, or *clicking.* (The mouse pitches in with a helpful clicking noise when you press its button.)

- The plural of mouse is *mice,* just like the ones cats chew on. It's not *mouses.*

- Fold-down airline trays don't have enough room for a laptop, a mouse, *and* a beverage, so laptoppers often substitute trackballs for mice. A *trackball* is a small *upside-down mouse* that clips to the keyboard. You roll the mouse's ball with your thumb to move the on-screen arrow. You use your other fingers to inadvertently spill your beverage.

- Trackballs must be *purchased.* You can't just turn your normal mouse upside down and use masking tape. (I already tried.)

- Most mice run in two modes: Microsoft-compatible mode or some funky third-party way. Microsoft created Windows, so you'll have fewer problems if you run the mouse in the Microsoft-compatible mode.

- Mice come in two breeds: bus and serial. Windows doesn't care which you have, so neither should you. And ignore the technical trivia listed in the sidebar "The breeds of mice."

- A mouse won't work by itself; it needs software called a *driver.* A driver listens to the mouse location information coming down the tail and puts the mouse's location in a special spot in the computer's memory. All your other programs can glance at that spot to see where you've pushed the mouse this time. For still more information on drivers, scurry to the section on installing drivers in Chapter 17.

- If your mouse doesn't work with Windows (it gets the shivers, it scurries around at random, or the arrow doesn't move), the driver (the software — not your hand) is probably to blame. Visit Chapter 17 for help.

The mouse arrow changes shape, depending on what it's pointing at in Windows. When it changes shape, you know that it's ready to perform a new task. Table 2-3 is a handy reference for the different uniforms the mouse pointer wears for different jobs.

The breeds of mice

A serial mouse and a bus mouse look the same; both are plastic things with tails stretching toward the computer's rear. When the tails reach the back of the computer, the serial and bus mice begin to differ. A serial mouse plugs into an oblong doodad called a *serial port.* Almost all computers come with a preinstalled serial port that nerds call *COM1.*

The tail from a bus mouse doesn't head for the serial port. Instead, it creeps into a special *card* that's plugged into a slot in the computer's *expan-*

sion bus. How did the card get there? Well, the person who sold you the computer took off the computer's case and plugged it in.

Also, some computers, such as IBM's PS/2 series, come with a mouse already built in.

You can install a serial mouse yourself by just plugging it into the serial port. If you buy a bus mouse, however, you'd better buy a bag of Doritos, too, so that you can bribe a computer guru to pull off your computer's case and slide that card in there.

Table 2-3   The Various Shapes of the Mouse Pointer

Shape	What It Points At	What to Do When You See It
⌖	Just about anything on-screen	Use this pointer for moving from place to place on-screen.
✛	A single window	Uh-oh. You've somehow selected the annoying size or move option from the Control menu. Moving the mouse or pressing the cursor-control keys now makes the current window bigger or smaller. Press Enter when you're done, or press Esc if you want to get away from this uncomfortable bit of weirdness.
↕	The top or bottom edge of a window	Hold down the mouse button and move the mouse back and forth to make the window grow taller or shorter. Let go when you like the window's new size.
↔	The left or right of a window	Hold down the mouse button and move the side mouse back and forth to make the window fatter or skinnier. Let go when you like the window's new size.
↖	The corner of a window	Hold down the mouse button and move the mouse anywhere to make the window fat, skinny, tall, or short. Let go when you're through playing.

Shape	What It Points At	What to Do When You See It
I	A program or box that accepts text (this pointer is called an I-beam)	Put the pointer where you want words to appear, click the button, and start typing the letters or numbers.
🖑	A word with a hidden meaning in the Windows help system	Click the mouse, and Windows will trot out some more helpful information about that particular subject.
⌛	Nothing (Windows is busy ignoring you)	Move the mouse in wild circles and watch the hourglass spin around until Windows catches up with you. This shape usually appears when you are loading files or copying stuff to a floppy disk.
⌛	Anything	Keep working. This pointer means Windows 95 is doing something in the background, so it might work a little more slowly.
?	Anything	By clicking on the little question mark found in the top, right corner of some boxes, you create this pointer. Click on confusing onscreen areas or helpful informational handouts.
⊘	Something forbidden	Let go of the mouse button and start over. (You're trying to drag something to a place it doesn't belong.)

 Don't worry about memorizing all the various shapes that the pointer takes on. The pointer changes shape automatically at the appropriate times. The shapes are described here so you won't think that your pointer's goofing off when it changes shape.

Cards and Monitors

The monitor is the thing you stare at all day until you go home to watch TV. The front of the monitor, called its *screen* or *display,* is where all the Windows action takes place. The screen is where you can watch the windows as they bump around, occasionally cover each other up, and generally behave like nine people eyeing a recently delivered eight-slice pizza.

Monitors have *two* cords so they won't be mistaken for a mouse. One cord plugs into the electrical outlet; the other heads for the *video card,* a special piece of electronics poking out from the computer's back. The computer tells the video card what it's doing; the card translates the events into graphics information and shoots it up the cable into the monitor, where it appears on-screen.

- ✔ Like herbivores and cellulose-digesting gut microorganisms, monitors and video cards come in symbiotic pairs. Neither can function without the other, and you buy them in matched sets so that they'll get along.

- ✔ Unlike other parts of the computer, the video card and monitor don't require any special care and feeding. Just wipe the dust off the screen every once in a while.

- ✔ Spray plain old glass cleaner on a rag and then wipe off the dust with the newly dampened rag. If you spray glass cleaner directly on the screen, it drips down into the monitor's casing, annoying the trolls who sleep under the bridge.

- ✔ Some glass cleaners contain alcohol, which can cloud the anti-glare screens found on some fancy new monitors. When in doubt, check your monitor's manual to see if glass cleaner is allowed.

- ✔ When you first install Windows, it interrogates the video card and monitor until they reveal their brand name and orientation. Windows almost always gets the right answer from them and sets itself up automatically so that everything works fine the first time.

- ✔ Windows may be dominating, but it's accommodating, too. It can handle a wide variety of monitors and cards. In fact, most monitors and cards can switch to different *modes,* putting more or fewer colors on-screen and shrinking the text so that you can cram more information onto the screen. Windows enables you to play around with all sorts of different video settings if you're in that sort of mood. (If you are, check out Chapter 10.)

- ✔ For such simple gadgets, monitors and cards command a dazzling array of nerdy terms. Ignore them all. Windows picks the appropriate video settings automatically and moves on to the hard stuff, like mouse drivers.

Some people describe their monitors as *boxy* or *covered with cat hair;* others use the following strange scientific terms:

Ignore these awful graphics terms

Pixel: A pixel is a fancy name for an individual dot on-screen. Everything on-screen is made up of bunches of graphic dots, or pixels. Each pixel is a different shade or color, which creates the image. (Squint up close and you may be able to make out an individual pixel.) Monochrome monitors are often called *gray-scale monitors* because their pixels can only show shades of gray.

Resolution: The resolution is the number of pixels on a screen — specifically, the number of pixels across (horizontal) and down (vertical). More pixels mean greater resolution: smaller letters and more information packed onto the same-sized screen. People with small monitors usually use 640 x 480 resolution. People with larger monitors often switch to 1024 x 768 resolution so that they can fit more windows on-screen.

Color: This term describes the number of colors the card and monitor display on-screen. The number of colors can change, however, depending on the current resolution. When the card runs at a low resolution, for example, it can use its leftover memory to display more colors. At super-duper-high 1024 x 768 resolution, you may see only 16 colors on-screen. With a lower resolution of 640 x 480 — and an expensive video card — you may be able to see 16.7 million colors. Windows runs fastest with 16 colors. (Windows looks the flashiest — especially if you're using Kodak PhotoCD — with 256 colors or more.)

Mode: A predetermined combination of pixels, resolution, and colors is described as a *graphics mode.* Right out of the box, Windows can handle the mode needs of most people. If the video card hails from a weird mode planet, you need a *driver* from the folks who made the card (see Chapter 17 for help).

You don't need to know any of this stuff. If you're feeling particularly modular, however, you can change the Windows graphics modes after reading Chapter 10.

Keyboards

Computer keyboards looks pretty much like typewriter keyboards with a few dark growths around the perimeter. In the center lie the familiar white typewriter keys. The grayish keys with obtuse code words live along the outside edges. They're described next.

Groups of keys

Obtuse code-word sorters divvy those outside-edge keys into key groups:

Function keys: These keys either sit along the top of the keyboard in one long row or clump together in two short rows along the keyboard's left side. Function keys boss around programs. For example, you can press F1 to demand help whenever you're stumped in Windows.

Numeric keypad: Zippy-fingered bankers like this thingy: a square, calculator-like pad of numbers along the right edge of most keyboards. (You have to press a key called Num Lock above those numbers, though, before they'll work. Otherwise, they're *cursor-control keys,* described next.)

Cursor-control keys: If you *haven't* pressed the magical Num Lock key, the keys on that square, calculator-like pad of numbers are the cursor-control keys. These keys have little arrows that show which direction the cursor will be moved on-screen. (The arrowless 5 key doesn't do anything except try to overcome its low self-esteem.) Some keyboards have a second set of cursor-control keys next to the numeric keypad. Both sets do the same thing. Additional cursor-control keys are Home, End, PgUp, and PgDn (or Page Up and Page Down). To move down a page in a word processing program, for example, you press the PgDn key.

More key principles

Other keyboard keys you need to be familiar with follow:

Shift: Just as on a typewriter, this key creates uppercase letters or the symbols %#@$, which make great G-rated swear words.

Alt: Watch out for this one! When you press Alt (which stands for *Alternate*), Windows moves the cursor to the little menus at the top of the current window. If you're trapped up there and can't get out, you probably pressed Alt by mistake. Press Alt again to free yourself.

Ctrl: This key (which stands for *Control*) works like the Shift key, but it's for weird computer combinations. For example, holding down the Ctrl key while pressing Esc (described next) brings up a special Windows Task List box that tracks down missing windows. (Check out "The Way-Cool Task List" section in Chapter 7.)

Esc: This key, which stands for *Escape,* was a pipe dream of the computer's creators. They added Esc as an escape hatch from malfunctioning computers. By pressing Esc, the user was supposed to be able to escape from whatever inner turmoil the computer was currently going through. Esc doesn't always work that way, but give it a try. It sometimes enables you to escape when you're trapped in a menu or a dastardly dialog box. (Those traps are described in Chapter 6.)

Scroll Lock: This one's too weird to bother with. Ignore it. (It's no relation to a *scroll bar,* either.) If a little keyboard light glows next to your Scroll Lock key, press the Scroll Lock key to turn it off. (The key's often labeled Scrl Lk or something equally obnoxious.)

Delete: Press the Delete key (sometimes labeled Del), and the unlucky charac-ter sitting to the *right* of the cursor disappears. Any highlighted information disappears as well. Poof.

Backspace: Press the Backspace key, and the unlucky character to the *left* of the cursor disappears. The Backspace key is on the top row, near the right side of the keyboard; it has a left-pointing arrow on it. Oh, and the Backspace key deletes any highlighted information, too.

If you've goofed, hold down Alt and press the Backspace key. This action undoes your last mistake in most Windows programs.

Insert: Pressing Insert (sometimes labeled Ins) puts you in Insert mode. As you type, any existing words are scooted to the right, letting you add stuff. The opposite of Insert mode is Overwrite mode, where everything you type replaces any text in its way. Press Insert to toggle between these two modes.

Ugly disclaimer: Some Windows programs — Notepad, Cardfile, Write, and Calendar — are always in Insert mode. There's simply no way to move to Overwrite mode, no matter how hard you pound the Insert key.

Enter: This key works pretty much like a typewriter's Return key but with a big exception. Don't press Enter at the end of each line. A word processor can sense when you're about to type off the edge of the screen. It herds your words down to the next line automatically. So just press Enter at the end of each paragraph.

You'll also want to press Enter when Windows asks you to type something — the name of a file, for example, or the number of pages you want to print — into a special box.

Caps Lock: If you've mastered the Caps Lock key on a typewriter, you'll be pleased to find no surprises here. (OK, there's one surprise. Caps Lock affects only your letters. It has no effect on punctuation symbols or the numbers along the top row.)

Tab: There are no surprises here, either, except that Tab is equal to five spaces in some word processors and eight spaces in others. Still other word proces-sors enable you to set Tab to whatever number you want. Plus, a startling Tab Tip follows.

Press Tab to move from one box to the next when filling out a form in Windows. (Sometimes these forms are called *dialog boxes.*)

- ✔ A mouse works best for most Windows tasks, like starting programs or choosing among various options. Sometimes the keyboard comes in handy, however. Windows comes with *shortcut keys* to replace just about anything you can do with a mouse. Sometimes pressing a few keys can be quicker than wading through heaps of menus with a mouse. (The shortcut keys are described in Chapter 5 in the section on when to use the keyboard.)

- ✔ If you don't own a mouse or a trackball, you can control Windows exclusively with a keyboard. But it's awkward, like when Freddy from *Nightmare on Elm Street* tries to floss his back molars.

Print Screen: The one, fun, weird code key

Windows fixed something dreadfully confusing about an IBM computer's keyboard: the Print Screen key (sometimes called PrtScr, Print Scrn, or something similar). In the old days of computing, pressing the Print Screen key sent a snapshot of the screen directly to the printer. Imagine the convenience!

Unfortunately, nobody bothered to update the Print Screen key to handle graphics. If a screen shows anything other than straight text, pressing the Print Screen key sends a wild jumble of garbled symbols to the printer. And, if the printer isn't connected, turned on, and waiting, the computer stops cold.

Windows fixes the Print Screen woes. Pressing the Print Screen key now sends a picture of the screen to a special place in Windows that is known as the *Clipboard*. When the image is on the Clipboard, you can *paste* it into your programs or save it to disk. You can even print the screen's picture if you paste the image from the Clipboard into Paintbrush, the Windows drawing program.

- ✔ With some computers, you have to hold down Shift while you press Print Screen, or you get just an asterisk on-screen. Not nearly as much fun.

- ✔ The Clipboard is described in Chapter 9.

Modems

Modems are the things those youngsters down the street use to break into the computer of a defense contractor and order tanks, billing them to your credit card number.

Although modems are surrounded by intrigue, they're really just little mechanical gadgets that translate a computer's information into squealing sounds that can be sent and received over plain, ordinary phone lines.

✔ The computers on both ends of the phone lines need modems in order to talk to each other.

✔ Modems need special *communications software* to make them work. Windows 95 comes with a communications program called HyperTerminal. The program is just waiting for you to buy a modem.

✔ Modems come in two breeds: *internal* and *external.* Internal modems come on special *cards* that must be buried inside the computer — a process best left to professional buriers.

✔ An external modem comes in its own little case. A cable runs from the modem's case to a *serial port,* or *COM port,* which is a special receptacle in the back of the computer. (Plugging an external modem into the port is easy, unless you have only one serial port and you've already plugged the mouse into it. Then it's time to drive back to the computer store, with your computer in the back seat, and tell the teenager to put another serial port in the computer when he's through setting a new high score.)

✔ Most people use modems to call Prodigy, CompuServe, and other *on-line services.* On-line services are huge computers stuffed with information like stock prices, weather updates, news, and *message areas,* where people can swap talk about flatware, UFOs, and how much the on-line service is costing them. (On-line services cost anywhere from $8.95 a month to more than $20 an hour, all charged to the user's credit card.)

✔ Windows 95 comes with Microsoft's entry into the online boxing ring: The Microsoft Network. It's not much different from America Online or CompuServe, actually. In fact, there's a big difference. Since it's brand new, it has very few members.

✔ For more information about CompuServe, call (800) 848-8199. For more information about Prodigy, call (800) PRODIGY. And, for more information about your credit rating, call those youngsters down the street.

Printers

Realizing that the paperless office still lies several years down the road, Microsoft made sure that Windows can shake hands and make enthusiastic gestures with more than 200 different types of printers. When you install Windows, you need to type in your printer's name. Windows checks its dossiers, finds your printer, and immediately begins speaking to it in its native language.

That's all there is to it. Unless, of course, your printer happens to be one of the several hundred printers *left off* the Windows master list. In that case, cross your fingers that your printer's manufacturer is still in business. You have to get a *driver* from the manufacturer before your prose can hit the printed page. (For information on printers, see Chapter 10.)

✔ You need to know the name and model number of your printer when you install Windows, or Windows snubs it. Windows can figure out what brands of computer parts are inside your case, but it can't figure out what's connected to the end of your printer cable.

✔ Printers must be turned on before Windows can print to them. (You'd be surprised how easily you can forget this little fact in the heat of the moment.)

✔ Windows prints in a WYSIWYG (what you see is what you get) format, which means that what you see on-screen is reasonably close to what you'll see on the printed page.

Networks

Only die-hard computer geeks have a computer network at home, and they deserve what they get. Ordinary people deal with networks only in business settings, where the networks can be safely ignored except when they crash, which is usually right before it's your turn at the next available teller.

Networks connect PCs so that employees can share information. They can all send stuff to a single printer, for example, or send messages to each other asking whether Marilyn has passed out the paychecks yet.

✔ You're probably on a network if you can answer "yes" to any of these questions: Can your coworkers and you share a printer, data, or messages without standing up or yelling across the room? Do you ever *log in* or *log out* on your computer? When your computer stops working, does everybody else's computer stop working, too?

✔ You can safely ignore networks. Most networks require a paid human attendant, usually that person with drained-looking eyes, slumped shoulders, and a mouth that's slightly open on one side.

✔ Another common name for network is *not work.*

✔ When they work, you need to deal with networks only when you first turn Windows on. For a description of this frivolity, see the section on networks in Chapter 4. And for even more frivolity, check out Chapter 20 for information about Windows for Workgroups.

Sound Cards (Making Barfing Noises)

For years, PC owners looked enviously at Macintosh owners — especially when their Macs ejected a disk. The Macintosh would simultaneously eject a floppy disk from its drive and make a cute barfing sound. Macs come with sound built in; they can barf, giggle, and make *really* disgusting noises that won't be mentioned here. (Any Mac owners will be happy to play them back for you.)

But the tight shirts at IBM decided there was no place for sound on a Serious Business Machine. Windows fixes that mistake, so now the accounting department's computers can barf as loudly as the ones in the art department down the hall.

✔ Before your computer can barf, it needs a *sound card.* A sound card looks just like a video card. In fact, all cards look alike: long, green, flat things that nestle into long flat slots inside the computer. Speakers plug into a sound card like a monitor plugs into a video card.

✔ Just as computers mimic IBM's original computer design, sound cards mimic the designs of three popular sound cards: AdLib, Sound Blaster, and Roland MPU-401. The AdLib and Roland cards are standards for playing music; the Sound Blaster design is a standard for playing music *and* for making noises.

✔ Windows works with these three standard sound cards. It works with other sound cards as well, as long as you get the right driver. Refer to the section in Chapter 17 on installing a driver.

✔ Windows comes with a pleasant chimes sound already included, but it doesn't have any barf noises. Most computer gurus can either find a copy for you or personally record one.

✔ Just like the Macintosh, Windows enables you to assign cool sounds to various Windows functions. For example, you can make your computer scream louder than you do when it crashes. For more information, refer to the section in Chapter 10 on making cool sounds with multimedia.

CD-ROM Drive Stuff

Most people think compact discs contain music. Nope. Compact discs contain numbers. That's all the information they can handle. The CD factory translates music into numbers, and the CD player translates those numbers back into music.

Computer nerds snapped up compact discs pretty quickly when they realized that they could store numbers, and many companies now sell their programs and information on compact discs. A single compact disc can hold more information than hundreds of floppy disks.

To use them, however, you have to buy a CD-ROM drive for the computer. The CD player with your stereo won't cut it. If you spend enough money, though, you can buy a CD-ROM drive that hooks up to your computer *and* plays music. Then you can sell the one attached to your stereo. It's getting old anyway.

- ✔ Compact discs can store a great deal of information, but they're notoriously slow in bringing it back up. They're even slower than floppy disks. Buy a comfortable chair.

- ✔ You can't write information to a compact disc. Only the people at the CD factory can write to it, and that's because they have an expensive machine. Compact discs can't ever be erased, either.

- ✔ Compact discs are spelled with a *c* to confuse people accustomed to seeing disks spelled with a *k*.

- ✔ Do you plan to use that new Kodak PhotoCD stuff or watch any fancy multimedia videos of Venus flytraps eating frogs? If so, you'll want Windows to display at least 256 colors on-screen. Chapter 10 shows you how to make Windows' video modes more palatable.

- ✔ Multimedia computers need a sound card and a CD-ROM drive; the drive alone isn't enough. It's the computer industry's special way of making people spend more money.

- ✔ Windows 95 has new technology called Autoplay. Just pop the CD into the CD-ROM drive, and Windows 95 automatically revs it up, whether the disc contains music, programs, or pictures of English gardens. It's one more step toward eliminating installation hassles.

Parts Required by Windows 95

Table 2-4 compares what Windows 95 asks for on the side of the box with what you *really* need before it works well.

Table 2-4	What Windows 95 Requires	
Computer Requirements Politely Recommended by Microsoft	*What Your Computer Really Needs to Run Windows 95*	*Why?*
2MB of memory (RAM)	At least 4MB of memory	Windows 95 crawls across the screen with only 2MB and moves much more comfortably with 4MB. If you plan to run several large programs at once, however, add 8MB or more. Power users might want to consider 12 or even 16MB.

Computer Requirements Politely Recommended by Microsoft	What Your Computer Really Needs to Run Windows 95	Why?
10MB of additional hard drive space	At least 120MB more than you needed to run Windows 3.1	That 10MB can hold Windows 95 but little else. Where do your programs go? Where do your files go? Some Windows programs want 10MB or 20MB of space just for themselves. Don't be afraid to buy a hard drive that's 500MB or larger.
A 386SX microprocessor	A 486DX or Pentium CPU	Compare Windows 95 running on a 386SX, 486SX, 486DX, and Pentium computer. The faster the computer, the less time you spend waiting for Windows 95 to do something exciting.
A 5¼-inch high-density floppy drive or a 3½-inch floppy drive	At least one high-density 3½-inch floppy drive	Most Windows programs come packaged on high-density, 3½-inch floppy disks. People with *low*-density disk drives find themselves mailing in coupons when they buy software so that they can get the low-density versions of the program.
Color VGA card	Accelerated color Super VGA card, VL-Bus card, or PCI bus card	Because Windows 95 tosses so many little boxes on-screen, get an accelerated high-resolution Super VGA card. Or if your computer has the right slots, get a local bus or PCI video card.
MS-DOS version 5.0 or later; Windows 3.0 or later	MS-DOS version 5.0 or later; Windows 3.0 or later	Microsoft is selling Windows 95 as an upgrade to its older products. Not upgrading an older version of Windows? Then you'll have to buy the more expensive version of Windows 95 at the software store.

(continued)

Table 2-4 *(continued)*		
Computer Requirements Politely Recommended by Microsoft	**What Your Computer Really Needs to Run Windows 95**	**Why?**
None	A 15-inch monitor or larger	The bigger your monitor, the bigger your desktop: Your windows won't overlap so much. Unfortunately, super-large monitors are super-expensive.
Miscellaneous	CD-ROM drive	No, you don't need a CD-ROM drive for Windows 95. But it's a *lot* easier to install off a compact disc than an awkward handful of floppy disks. And isn't it time you joined the multimedia explosion, anyway?
Miscellaneous	Modem	You don't *need* a modem, but without one you can't dial up The Microsoft Network (dubbed MSN) — the on-line service that comes packaged with Windows 95. (And isn't it time you joined the Internet explosion, anyway?)

Your Computer's Parts

Use the handy list on the following page to write down all the parts of your computer. You'll probably need to know them later on, if only to read this list to the technical support person on the other end of the phone:

Chapter 3

Out of the Box and onto the Hard Drive (Installation Chores)

. . . .

In This Chapter

▶ Turning on the computer

▶ Deciding whether to install Windows 95 over your old version of Windows

▶ Installing Windows 95

▶ Taking the tutorial

▶ Leaving the Setup program

▶ Turning off the computer

. . . .

*I*nstalling software means copying the program from the disks in the box onto the hard drive inside your PC. Unfortunately, it usually also means hours of tinkering until the newly installed software works correctly with your particular computer, printer, disk drives, and internal organs. Because of the frustration potential, installation chores should usually be left to a certified computer guru. Gurus like that sort of stuff. (They even like the smell of freshly copied floppy disks.)

Luckily, Microsoft took mercy on Windows 95 beginners. It designed Windows 95 to install itself. Just slide the first disk into the disk drive and type a magic word. After that, keep feeding disks into the computer when it asks for a new one.

Remove the first floppy disk before trying to slide in the next one, and you'll be fine.

This chapter walks you through the installation process. You see how easy Microsoft made this chore, and you find out where else in the book you can turn if you need further information.

Turning On the Computer

The first step is to look for the computer's *power* switch. It's usually the largest switch on the computer. Sometimes it's red and important-looking.

> ✔ Put your ear next to the computer's case: If the computer is not making any noise, it's either turned off or broken. Flip its power switch to the opposite direction, and it will either jump to life or stay broken (or stay unplugged, which is why it always works in the repair shop).

> ✔ When a computer is first turned on, it makes a grinding sound, several clicking noises, and a whirring sound. Then it flashes long strings of code words on-screen. You can safely ignore the words unless you're reading them to a technical support person over the telephone.

Turning the computer off and then turning it on again can send devastating jolts of electricity through the computer's tender internal organs. Turn the computer on in the morning and off when you're finished for the day. Some sensitive people even leave their computers turned on all the time to spare them that morning power jolt.

And never turn the computer off while it's running Windows 95 or any other program. Doing so can destroy data and damage your programs. If the computer is doing something weird, like freezing up solid, try the less disastrous disciplinary measures described in Chapter 17.

> ✔ Finally, when installing Windows 95, tell it to keep your old version of Windows hanging around, as described in Step 8 of the following numbered list. Windows 95 then compresses your old Windows version and hides it in a secret directory on your hard drive. Later, after you've had time to play with Windows 95, you can tell Windows 95 to purge your old version for good. (Or, if Windows 95 doesn't meet your needs, you can tell it to resurrect your old version, removing itself in the process.)

Removing the Wrapper from the Box

Pick up the box that contains the Windows 95 software and look for where the plastic bunches up in the corners. With your incisors, bite into that little chunk of bunched-up plastic and give it a good tug. Repeat this procedure a few times until you've created a finger-sized hole. Then peel back the plastic until the box is free.

Should you install Windows 95 over your old version of Windows?

Should you copy this new version of Windows 95 over your older, faithful version of Windows 3.1 — a version that serves you so well except when it crashes?

Yeah, go ahead. The new version won't wipe out the important parts of the old version. The desktop will have the same programs as before. In fact, if you don't install Windows 95 over your old version of Windows, you'll have to reinstall all your old programs by hand.

To be on the safe side, copy your important data files to floppy disks before you begin. You've prob-ably been backing up your work anyway, so doing it shouldn't take long.

✔ If you *haven't* been copying your important files to floppy disks for safekeeping, head to the store and ask for a tape backup unit that's compatible with Windows 95.

✔ If you're the extra-cautious sort, you can in-stall the new version of Windows 95 into a separate directory and try it out for a while. I did. After 15 minutes or so, I deleted the old version because it was just cluttering up my hard drive.

Installing Windows 95

Forget those awkward experiences setting up metal Christmas trees or listening to your car make funny noises. Windows 95 caters to beginners with an installa-tion program that checks under your PC's hood and sets itself up automatically, adjusting the fluid levels as needed.

Here's how to pull into the full-service lane:

First, make sure that your computer's turned on; then make sure that anything plugged into your computer is turned on, as well. That includes modems, printers, compact disc drives, yogurt makers, and other goodies. Plug in your joysticks, too; Windows 95 finally recognizes them. Hurrah!

If you are using DOS 5.0 or an earlier version, make sure that you've made a boot disk that contains a copy of SYS.COM. You'll need this in case you ever want to uninstall Windows 95, as described in the Appendix at the back of this book.

1. **Start your current version of Windows, put your Windows 95 Installa-tion disk in drive A (or in your CD-ROM drive if you're installing from a compact disc), and then open the Program Manager's Run box.**

Never used Program Manager's secret Run box before? Then click on File from along the top of Program Manager, as shown in Figure 3-1, and choose Run from the menu that drops down.

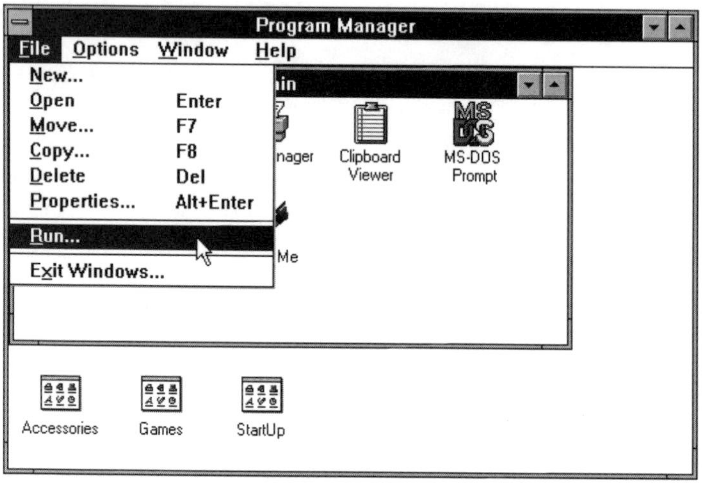

Figure 3-1:
Click on File
in Program
Manager
and choose
Run from the
menu.

If you don't have any version of Windows installed on your computer, you need to do *two* things. First, bring up a DOS prompt (that C:\> thing), and second, find your old Windows disks. See, Windows 95 is an *upgrade* — if you aren't installing it over an old version, then you need to buy the expensive, non-upgrade version of Windows 95.

2. **Type** A:\SETUP **in the box that appears, as shown in Figure 3-2, and click on the OK button.**

If you're installing Windows 95 from a compact disc, however, the process is a little different. You need to change the drive letter, and add **WIN95** to the mix. For example, if your CD-ROM drive is drive E, type this in the box shown in Figure 3-2:

```
E:\WIN95\SETUP
```

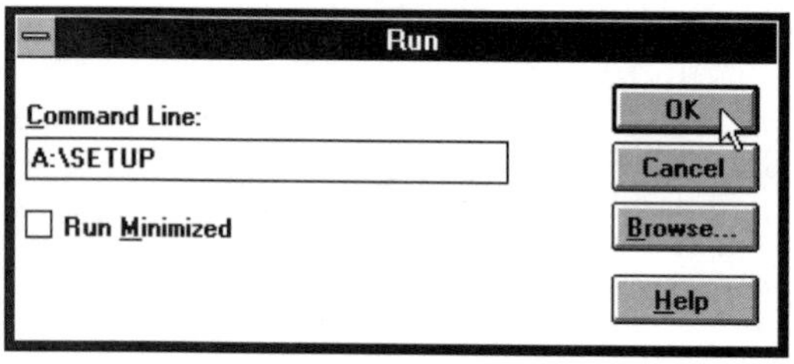

Figure 3-2:
Type
A:\SETUP
and click on
OK to load
the
Windows 95
installation
program.

Or, if you're installing Windows 95 straight from DOS, type this at the DOS prompt and press Enter:

```
A:\>SETUP
```

Your first taste of Windows 95 leaps to the screen. The window merely announces that Windows 95 will check your hard disk for any problems before continuing (see Figure 3-3). It also breaks the news that you might be sitting in front of your computer for anywhere from 30 minutes to an hour, depending on how smoothly the installation process goes.

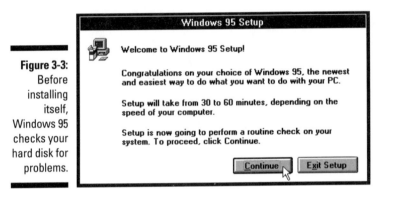

Figure 3-3:
Before
installing
itself,
Windows 95
checks your
hard disk for
problems.

3. Click on Continue, and Windows 95 checks your hard disk.

If Windows 95 finds anything wrong with your hard disk, it says so, and promptly fixes the problem. Usually, however, everything is fine, and Windows 95 moves on to Step 4.

If Windows 95 said it found something weird, you may want to click on the Details button to see what's up. You can usually get away with clicking on the Continue button and pressing forward, however. Windows 95 prepares its own computerized "computer guru" that helps install itself on your computer. If you're installing Windows 95 from floppy disks, Windows 95 occasionally asks you to insert the next disk, so be prepared by keeping all the disks on the desk in front of you.

But first, be prepared for the legalese Windows 95 tosses in your face, as described in Step 4.

4. Click on Yes on the software agreement.

Here's where Microsoft tosses you a stumper, shown in Figure 3-4. Unless you agree to abide by Microsoft's special Windows 95 terms, the install process simply stops and leaves the room like a surly bellhop who only got a dollar tip. Promise to play by Microsoft's rules and click on the Yes button.

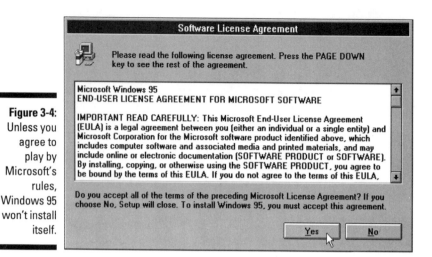

Figure 3-4:
Unless you agree to play by Microsoft's rules, Windows 95 won't install itself.

5. If Windows 95 asks you to close down any currently running programs, do so. Then click on the OK button.

The Windows 95 Installation program works hard, and it wants the computer all to itself, as shown in Figure 3-5. If you're running any other programs in the background, shut them down before going further.

Don't have an earlier version of Windows on your hard drive? Then Windows 95 asks you to insert the first disk from your *old* version of Windows into a disk drive so it can verify that you're merely upgrading an older version of Windows. Without that older version of Windows you won't be able to install the Windows 95 upgrade, unfortunately. Better head back to the store for the more expensive version of Windows 95 that doesn't require an older version of Windows.

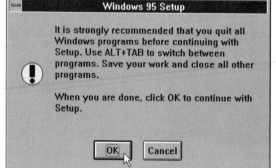

Figure 3-5:
Don't run any other programs while installing Windows 95.

Legal gibberish and licensing terms that leap out during the installation

By clicking on the Yes button, you're essentially telling Microsoft that you've agreed to the following things:

- ✔ You won't take Windows 95 apart to see how it works.

- ✔ You won't rent out your copy of Windows 95, or give copies away to friends.

- ✔ If you've been using a special "preview" copy of Windows 95, you promise to destroy that

version after a year (or whenever Microsoft tells you, whichever comes first).

- ✔ Finally, you understand you're the one punching the keyboard, so Microsoft isn't responsible if the software completely destroys your computer, your business, your data, and your love life.

Welcome to Windows 95!

Don't know whether you're running any other programs? Then press Ctrl+Esc, and the Windows 3.1 Task List will list all the currently running programs. The list should contain only Program Manager and Windows 95 Setup. If you see another program listed, click on its name and then click on the Task List's End Task button to shut it down.

6. When the Windows 95 Setup Wizard appears, press Enter (or click on the button marked Next) to continue.

As shown in Figure 3-6, Windows 95 explains that installation takes three steps: It gathers information about the computer, copies the files that your particular computer needs, and then restarts the computer to see whether it copied the right files over. Windows 95 replaces your old versions of Windows and DOS in the process.

See the buttons marked Back and Next along the bottom of the window? Throughout the next few steps, you'll be able to click the Back button to go back to your last step. So don't feel that you've blown it if you accidentally click on the Next button before you're ready or if you want to go back and change something. Just click on the Back button, and Windows 95 will go back a step.

7. Click on the Next button to choose the C:\WINDOWS directory.

Your best bet is to leave the directory at the recommended choice, C:\WINDOWS (see Figure 3-7). This directory is where most programs expect to find Windows, and installing Windows 95 elsewhere can cause problems down the road.

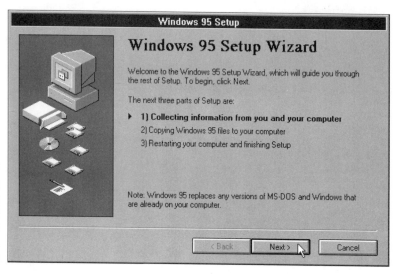

Figure 3-6:
Installing
Windows 95
takes three
steps.

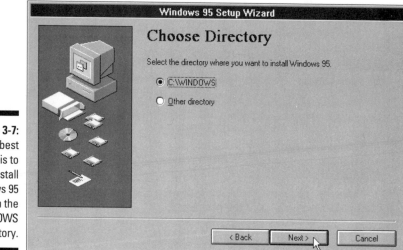

Figure 3-7:
Your best
bet is to
install
Windows 95
in the
C:\WINDOWS
directory.

After you click Next, Windows probes your hard drive, making sure that it has enough room to fit all the incoming files.

8. Click on the Next button so Windows 95 will save your old versions of DOS and Windows in case something goes wrong.

Although Windows 95 replaces your old versions of DOS and Windows, it doesn't necessarily scrape them off your hard drive. By leaving the Yes button selected and simply clicking Next (see Figure 3-8), Windows 95 compresses your old versions of DOS and Windows into a 6MB file and puts them in a hidden place on your hard drive.

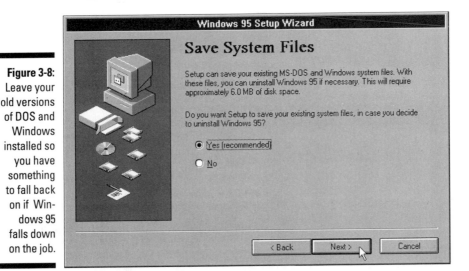

Figure 3-8:
Leave your
old versions
of DOS and
Windows
installed so
you have
something
to fall back
on if Win-
dows 95
falls down
on the job.

(Later on, if you decide Windows 95 really *does* work better than your old versions of Windows and DOS, you can tell Windows 95 to delete that 6MB file for you.)

9. **Click on the Next button to choose the Typical setup.**

Just clicking on the Next button, as seen in Figure 3-9, tells Windows 95 to install the most typical files your computer needs. This decision isn't as difficult as it might seem for one big reason: Windows 95 makes it really easy to go back and add programs you might have left off during the install process.

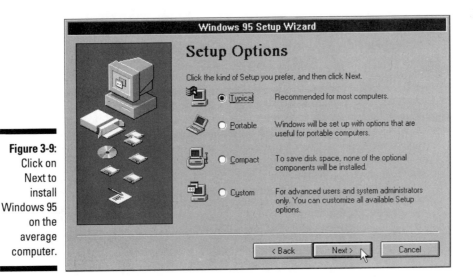

Figure 3-9:
Click on
Next to
install
Windows 95
on the
average
computer.

If you're installing Windows 95 on a laptop, choose the Portable setup. If your hard disk is itty-bitty (less than 60 megabytes), choose the Compact setup. If you're a computer guru who's simply testing this book for a friend, choose Custom for more advanced options.

10. **Type your name, press Tab, type your company name, and click on Next.**

Type your name and company, as shown in Figure 3-10. Windows 95 registers the software in your name. If you misspell your name or company and Windows 95 jumps to the next page before you can correct it, click on the Back button. Windows 95 gives you a second chance.

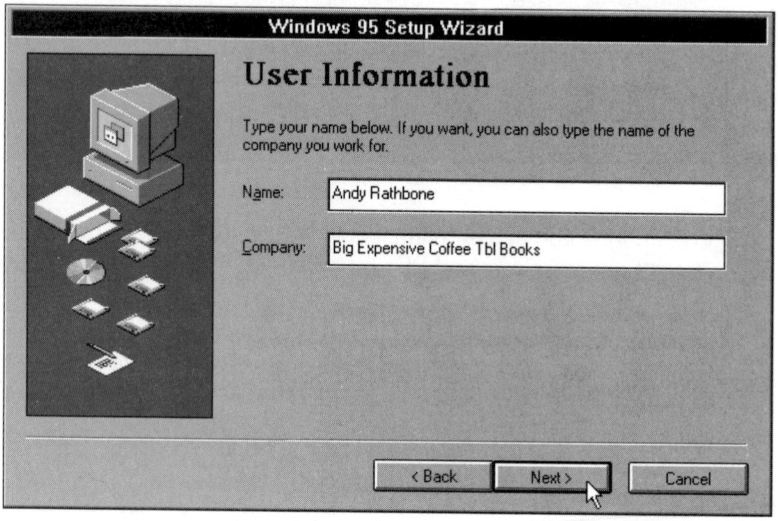

Windows 95 Setup Wizard

User Information

Type your name below. If you want, you can also type the name of the company you work for.

Name: | Andy Rathbone

Company: | Big Expensive Coffee Tbl Books

[< Back] [Next >] [Cancel]

Figure 3-10: Press Tab to move from the Name box to the Company box.

11. **If you're installing Windows 95 from a compact disc, type the CD's special "key number" into the box and click Next, as shown in Figure 3-11.**

12. **Click in the boxes next to any special computer parts you have and then click on Next.**

Some software puts all the burden on you. *You* have to remember what's installed inside your computer, as well as the equipment's brand name, switch settings, and any other bothersome details. Windows 95 doesn't mind searching inside your computer for all that information, but it needs a little help. If you know your computer uses any of the equipment listed in the Setup Wizard box, click on the little check box next to that equipment. The box in Figure 3-12, for example, tells Windows 95 that the computer has a sound card installed.

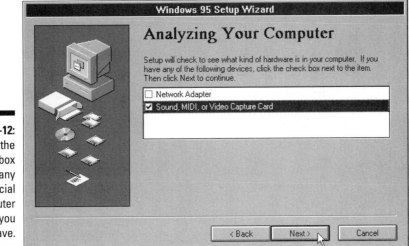

Figure 3-11:
If installing
Windows 95
from a
compact
disc, type
the CD's
special "key
number"
into the box
and click on
Next.

Figure 3-12:
Click in the
little box
next to any
special
computer
parts you
have.

After choosing your special parts, click on the Next button. Windows 95 will try to figure out what's inside your computer, a relatively time-consuming process shown in Figure 3-13.

If Windows 95 gets lost while poking around inside your computer, and the computer just sits there looking stupid for 10 or 15 minutes, reach for that off switch. (Don't try the Ctrl+Alt+Delete trick that usually works.) When you start over at Step 1, Windows 95 lets you choose its Safe Recovery process, where you both try to figure out what went wrong.

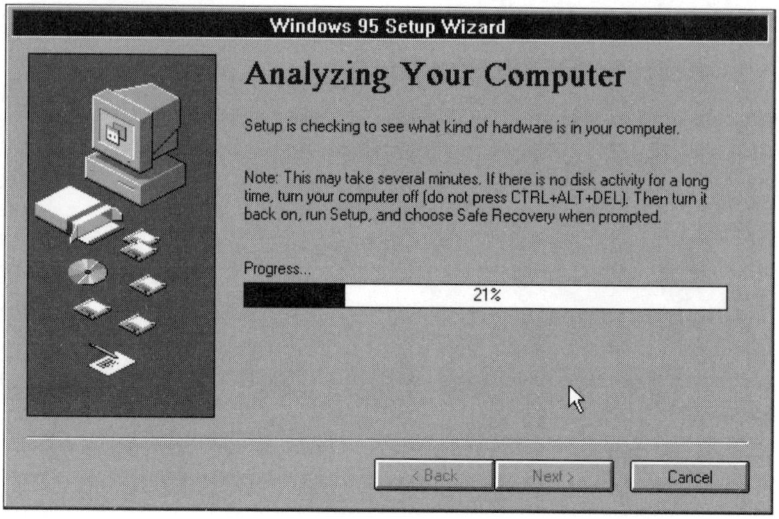

Windows 95 Setup Wizard

Analyzing Your Computer

Setup is checking to see what kind of hardware is in your computer.

Note: This may take several minutes. If there is no disk activity for a long time, turn your computer off (do not press CTRL+ALT+DEL). Then turn it back on, run Setup, and choose Safe Recovery when prompted.

Progress...

21%

< Back   Next >   Cancel

Figure 3-13: Windows 95 usually guesses correctly when trying to figure out what parts are inside your computer.

13. **Click in the appropriate boxes if you'd like Windows 95 to include The Microsoft Network, Microsoft Mail, or Microsoft Fax. Then click Next.**

Sick of the Information Superhighway yet? If not, you might want to try Microsoft's online entry: The Microsoft Network. Microsoft is starting its own online service and it wants you to drop by with your modem.

Microsoft Fax can send and receive faxes on computers that contain fax modems, and Microsoft Mail software helps people organize their electronic mail (especially if they correspond mostly on The Microsoft Network).

Not sure whether to install The Microsoft Network, Microsoft Mail, or Microsoft Fax? Then don't bother. Later on down the road, you can head to the Control Panel's Add/Remove Programs button and install the programs (when you have more time on your hands).

14. **Click on Next. Windows 95 installs the recommended components.**

Let Windows 95 install its recommended components; you can go back later and install some extra goodies, like a Windows 95 Tour that explains some of the new features in Windows 95. For now, just click on the Next button, shown in Figure 3-14, and concentrate on getting Windows 95 up and running.

15. **Click on the Next button to tell Windows 95 to create a startup disk.**

Windows 95 recommends that you create a startup disk, which lets you boot your computer when Windows 95 is giving you grief (see Figure 3-15). It's a wise precaution, so go for it. In fact, when a computer guru comes over to bail you out of a mess, he or she will be relieved to see that startup disk sitting next to the computer. You'll have a better chance of getting your computer back on its feet when talking to the technical support people if you have a startup disk handy.

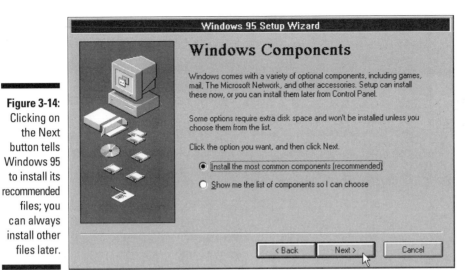

Figure 3-14:
Clicking on the Next button tells Windows 95 to install its recommended files; you can always install other files later.

Figure 3-15:
Follow Windows 95's recommendation and create a startup disk.

16. Click on Next to continue, or click on Back to review your settings.

Not sure you've clicked on all the right things so far? Now's your chance to click on the Back buttons to check your past choices. When everything looks good, click on the Next button to continue.

17. Label a disk "Windows 95 startup disk," put it in drive A, and click on OK.

You can get away with labeling the disk something else, but you won't get away with using Drive B. That drive simply doesn't work for startup disks. Click on the OK button to make the disk, as shown in Figure 3-16.

Figure 3-16:
The startup
disk needs
to go in
drive A;
drive B
won't work.

Any existing files on your floppy disk are deleted when Windows 95 makes
the startup disk. Don't use a disk with important files on it.

**18. After Windows 95 finishes making the startup disk, remove the disk and
click on OK.**

Not much explanation needed here. It's a long step, though: Windows 95
now begins copying all the right files onto your computer's hard drive.
With more than 20 disks, it's a rather ho-hum process. Feel free to watch
the screen so you won't miss Windows 95 telling you how great it is, as
shown in Figure 3-17. Yawn.

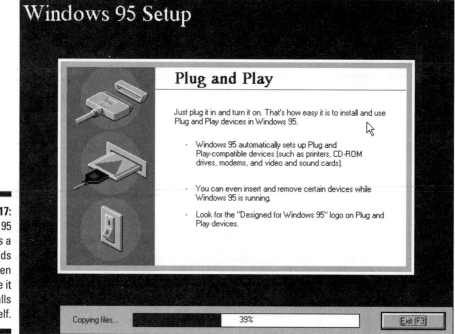

Figure 3-17:
Windows 95
flashes a
series of ads
on-screen
while it
installs
itself.

It wants to know what kind of Printer I have!

If you're installing Windows 95 over Windows 3.1, Windows 95 gets your printer information from Windows 3.1. But if you're installing Windows 95 from scratch, you'll need to enter the Printer's brand name when Windows 95 asks for it during the installation process.

When the Printer Wizard asks for the printer information, push the Page Down key and cursor keys until you've highlighted your printer's manufacturer. Press Tab and then use the Page Down key and cursor keys to highlight your printer's model.

Printer not listed? Then check your printer's manual to see what brand of printer it *emulates*, or copies. Many printers say they're compatible with Hewlett-Packard LaserJet II printers, for example, so you could choose that printer's name from the list. Then click on Next.

Choose the LPT1: option (almost all printers use that LPT1: option) and click on Next again.

Unless you want to change the printer's on-screen name, feel free to click on the Next button on the Printer Name page. See, Windows 95 lists your printer by its brand name in menus. If you're feeling generic — and have only one printer — feel free to change the printer's name to something simple, like "Printer," before clicking on Next. That's especially helpful if your printer has an exceptionally long brand name that might look weird on menus or bump into neighboring icons.

Click on Finish. Windows 95 tests your printer by sending it a sample page. If you have time, go ahead and have Windows 95 test your printer so that you can make sure that everything's set up right. If your toast is starting to burn in the kitchen, don't bother with the test page. You can always test it later.

Windows 95 will ask you to insert the appropriate disks so it can copy the right printer files to your computer, and you'll be through.

19. **Click on the Finish button.**

When Windows 95 thinks it's copied enough files onto your computer, it asks you to click on the Finish button. That tells Windows 95 to restart your computer, load Windows 95, and see whether everything works.

If Windows 95 can't even muster up the strength to restart your computer — it just sits there without making noise — wait a good ten or fifteen minutes and then turn it off. Count to 30 slowly, and then turn it back on.

Windows 95 will come back with a screen saying it's setting up for the first time. Twiddle your thumbs — it takes a while.

20. **Click on your time zone and press Enter.**

As shown in Figure 3-18, Windows 95 sometimes assumes that everybody lives in Dublin, Edinburgh, or London. If you live somewhere else, click on that spot on the on-screen map. The map will move, listing the appropriate time zone for that area. When it's listing the right time zone, press Enter or click on the Apply button, followed by the OK button.

Oh, and if you're on daylight savings time, click in the box next to "Automatically adjust clock for daylight saving changes."

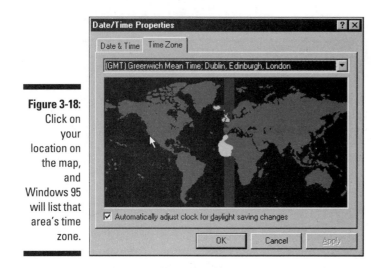

Figure 3-18:
Click on
your
location on
the map,
and
Windows 95
will list that
area's time
zone.

If you need to set your computer's date and time, click on the Date & Time tab at the top of the screen. Then click on the correct dates and times using the on-screen calendar and clock. Done? Click on the OK button at the bottom of the screen.

Windows will make some last checks to finalize settings and then leave you with the opening screen, shown in Figure 3-19.

21. **Did you tell Windows 95 to install The Microsoft Network, Microsoft Mail, or Microsoft Fax? Then follow the on-screen instructions to make Windows 95 install an "Inbox" for your online chatter.**

Microsoft Exchange puts an "Inbox" on your Windows 95 desktop, where you can send and receive electronic mail and faxes. Windows 95 can set up Microsoft Fax, Microsoft Mail, and The Microsoft Network to work with the Inbox, but if you want to use any other online services, Microsoft makes you set them up yourself.

22. **Click on the What's New button for some basic tips on getting Windows 95 to do something.**

If you've gotten this far, you've done it: You've successfully installed Windows 95.

Click on the button marked What's New for a quick look at the new goodies in Windows 95 (refer to Figure 3-19). If you have a modem, clicking on the Online Registration button lets you give Microsoft your name and address so that they can send you junk mail about new software.

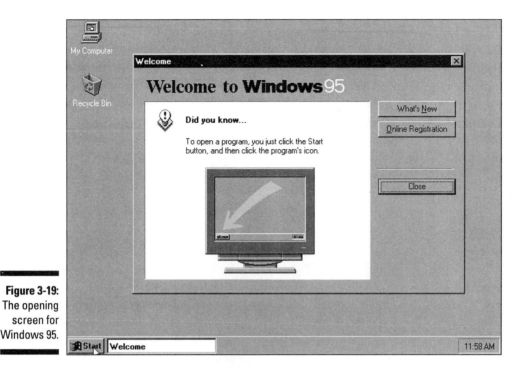

Figure 3-19:
The opening
screen for
Windows 95.

Leaving Windows 95

After you're finished with Windows 95 and ready to turn off your computer, click on the Start button, located near the lower-left corner of the screen. When the menu sprouts upward, click on the Sh<u>u</u>t Down option.

A window pops up, leaving you three options:

- ✔ **Shut down the computer:** Choose this option if you want to turn off your computer for the day and do something more constructive.

- ✔ **Restart the computer:** This option works well if Windows 95 is acting funny; it tells Windows 95 to shut down and then come back to life, hopefully in a better mood.

- ✔ **Restart the computer in <u>MS-DOS</u> mode:** Chances are you'll never have to use this option — unless you're trying to run a DOS program that just won't run when all the Windows 95 graphics are waiting in the background. (Type **exit** at the DOS prompt to make the prompt disappear and the windows reappear.)

Turning Off the Computer

If you're finished computing for the day — and you've told Windows 95 to shut down — turn off the computer. Find that switch you used to turn it on and flick it the other way. (Or, if it's a push button, give it another push.)

Never turn off the computer while Windows 95 is running. Use the Windows 95 Shut Down command, described in the preceding section, and wait until Windows 95 flashes a message on-screen saying that it's safe to turn off your computer.

The 5th Wave   By Rich Tennant

SO POORLY DOCUMENTED IS THE SOFTWARE THAT ROY IS BETA TESTING THAT HE FAILS TO NOTICE THAT THE GAME RULES TO "TWISTER" HAVE ACCIDENTALLY BEEN INCLUDED.

Chapter 4

Windows 95 Stuff Everybody Thinks You Already Know

· ·

In This Chapter

▶ Explanations of terms you need to understand in order to use Windows 95

▶ Information on where to look for more details on the topics that are introduced

· ·

*W*hen Windows first hit the market in 1985, it failed miserably. The weakling computers of the day burst their pectorals over its fancy graphics. In addition, Windows was slow and dorky looking with ugly colors.

Today's computers have Jean-Claude-Van-Damme arms: They can easily whip Windows into shape. With faster computers, perseverance, and a dozen fashionably healthy new color schemes, such as Celery, Tan, and Wheat, Windows has turned into a trendy best-seller.

But because it has been around for so long, a lot of computer geeks have had a head start. To help you catch up, this chapter is a tourist's guidebook to those Windows words the nerds have been batting around for ten years.

Backing Up a Disk

Computers store *bunches* of files on their hard drives. And that multitude of files can be a problem. When the computer's hard drive eventually dies, it takes all your files down with it. Pfffffft. Nothing left.

Computer users who don't like anguished *pfffffft* sounds *back up* their hard drives religiously. They do so in two different ways.

Some people copy all their files from the hard disk to a bunch of floppy disks. Although custom-written backup programs make this task easier, it's still a time-consuming chore. Who wants to spend half an hour backing up computer files *after* finishing work?

Other people buy a *tape backup* unit. This special computerized tape recorder either lives inside your computer like a floppy disk or plugs into the computer's rear. Either way, the gizmo tape records all the information on your hard disk. Then, when your hard disk dies, you still have all your files. The faithful tape backup unit plays back all your information onto the new hard drive. No scrounging for floppy disks.

- ✔ Windows 95 comes with Microsoft Backup, a program that automatically copies files from your hard disk to floppy disks. Unfortunately, you need to feed floppy disks to the computer until it's through copying everything. Yawn.

- ✔ The program can also copy your files to a tape backup unit, if you've finally decided to buy one.

- ✔ If your current backup program doesn't claim to be "Windows 95 compatible," don't use it. Old backup programs won't know how to back up files using the new Windows 95 file format of more than eight characters. If you try to use an old backup program with Windows 95, the backup won't be reliable.

- ✔ Windows 95 doesn't automatically install the Backup program onto your hard drive. To put it there yourself, use the Control Panel's Add/Remove Programs icon, described in Chapter 13. Once Backup has been added to your hard drive, you can load it by clicking on the Start button, clicking on Programs, then Accessories, and then System Tools; the word *backup* should be near the top of the final menu.

- ✔ The average cost of a tape backup unit runs from $150 to $400, depending on the size of your computer's hard drive. Some people back up their work every day, using a new tape for each day of the week. If they discover on Thursday that last Monday's report had key concepts, they can pop Monday's tape into the backup unit and grab the report.

Clicking

Computers make plenty of clicking sounds, but only one click counts: the one that occurs when you press a button on a mouse. You'll find yourself clicking the mouse hundreds of times in Windows 95. For example, to push the on-screen button marked Push Me, you move the mouse until the pointer rests over the Push Me button and click the mouse button.

✔ When you hear people say, "Press the button on the mouse," they leave out an important detail: *Release* the button after you press it. Press the button with your index finger and release it, just as you press a button on a touch-tone phone.

✔ Most mice have 2 buttons; some have 3, and some esoteric models for traffic engineers have more than 32. Windows 95 listens mostly to clicks coming from the button on the *left* side of your mouse. It's the one under your index finger if you're right-handed (or if you're left-handed and lucky enough to find a left-handed mouse). Refer to Chapter 10 for more mouse button tricks.

✔ Windows 95 listens to clicks coming from both the left *and* the right buttons on your mouse. Windows 3.1 listens only to clicks coming from the button on the *left* side of your mouse.

✔ Like Windows 95, most Windows 95 applications also listen to clicks coming from the *right* button as well as from the *left* button.

✔ Don't confuse a *click* with a *double-click*. For more rodent details, see "The Mouse," "Double-Clicking," and "Pointers/Arrows," later in this chapter. The insatiably curious can find even more mouse stuff in Chapter 2.

The Command Line

The *command line* is a macho place where you can type stern code words to boss the computer around. The most famous command line comes with DOS, and it looks like this:

```
C:\> MYPROGRAM
```

When you type a program's name at the command line, DOS rummages around, looking for that program. If DOS succeeds, it loads the program and brings it to the screen for your working pleasure. If it doesn't find it, it burps back with the following bit of ugliness:

```
Bad command or file name
```

✔ The most common reason DOS burps back is because you've spelled the file's name wrong. It's more critical than an English teacher with a hair bun. You must be exact.

✔ Don't confuse the command line with the DOS prompt, although the two usually go hand in hand. The *command line* is the information you type next to the DOS prompt. The *DOS prompt* is the thing you'll find described if you move your eyes to the section "The DOS Prompt."

✔ For the most part, Windows 95 replaces typing stuff at the command line with a more pleasant way of computing: pressing buttons or clicking on pictures. You'll find a command line hidden in the Start button's menu, however, if you want to boss your computer around that way. Just click on the <u>R</u>un button. For more information, see "Graphical User Interfaces."

The Cursor

Typewriters have a little mechanical arm that strikes the page, creating the desired letter. Computers don't have little mechanical arms (except in science fiction movies), so they have *cursors:* little blinking lines that show where that next letter will appear in the text.

✔ Cursors appear only when Windows 95 is ready for you to type text, numbers, or symbols — usually when you write letters or reports.

✔ The cursor and the mouse pointer are different things that perform different tasks. When you start typing, text appears at the cursor's location, not at the pointer's location.

✔ You can move the cursor to a new place in the document by using the keyboard's *cursor-control keys* (the keys with little arrows). You also can point to a spot with the mouse pointer and click the button. The cursor leaps to that new spot.

You can distinguish between the cursor and the mouse pointer with one look: Cursors always blink steadily; mouse pointers never do.

For more information, check out "Pointers/Arrows" in this chapter or Table 2-3 in Chapter 2.

Defaults (and the Any Key)

Finally, a computer term that can be safely ignored. Clap your hands and square dance with a neighbor! Here's the lowdown on the, er, hoedown: Some programs present a terse list of inexplicable choices and casually suggest that you choose the only option that's not listed: the *default option.*

Don't chew your tongue in despair. Just press Enter.

Those wily programmers have predetermined what option works best for 99 percent of the people using the program. So, if people just press Enter, the program automatically makes the right choice and moves on to the next complicated question.

- ✔ The default option is similar to the oft-mentioned *Any key* because neither of them appears on your keyboard (or on anybody else's, either — no matter how much money they paid).

- ✔ *Default* can also be taken to mean *standard option* or *what to select when you're completely stumped.* For example, "Strangers riding together in elevators will stare at their shoes by default."

- ✔ When a program says to press any key, simply press the spacebar. (The Shift keys don't do the trick, by the way.)

Desktop (and Wallpapering It)

To keep from reverting to revolting computer terms, Windows 95 uses familiar office lingo. For example, all the action in Windows 95 takes place on the Windows 95 desktop. The *desktop* is the background area of the screen where all the windows pile up.

Windows 95 comes with a drab green desktop. To jazz things up, you can cover the desktop with pictures, or *wallpaper.* Windows 95 comes with several pictures you can use for wallpaper (and Chapter 10 can help you hang it up).

You can customize the wallpaper to fit your own personality: pictures of little kittens, for example, or eggbeaters. You can draw your own wallpaper with the built-in Windows 95 Paint program. Paint saves your work in the required wallpaper format: a special *bitmap* file ending in the letters BMP.

Directories

In your everyday paper world, files are stored in folders in a cabinet. In the computer world, files are stored in a *directory* on a disk. Dusty old file cabinets are boring, but directories are even more dreadfully boring: They'll *never* hold any forgotten baseball cards.

So Windows 95 swapped metaphors. Instead of holding files in directories, Windows 95 holds files in folders. You can see the little pictures of the folders on your monitor.

The folders in Windows 95 are *really* just directories, if you've already grown used to working with directories.

Maintaining files and working with folders can be painful experiences, so they're explained in Chapter 12. In the meantime, just think of folders and directories as separate work areas to keep files organized. Different directories and folders hold different projects; you move from directory to directory as you work on different things with your computer.

- ✔ A file cabinet's Vegetables folder can have an Asparagus folder nested inside for organizing material further.
- ✔ Technically, a folder in a folder is a nested *subdirectory* that keeps related files from getting lost. For example, you can have folders for Steamed Asparagus and Raw Asparagus in the Asparagus folder, which lives in the Vegetable folder.

The DOS Prompt

Some people haven't switched to the newer, Windows breed of programs. They're still using the programs they bought several years ago, back when it was trendy to use a DOS program. Luckily, Windows 95 cannot only run DOS programs, but it can provide a DOS prompt for the needy. Click on the Start button, click on the word <u>P</u>rograms, and click on MS-DOS Prompt from the menu.

The DOS prompt rhymes with *the boss chomped,* and it's a symbol that looks somewhat like this:

```
C:\>
```

Type the name of your program at the DOS prompt, press Enter, and the program will begin.

If you've been rudely dumped at the DOS prompt, you can scoot quickly to Windows 95 by typing the following no-nonsense word:

```
C:\> EXIT
```

That is, you type **EXIT** (lowercase works too) and follow it with a press of the Enter key.

To appease the DOS hounds, Windows 95 waits in the background while you run a DOS session.

Double-Clicking

Windows 95 places a great significance on something pretty simple: pressing a button on the mouse and releasing it. Pressing and releasing the button once is known as a *click*. Pressing and releasing the button twice in rapid succession is a *double-click*.

Windows 95 watches carefully to see whether you've clicked or double-clicked on its more sensitive parts. The two actions are completely different.

   ✔ A click and a double-click mean two different things to Windows programs. They're not the same.

   ✔ A double-click can take some practice to master, even if you have fingers. If you click too slowly, Windows 95 thinks you're clicking twice — not double-clicking. Try clicking a little faster next time, and Windows 95 will probably catch on.

   ✔ Can't click fast enough for Windows 95 to tell the difference between a mere click and a rapid-fire double-click? Then grab the office computer guru and say that you need to have your Control Panel called up and your clicks fixed. If the guru is at the computer store, tiptoe to the section on tinkering with the Control Panel in Chapter 10.

Dragging and Dropping

Although the term *drag and drop* sounds as if it's straight out of a hitman's handbook, it's really a nonviolent mouse trick in Windows 95. Dragging and dropping is a way of moving something — say, a picture of an egg — from one part of your screen to another.

To *drag*, put the mouse pointer over the egg and *hold down* the mouse button. As you move the mouse across your desk, the pointer drags the egg across the screen. Put the pointer/egg where you want it and release the mouse button. The egg *drops*, uncracked. (If you held down the *right* mouse button while dragging, Windows 95 will toss a little menu in your face, asking if you're sure you want to move that egg across the screen.)

For more mouse fun, see "Clicking," "Double-Clicking," "The Mouse," "Pointers/ Arrows," and, if you're not yet weak at the knees, the information on the parts of your computer in Chapter 2.

Drivers

Although Windows 95 does plenty of work, it hires help when necessary. When Windows 95 needs to talk to unfamiliar parts of your computer, it lets special *drivers* do the translation. A driver is a piece of software that enables Windows 95 to communicate with parts of your computer.

Hundreds of computer companies sell computer attachables, from printers to sound cards to sprinkler systems. Microsoft requires these companies to write drivers for their products so that Windows 95 knows the polite way to address them.

  ✔ Sometimes computer nerds say that your *mouse driver* is all messed up. They're not talking about your hand, even though your hand is what steers the mouse. They're talking about the piece of software that helps Windows 95 talk and listen to the mouse.

  ✔ New versions of Windows 95 often require new drivers. If you send a begging letter to the company that made your mouse, the company may mail you a new, updated driver on a floppy disk. Occasionally, you can get these new drivers directly from Microsoft or from the wild-haired teenager who sold you your computer. Find a computer guru to install the driver, however, or check out the section on installing drivers in Chapter 17.

Files

A *file* is a collection of information in a form that the computer can play with. A *program file* contains instructions telling the computer to do something useful, like adding up the number of quarters the kids spent on Sweet Tarts last month. A *data file* contains information you've created, like a picture of a steak knife you drew in the Windows 95 Paint program.

  ✔ Files can't be touched or handled; they're invisible, unearthly things. Somebody figured out how to store files as little magnetic impulses on a round piece of specially coated plastic, or *disk.*

  ✔ A file is referred to by its *filename.* DOS makes people call files by a single word containing no more than eight characters. For example, FILENAME could be the name of a file, as could REPORT, SPONGE, or X. Yes, it's difficult to think up descriptive filenames in DOS.

  ✔ It's so difficult that Windows 95 finally broke the barrier: It lets you call files by bunches of words, as long as they don't total more than 255 characters.

✔ Filenames have optional *extensions* of up to three letters that usually refer to the program that created them. For example, the Windows 95 Paint program automatically saves files with the extension BMP. Microsoft realized that most people don't care about file extensions, so Windows 95 no longer lists a file's extension when it's displaying filenames. Windows 3.1, however, does list file extensions when loading or saving files.

✔ Filenames still have more rules and regulations than the Jacuzzi at the condo's clubhouse.

✔ For more information than you'll ever want to know about filenames, flip to Chapter 12.

Graphical User Interfaces

The way people communicate with computers is called an *interface.* For example, the *Enterprise*'s computer used a *verbal interface.* Captain Kirk just told it what to do.

DOS uses a *command line interface.* People type *commands* into the computer, and the computer either digests them or tosses them back in confusion.

Windows 95 uses a *graphical user interface.* People talk to the computer through *graphical symbols,* or pictures. A graphical user interface works kind of like Travel Kiosks at airports — you select some little button symbols right on the screen to find out which hotels offer free airport shuttles.

✔ A graphical user interface is called a *GUI,* pronounced *gooey,* as in *Huey, Dewey, Louie,* and *GUI.*

✔ Despite what you read in Microsoft's full-page ads, Windows 95 isn't the only GUI for a personal computer. OS/2 Warp and Tandy's Deskmate are both GUIs (pronounced *gooeys,* as in *Those are Huey's GUIs*).

✔ The little graphical symbols or buttons in a graphical user interface are called *icons.*

✔ Sooner or later, computers will be capable of speaking to us. A few of today's more expensive computers can actually speak a few words, but even they stumble when asked to comment on the sacrifice of Isaac in Kierkegaard's *Fear and Trembling.*

Hardware and Software

Alert! Alert! Fasten your seat belt so you don't slump forward when reading about these two particularly boring terms: hardware and software.

Your CD player is *hardware;* so are the stereo amplifier, speakers, and batteries in the boom box. By itself, the CD player doesn't do anything but hum. It needs music to disturb the neighbors. The music is the *software,* or the information processed by the CD player.

- Now you can unfasten your seat belt and relax for a bit. Computer *hardware* refers to anything you can touch, including hard things like a printer, a monitor, disks, and disk drives.

- *Software* is the ethereal stuff that makes the hardware do something fun. A piece of software is called a *program.* Programs come on disks (or CDs, too, if you've anted up for the latest computer gear).

- Software has very little to do with lingerie.

- When somber technical nerds (STNs) say, "It must be a hardware problem," they mean that something must be wrong with your computer itself: its disk drive, keyboard, or central processing unit (CPU). When they say, "It must be a software problem," they mean that something is wrong with the program you're trying to run from the disk.

Here's how to earn points with your computer gurus: When they ask you the riddle, "How many programmers does it take to change a light bulb?" pretend that you don't know this answer: "None; that's a hardware problem."

Icons

An *icon* is a little picture. Windows 95 fills the screen with little pictures, or icons. You choose among them to make Windows 95 do different things. For example, you'd choose the Printer icon, the little picture of the printer, to make your computer print something. Icons are just fancy names for cute buttons.

- Windows 95 relies on icons for nearly everything, from opening files to releasing the winged monkeys.

- Some icons have explanatory titles, like Open File or Terrorize Dorothy. Others make you guess that the Little Juggling Man icon opens the network mail system.

- For more icon stuff, see "Graphical User Interfaces" earlier in this chapter.

Kilobytes, Megabytes, and So On

Figuring out the size of a real file folder is easy: Just look at the thickness of the papers stuffed in and around it. But computer files are invisible, so their size is measured in bytes (which is pronounced like what Dracula does).

A *byte* is pretty much like a character or letter in a word. For example, the word *sodium-free* contains 11 bytes. (The hyphen counts as a byte.) Computer nerds picked up the metric system a lot more quickly than the rest of us, so bytes are measured in kilos (1,000), megas (1,000,000), and gigas (way huge).

A page of double-spaced text is about 1,000 bytes, known as 1 kilobyte, which is often abbreviated as 1K. One thousand of those kilobytes is a megabyte, or 1MB. Your computer's hard drive is full of bytes; most hard drives today contain between 80MB and 500MB.

✔ Depending on how much money you paid, your floppy disks can hold from 360 kilobytes to 2.8 megabytes (2,800 kilobytes).

✔ All files are measured in bytes, regardless of whether they contain text. For example, that leafy background art some people put on their Windows 95 desktop takes up 15,118 bytes. (For information on changing to a leafy desktop, see Chapter 10.)

✔ The Windows 95 Explorer or My Computer windows can tell you how many bytes each of your files consumes. To find out more, check out the information on the Explorer in Chapter 12. (Or click on the file's name with your right mouse button, and choose Properties from the menu that pops up.)

One kilobyte doesn't *really* equal 1,000 bytes. That would be too easy. Instead, this byte stuff is based on the number two. One kilobyte is really 1,024 bytes, which is 2 raised to the 10th power, or 2^{10}. (Computers love mathematical details, especially when there's a 2 involved.) For more byte-size information, see Table 4-1.

Table 4-1	Ultra-Precise Details from the Slide-Rule Crowd		
Term	*Abbreviation*	*Rough Size*	*Ultra-Precise Size*
Byte		1 byte	1 byte
Kilobyte	K or KB	1,000 bytes	1,024 bytes
Megabyte	M or MB	1,000,000 bytes	1,048,576 bytes
Gigabyte	G or GB	1,000,000,000 bytes	1,073,741,824 bytes

Loading, Running, Executing, and Launching

Files are yanked from a file cabinet and placed onto a desk for easy reference. On a computer, files are *loaded* from a disk and placed into the computer's memory so you can do important stuff with them. You can't work with a file or program until it has been loaded into the computer's memory.

When you *run, execute,* or *launch* a program, you're merely starting it up so you can use it. *Load* means pretty much the same thing, but some people fine-tune its meaning to describe when a program file brings in a data file.

> ✔ The Windows 95 Start button enables picture lovers to start programs by using icons. The Windows 95 Explorer enables text-and-word lovers to start programs by clicking on their names in a list (although Explorer lets you click on icons too, if you prefer).
>
> ✔ If you're feeling particularly bold, you can load programs by using the command line hidden in the Start button as well. For the full dirt, check out the information on the Start button in Chapter 11 and the information on the Explorer in Chapter 12.

Memory

Whoa! How did this ugly memory stuff creep in here? Luckily, it all boils down to one key sentence:

The more memory a computer has, the more pleasantly Windows 95 behaves.

> ✔ Memory is measured in bytes, just like a file. Most computers have at least 640 kilobytes, or 640K, of memory.
>
> ✔ Windows 95 requires 386-class computers to have at least 4 megabytes, or 4MB, of memory or it won't even bother to come out of the box.

Memory and hard disk space are both measured in bytes, but they're two different things: *Memory* is what the computer uses for quick, on-the-fly calculations when programs are up and running on-screen. *Hard disk space* is what the computer uses to store unused files and programs.

Everybody's computer contains more hard disk space than memory because hard disks — also known as *hard drives* — are a great deal cheaper. Also, a hard disk remembers things even when the computer is turned off. A computer's memory, on the other hand, is washed completely clean whenever someone turns it off or pokes its reset button.

The Mouse

A *mouse* is a smooth little plastic thing that looks like Soap on a Rope. It rests on a little roller, or *ball,* and its tail plugs into the back of the PC. When you push the mouse across your desk, the mouse sends its current location through its tail to the PC. By moving the mouse around on the desk, you move a corresponding arrow across the screen.

You can wiggle the mouse in circles and watch the arrow make spirals. Or, to be practical, you can maneuver the on-screen arrow over an on-screen button and click the mouse button to boss Windows 95 around. (Refer to "Clicking," "Double-Clicking," and "Pointers/Arrows," and, if you haven't run out of steam, turn to Chapter 2 for information on the parts of your computer.)

Multitasking and Task Switching

Windows 95 can run two or more programs at the same time, but computer nerds take overly tedious steps to describe the process. So skip this section because you'll never need to know it.

Even though the words *task switching* and *multitasking* often have an exclamation point in computer ads, there's nothing really exciting about them.

When you run two programs, yet switch back and forth between them, you're *task switching.* For example, if Jeff calls while you're reading a book, you put down the book and talk to Jeff. You are task switching: stopping one task and starting another. The process is similar to running your word processor and then stopping to look up a phone number in the handy Windows 95 Cardfile.

But when you run two programs simultaneously, you're *multitasking.* For example, if you continue reading your book while listening to Jeff talk about the Natural History Museum's new Grecian urns, you're multitasking: performing two tasks at the same time. In Windows 95, multitasking can be playing its solitaire game while you print something in the background.

These two concepts differ only subtly, and yet computer nerds make a big deal out of the difference. Everybody else shrugs and says, "So what?"

Networks

Networks connect PCs with cables so that employees can share equipment and information. Employees can all send stuff to one printer, for example, or they can send messages back and forth talking about Jane's new hairstyle.

Just be glad that you, as a Windows 95 beginner, are safely absolved from knowing anything about networks. Leave network stuff to that poor person in charge.

Pointers/Arrows

This one sounds easy at first. When you roll the mouse around on your desk, you see a little arrow move around on-screen. That arrow is your *pointer,* and it is also called an *arrow.* (Almost everything in Windows 95 has two names.)

The pointer serves as your *electronic index finger.* Instead of pushing an on-screen button with your finger, you move the pointer over that button and click the left button on the mouse.

So what's the hard part? Well, that pointer doesn't always stay an arrow. Depending on where the pointer is located on the Windows 95 screen, it can turn into a straight line, a two-headed arrow, a four-sided arrow, a little pillar, or a zillion other things. Each of the symbols makes the mouse do something slightly different. Luckily, you'll find these and other arrowheads covered in Chapter 2.

Plug and Play

Historically, installing new hardware devices has required substantial technical expertise to configure and load hardware and software. Basically, that means only geeks could figure out how to fix their computers and add new gadgets to them.

So a bunch of computer vendors hunched together around a table and came up with *Plug and Play* — a way for Windows 95 to set up new gadgets for your computer automatically, with little or no human intervention. You plug in your latest gadget and Windows 95 "interviews" it, checking to see what special settings it needs. Then Windows 95 automatically flips the right switches.

Because Windows 95 keeps track of which switches are flipped, none of the parts argue over who got the best settings. Better yet, users don't have to do anything but plug the darn thing into their computers and flip the On switch.

- ✔ Of course, it couldn't be *that* simple. Only gadgets that say "Plug and Play" on the box allow for this automatic switch flipping. With the others, you'll probably have to flip the switches yourself. But at least they'll still work.

- ✔ Plug-and-play laptops can work well with "docking stations." For example, when you plug the laptop into the docking station, Windows 95 automatically detects the new monitor, keyboard, mouse, sound card, and whatever other goodies the owner could afford. Then Windows 95 automatically sets itself up to use those new goodies — without the owner having to fiddle with the settings.

- ✔ Some people call Plug and Play "PNP."

- ✔ Other, more skeptical, people refer to Plug and Play as "Plug and Pray." (It's still rather new technology.)

Programs/Applications

Most people call a computer program a *program*. In Windows, programs are called *applications*.

- ✔ I dunno why.

- ✔ Those free programs that came with Windows (HyperTerminal, WordPad, Phone Dialer, and so on) aren't called programs or applications. They're called *Windows applets*.

- ✔ For the record, DOS programs are *programs*. Windows programs are *applications*. And the programs that came with Windows are *applets*.

- ✔ This book uses the terms *program* and *application* interchangeably. And it hardly uses the name *applet* at all because it sounds so funny.

Quitting or Exiting

When you're ready to throw in the computing towel and head for greener pastures, you need to stop, or quit, any programs you've been using. The terms *quit* and *exit* mean pretty much the same thing: making the current program on-screen stop running so you can go away and do something a little more rewarding.

Luckily, exiting Windows 95 programs is fairly easy because all of them are supposed to use the same special exit command. You simply click on the little X in the upper-right corner of the program's window. Or, if you prefer using the keyboard, you hold down the Alt key (either one of them, if you have two) and press the key labeled F4. (The F4 key is a *function key;* function keys are either in one row along the top of your keyboard or in two rows along its leftmost edge.)

Don't quit a program by just flicking off your computer's power switch. Doing so can foul up your computer's innards. Instead, you must leave the program responsibly so that it has time to perform its housekeeping chores before it shuts down.

✔ When you press Alt+F4 or click on the little X in the upper-right corner, the program asks whether you want to save any changes you've made to the file. Normally, you click on the button that says something like "<u>Y</u>es, by all means save the work I've spent the last three hours trying to create." (If you've muffed things up horribly, click on the <u>N</u>o button. Windows 95 disregards any work you've done and lets you start over from scratch.)

✔ If by some broad stretch of your fingers you press Alt+F4 by accident, click on the button that says Cancel, and the program pretends that you never tried to leave it. You can continue as if nothing happened.

✔ The Alt+F4 trick doesn't work for a DOS program — even if it's running in its own window. You must exit the DOS program by using its own exit keys. Complicated? Well, yes. That's why people are switching to Windows.

✔ Windows 3.1 programs have a square button in their uppermost left corner that looks like an aerial view of a single-slot toaster. Double-clicking on that toaster exits the program. Windows 95 still lets you close most Windows programs by either double-clicking in their uppermost left corner (although the programs don't have that toaster anymore). However, it's usually easier to single-click on the X in the program's uppermost *right* corner. But either action tells the program that you want to close it down.

✔ Save your work before exiting a program or turning off your computer. Computers aren't smart enough to save it automatically.

<u>S</u>ave Command

Save means to send the work you've just created on your computer to a disk for safekeeping. Unless you specifically save your work, your computer thinks you've just been fiddling around for the past four hours. You need to specifically tell the computer to save your work before it will safely store the work on a disk.

Thanks to Microsoft's snapping leather whips, all Windows 95 programs use the same <u>S</u>ave command, no matter what company wrote them. Press and release the Alt, F, and S keys in any Windows 95 program, and the computer saves your work.

If you're saving something for the first time, Windows 95 asks you to think up a filename for the work and pick a folder (which is really a directory) to stuff the new file into. Luckily, this stuff's covered in Chapter 5 in the section, "Saving Your Work."

- ✔ You can save files to a hard disk or a floppy disk.

- ✔ If you prefer using the mouse to save files, click on the word <u>F</u>ile from the row of words along the top of the program. When a menu drops down, click on the word <u>S</u>ave.

- ✔ Choose descriptive filenames for your work. Windows 95 gives you 255 characters to work with, so a file named "June Report on Squeegee Sales" will be easier to relocate than one named "Stuff."

- ✔ Some programs, like Microsoft's Word for Windows, have an *autosave* feature that automatically saves your work every five minutes or so.

Save <u>A</u>s Command

Huh? Save as *what?* A chemical compound? Naw, the Save <u>A</u>s command just gives you a chance to save your work with a different name and in a different location.

Suppose that you open the OHGOLLY.TXT file in your STUFF directory and change a few sentences around. You want to save the changes, but you don't want to lose the original stuff. So you select Save <u>A</u>s and type in the new name, OHGOLLY2.TXT.

- ✔ The Save <u>A</u>s command is identical to the <u>S</u>ave command when you're first trying to save something new: You can choose a fresh name and location for your work.

- ✔ Female armadillos have exactly four babies at a time, and they're always the same sex.

Shortcuts

The shortcut concept is familiar to most people: Why bother walking around the block to get to school, when a shortcut through Mr. McGurdy's backyard can get you there twice as fast?

It's the same with Windows 95. Instead of wading through a bunch of menus to get somewhere, you can create a shortcut and assign it to an icon. Then, when you double-click on the Shortcut icon, Windows 95 immediately takes you there and loads the file.

You can create a shortcut to your word processor, for example, and leave the shortcut icon sitting on your desktop within easy reach. A *shortcut* is simply a push button that loads a file or program. You can even make shortcuts for accessing your printer or a popular folder.

- ✔ The ever-helpful Start button automatically makes a shortcut to the last 15 documents you've opened. Click on the Start button, click on the word Documents, and you'll see shortcuts waiting for you to discover them.

- ✔ Unfortunately, the Start button only keeps track of the last 15 documents you've opened. If you're looking for the *16th* one, you won't find a shortcut waiting. Also, not all programs tell the Start button about recently opened documents; the shortcuts then don't appear on the list. (It's not your fault, if that makes you feel better.)

- ✔ A shortcut in Windows 95 is the same thing that an icon used to be in Windows 3.1 Program Manager: a push button that starts a program. If you delete a shortcut, you haven't deleted the program; you've just removed a button that started that program.

Temp Files

Like children who don't put away the peanut butter jar, Windows 95 also leaves things lying around. They're called *temp files* — secret files Windows 95 creates to store stuff in while it's running. Windows 95 normally deletes them automatically when you leave the program. It occasionally forgets, however, and leaves them cluttering up your hard drive. Stern lectures leave very little impression.

- ✔ Temp files usually (but not always) end with the letters TMP. Common temp filenames include ~DOC0D37.TMP, ~WRI3F0E.TMP, the occasional stray ~$DIBLCA.ASD, and similar looking files that start with the wavy ~ thing. (Some people call it a *tilde.*)

✔ If you exit Windows 95 the naughty way — by just flicking the computer's off switch — Windows 95 won't have a chance to clean up its temp file mess. If you keep doing it, you'll eventually see hundreds of TMP files lying around your hard drive. Be sure to exit Windows 95 the Good Bear way: by clicking the Start button and choosing S̲hut down from the menu that pops up.

The Windows

DOS programs completely fill your screen; only one fits on-screen at one time. Windows 95, however, enables you to run several programs at the same time by placing them in *windows*. A window is just a little box.

You can move the boxes around. You can make them bigger or smaller. You can make them fill your entire screen. You can make them turn into little icons at the bottom of your screen. You can spend hours playing with windows. In fact, most frustrated new Windows 95 users do.

✔ You can put as many windows on-screen as you want, peeping at all of them at the same time or just looking into each one individually. This activity appeals to the voyeur in all of us.

✔ For instructions on how to retrieve a lost window from the pile, head immediately to Chapter 8.

✔ When a DOS program runs *as a window* in Windows 95, it won't fill the whole screen. Windows 95 shrinks it a little so you can see other windows sitting around it.

Part II
Making Windows 95 Do Something

The 5th Wave   By Rich Tennant

GLOVES

And, of course, we have a version for Windows.

In this part . . .

Windows 95 is more fun than a plastic snap-together stegosaurus from the bottom of a Cracker Jack box. It's especially fun to show friends the built-in screen savers, like the one that straps you into a starship and cruises toward the fifth quadrant's snack shop at warp speed. You can even adjust the ship's speed by using the Control Panel.

Unfortunately, some spoil-sport friend will eventually mutter the words that bring everything back to Earth: "Let's see Windows 95 do something useful, like balance a checkbook or teach the kids to rinse off their plates and put them in the dishwasher."

Toss this eminently practical part at them to quiet 'em down.

Chapter 5

Starting Windows 95

• •

In This Chapter

▶ Revvin' up Windows 95

▶ Starting a program

▶ Finding the secret pull-down menus

▶ Loading a file

▶ Putting two programs on the screen

▶ Using the keyboard

▶ Printing your work

▶ Saving your work

▶ Quitting Windows 95

• •

*H*old on to your hat! Then try to type at the same time. No, let the hat fly by the wayside because this is a hands-on Windows 95 chapter that demonstrates some dazzling special effects. First, you make Windows 95 leap to your screen, ready to load a program!

Then, at the click of the mouse, you launch a second program, running at the same time as the first! Plus, you learn secret magic tricks to bypass the mouse and use the keyboard instead!

Finally, you learn how to print your work so you'll have some hard copy to show those doubting friends of yours.

Oh, and you learn to save your work so you can find it again the next day. So warm up those fingers, shake out your sleeves, and get ready for action. . . .

Revvin' Up Windows 95

If your PC came with Windows 95 already installed, Windows 95 probably leaps to your screen automatically when you first turn on the computer. If not, perhaps some evil soul left you at a DOS prompt. Try opening the cage door manually by typing the following command at the `C:\>` prompt:

```
C:\> EXIT
```

That is, you type **EXIT** (lowercase works, too) and follow it with a deft press of the Enter key.

If Windows 95 has been installed on your computer, a chore described in Chapter 3, it will pop up on the screen, and its Start button will be ready for action. Windows 95 is like an elevator that moves around your computer, and the Start button is like a panel of elevator buttons. By pushing the Start button, you tell Windows 95 where to go and what to do.

✔ When you start Windows 95, you might hear a triumphant *Ta-Da!* sound coming from the computer's sound card. If you don't have a sound card, you don't hear anything but a strong inner urge driving you toward the computer store's sound-card aisles. (Sound cards range in price from $75 to $250.)

✔ Because Big Business doesn't want to hear cool Ta-Da sounds coming from employees' computers, Windows 95 doesn't automatically turn on its sound options when first installed. You might have to activate the sounds yourself by choosing the Sounds icon from the Control Panel and choosing a new sound Scheme, a not-too-laborious process described in Chapter 10.

✔ If you're still using Windows 3.1, try starting it up by typing the word **WIN** at the DOS prompt. Microsoft chose the program name WIN because it's such an eager, positive-sounding command, like something from a best-selling *You Can Be a Success Despite Your Chin* paperback.

Starting your favorite program

When Windows 95 first takes over your computer, it turns your screen into a desktop. However, the desktop is merely a fancy name for a plate of buttons with labels underneath them. Click on a button, and programs hop to the screen in their own little windows. Click on the Start button in the bottom, left-hand corner of the screen, and you'll have even more buttons to choose from, as seen in Figure 5-1.

Figure 5-1:
The Start
button in
Windows 95
hides
dozens of
menus for
starting
programs.

Because the buttons have little pictures on them, they're called *icons.* (No relation to the icons favored by the Byzantine emperors in the eighth and ninth centuries A.D. They still used DOS back then.)

Icons offer clues to the program they represent. For example, the icon of the Inbox with mail stands for Microsoft Exchange, a program that lets people send and receive mail on their computers.

See the dark bar shading the Windows Explorer icon's title in Figure 5-1? The bar means that the Windows Explorer program is *highlighted:* It's queued up and ready to go. If you press the Enter key while the Windows Explorer is highlighted, Explorer hops to the forefront. (Don't press Enter, though, because Explorer is too boring to play with right now.)

Look at the little arrow sitting by itself in the corner of your screen. Roll your mouse around until that arrow hovers over the button that says Start.

Click your mouse button, and the Start menu pops up on the screen, as seen in Figure 5-2. Next, click on the Programs button, and another menu full of buttons shoots out, as seen in Figure 5-3. Click on Accessories to see yet another menu, seen in Figure 5-4. Click on Games to see the last menu on the chain. And, if you're not too exhausted, click on FreeCell to check out Windows 95's great solitaire game.

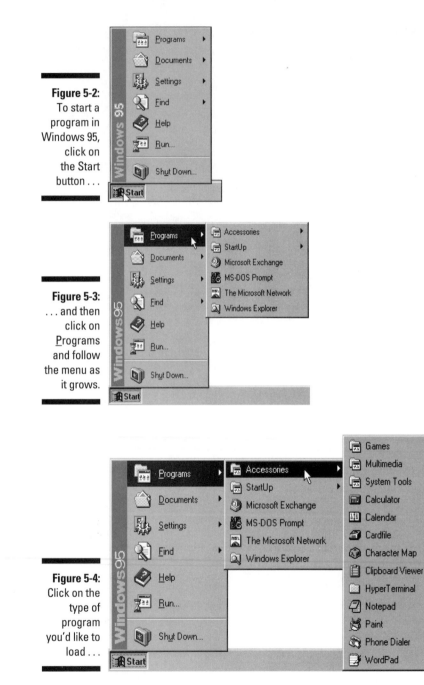

Figure 5-2:
To start a program in Windows 95, click on the Start button . . .

Figure 5-3:
. . . and then click on Programs and follow the menu as it grows.

Figure 5-4:
Click on the type of program you'd like to load . . .

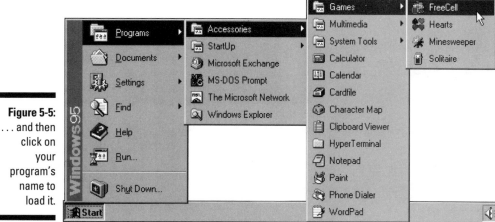

Figure 5-5:
... and then
click on
your
program's
name to
load it.

✔ The Start button is just a big panel of buttons. When you press one of the buttons by pointing at it and clicking with the mouse, the program as-signed to that button heads for the top of the screen and appears in a little window.

✔ You don't have to click your way through all those buttons hiding beneath the Start button. Click on the Start button and then just hover your mouse pointer over the other menu areas you'd like to have opened up. Windows 95 opens them without even waiting for your clicks.

✔ Icons can stand for files as well as for programs. Clicking on the Docu-ments button usually brings up shortcut buttons that take you to 15 of your most recently used documents.

✔ Microsoft has already set up the Start button to include icons for the most popular programs and files Windows 95 found as it installed itself on your computer — stuff like 1-2-3 and WordPerfect. If you want to add some other programs and files, however, check out the section in Chapter 11 on customizing your Start button.

✔ If you're kind of sketchy about all this *double-click* stuff, head back to the section in Chapter 2 on your mouse and that double-click stuff.

✔ Despise mice? You don't need a mouse for the Start button. Hold down the Ctrl key and press the Esc key to make the Start menu appear. Then push your arrow keys to navigate the various menus. Highlighted the program you want? Push Enter, and the program begins to run.

✔ If the icon you're after in the Start menu has a little black bar around its name, then it's *highlighted.* If you just press the Enter key, the highlighted program will load itself into a little window. Or you can still double-click on it to load it. Windows 95 lets you do things in a bunch of different ways.

> ✔ This chapter gives you just a quick tour of Windows 95. You can find glowing descriptions of the Start button in Chapter 11.

Pull-Down Menus

Windows 95, bless its heart, makes an honest effort toward making computing easier. For example, the Start button puts a bunch of options on the screen in front of you. You just choose the one you want, and Windows 95 takes it from there.

But if Windows 95 put all its options on the screen at the same time, it would look more crowded than a 14-page menu at the House of Hui restaurant. To avoid resorting to fine print, Windows 95 hides some menus in special locations on the screen. When you click the mouse in the right place, more options leap toward you, like Sparky, the friendly Dalmatian.

For example, load Windows word processing program, WordPad, by clicking on the Start button and clicking on WordPad from the Accessories menu (which is hiding in the Programs menu, by the way).

See the row of words beginning with File that rests along the top edge of WordPad? You'll find a row of words across the top of just about every Windows 95 program. Move your mouse pointer over the word File and click.

A menu opens from beneath File. This menu is called a *pull-down menu,* if you're interested, and it looks like what you see in Figure 5-6.

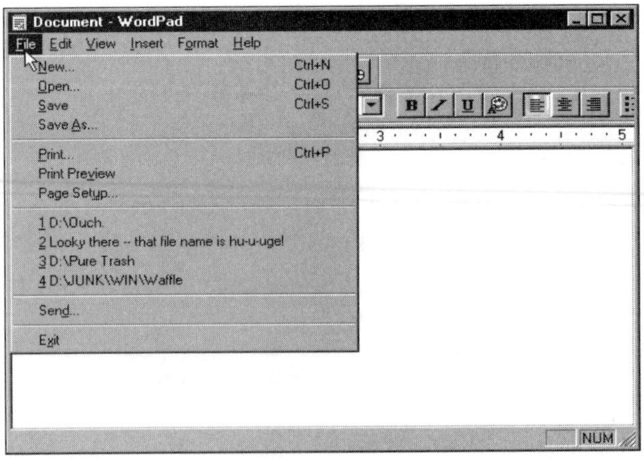

Figure 5-6:
Click on a word along the top of any window to reveal a secret pull-down menu.

> ✔ Pull-down menus open from any of those key words along the top of a window. Just click the mouse on the word, and the menu tumbles down like shoeboxes falling off a closet shelf.

✔ To close the menu, go back up and click the mouse again, but click it someplace away from the menu.

✔ Different Windows 95 programs have different words across the menu bar, but almost all of the bars begin with the word File. The File pull-down menu contains file-related options, like Open, Save, Print, and Push Back Cuticles.

✔ You'll find pull-down menus sprinkled liberally throughout Windows 95.

Loading a file

First, here's the bad news: Loading a file into a Windows 95 program can be a mite complicated sometimes. Second, *loading* a file means the same thing as *opening* a file.

Now that those trifles have been dispensed with, here's the good news: All Windows 95 programs load files in the exact same way. So, after you learn the proper etiquette for one program, you're prepared for all the others!

Here's the scoop: To open a file in any Windows 95 program, look for the program's *menu bar,* that row of important-looking words along its top. Because you're after a *file*, click on File.

A most-welcome pull-down menu descends from the word File. The menu has a list of important-looking words. Because you're trying to *open* a file, move the mouse to the word Open and click once again.

Yet another box hops onto the screen, as shown in Figure 5-7, and you'll see this box named *Open* appear over and over again in Windows 95.

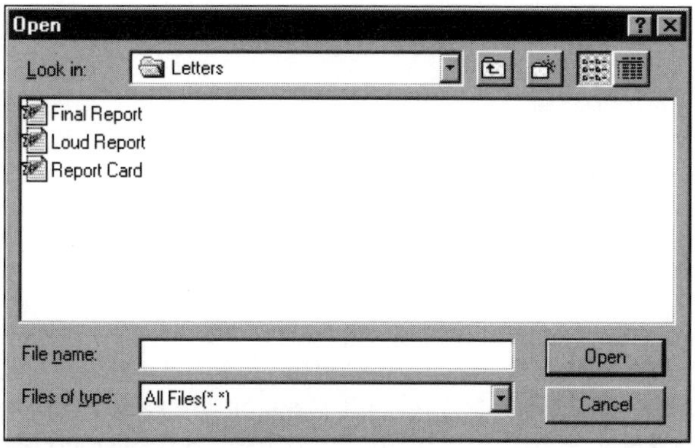

Figure 5-7:
Almost
every
Windows 95
program
tosses this
box at you
when you
load or save
a file.

Open	? ✕
Look in: 📁 Letters	▼ ⬆ 🗂 ▦ ▦

📄 Final Report
📄 Loud Report
📄 Report Card

File name:	_____	Open
Files of type:	All Files(*.*) ▼	Cancel

See the list of file names inside the box? Point at one of them with the mouse, click the button, and that file's name will show up in the box called File name. Click on the Open button, and WordPad will open the file and display it on the screen. If you don't have a mouse, press the Tab key until a little square appears around one of the file's names. Then press the arrow keys until the file you want is highlighted, and press Enter.

You've done it! You've loaded a file into a program! Those are the same stone steps you'll walk across in any Windows 95 program, whether it was written by Microsoft or by the teenager down the street. They all work in the same way.

✔ You can speed things up by simply double-clicking on a file's name; that tells Windows 95 to load the file as well. Or you can click on the name once to highlight it (it turns black) and then press the Enter key. Windows 95 is full of multiple options like that. (Different strokes for different folks and all.)

✔ If you've changed an open file, even by an accidental press of the spacebar, WordPad takes it for granted that you've changed the file for the better. When you try to load another file, WordPad cautiously asks whether you want to save the changes you've made to the current file. Click on the <u>N</u>o button unless you do, indeed, want to save that version you've haphazardly changed.

✔ The Open box has a bunch of options in it. You can open files that are stored in different folders or on other disk drives. You can also call up files that were created by certain programs, filtering out the ones you won't be needing. All this Open box stuff is explained in Chapter 6.

✔ Now here's some more bad news: Only Windows 95 programs can handle long filenames. If you're using Windows 3.1 programs in Windows 95, you'll still be stuck with the old versions of the Open and Save boxes, and the long filenames won't work right in these programs.

✔ If you're still a little murky on the concepts of *files, folders, directories,* and *drives,* flip to Chapter 12 for an explanation of the Explorer.

Putting two programs on-screen simultaneously

After spending all your money for Windows 95 and a computer powerful enough to cart it around, you're not going to be content with only one program on your screen. You want to *fill* the screen with programs, all running in their own little windows.

How do you put a second program on the screen? Well, if you've opened WordPad by double-clicking on its icon in the Start button's menu, then you're probably already itching to load FreeCell, the solitaire game. Simply click on the Start button, and start moving through the menus, as described in the Starting Your Favorite Program section earlier in this chapter.

✔ This section is intentionally short. When working in Windows 95, you almost always have two or more programs on the screen at the same time. There's nothing really special about it, so there's no need to belabor the point here.

✔ The special part comes when you move information between the two programs, which is explained in Chapter 9.

✔ If you want to move multiple windows around on the screen, then move yourself to Chapter 7.

✔ If you've started up FreeCell, you're probably wondering where the WordPad window disappeared to. It's now hidden behind the FreeCell window. To get it back, check out the information on retrieving lost windows in Chapter 8. (Or, if you see a button called WordPad along the bottom of your screen, click on it.)

✔ To switch between windows, just click on them. When you click on a window, it immediately becomes the *active* window — the window where all the activity takes place. For more information on switching between windows, switch to Chapter 7.

✔ Can't find FreeCell? Unfortunately, Windows 95 doesn't automatically install FreeCell on everybody's computers. To correct this oversight, use the Control Panel's Add/Remove Programs icon, as described in Chapter 10.

Using the Keyboard

It's a good thing Microsoft doesn't design automobiles. Each car would have a steering wheel, a joystick, a remote control, and handles on the back for people who prefer to push. Windows 95 offers almost a dozen different ways for you to perform the most simple tasks.

For example, check out the top of any window where that important-looking row of words hides above secret pull-down menus. Some of the words have certain letters underlined. What gives? Well, it's a secret way for you to open their menus without using the mouse. This sleight-of-hand depends on the Alt key, that dark key resting next to your keyboard's spacebar.

Press (and release) the Alt key and keep an eye on the row of words in the WordPad *menu bar*. The first word, File, darkens immediately after you release the Alt key. You haven't damaged it; you've selected it, just as if you'd clicked on it with the mouse. The different color means that it's highlighted.

Now, see how the letter V in View is underlined? Press the letter V, and the pull-down menu hidden below View falls recklessly down, like a mushroom off a pizza.

That's the secret underlined-letter trick! And pressing Alt and V is often faster than plowing through a truckload of mouse menus — especially if you think that the whole mouse concept is rather frivolous, anyway.

- ✔ You can access almost every command in Windows 95 by using the Alt key rather than a mouse. Press the Alt key, and then press the key for the underlined letter. That option, or command, then begins to work.

- ✔ If you've accidentally pressed the Alt key and find yourself trapped in Menu Land, press the Alt key again to return to normal. If that doesn't work, try pressing the Esc key.

- ✔ As pull-down menus continue to appear, you can keep plowing through them by selecting underlined letters until you accomplish your ultimate goal. For example, pressing Alt and then V brings down the Yiew pull-down menu. Pressing R subsequently activates the Ruler option from the View menu and immediately turns off the Ruler from the top of the word processor's screen. (If you liked the Ruler, press Alt, V, and R again to toggle the Ruler back on.)

When you see a word with an underlined letter in a menu, press and release your Alt key. Then press that underlined letter to choose that menu item.

Printing Your Work

Eventually, you'll want to transfer a copy of your finely honed work to the printed page so you can pass it around. Printing something from any Windows 95 program (or application, or applet, whatever you want to call it) takes only three keystrokes. Press and release the Alt key and then press the letters F and P. What you see on your screen will be whisked to your printer.

Pressing the Alt key activates the words along the top, known as the *menu bar.* The letter F wakes up the File menu, and the letter P tells the program to send its stuff to the printer — pronto.

- ✔ Alternatively, you can use the mouse to click on the word File and then click on the word Print from the pull-down menu. Depending on the RPM of your mouse ball and the elasticity of your wrist, both the mouse and the keyboard method can be equally quick.

- ✔ If nothing comes out of the printer after a few minutes, try putting paper in your printer and making sure that it's turned on.

- ✔ When you print something in Windows 95, you're actually activating yet another program which sits around and feeds stuff to your printer. You may see the program as a little icon at the bottom of your screen. If you're curious about the new printing process, check out the section in Chapter 9 that covers it.

✔ Some programs, like WordPad, have a little picture of a printer along their top. Clicking on that printer icon is a quick way of telling the program to shuffle your work to the printer.

Saving Your Work

Any time you've created something in a Windows 95 program, be it a picture of a spoon or a letter to the *New York Times* begging for a decent comics page, you'll want to save it to disk.

Saving your work means placing a copy of it onto a disk, be it the mysterious hard disk inside your computer or a floppy disk, one of those things you're always tempted to use as beverage coasters. (Don't try it, though.)

Luckily, Windows 95 makes it easy for you to save your work. You need only press three keys, just as if you were printing your work or opening a file. To save your work, press and release the Alt key, press F, and then press S.

If you prefer to push the mouse around, click on File from the Windows 95 menu bar. When the secret pull-down menu appears, click on Save. Your mouse pointer turns into an hourglass, asking you to hold your horses while Windows 95 shuffles your work from the program to your hard disk or a floppy disk for safekeeping.

That's it!

✔ If you're saving your work for the first time, you'll see a familiar-looking box: It's the same box you see when opening a file. See how the letters in the File name box are highlighted? The computer is always paying attention to the highlighted areas, so anything you type will appear in that box. Type in a name for the file and press Enter.

✔ If Windows 95 throws a box in your face saying something like This filename is not valid, then you haven't adhered to the ridiculously strict filename guidelines discussed in Chapter 12.

✔ Just as files can be loaded from different directories and disk drives, they can be saved to them as well. You can choose between different directories and drives by clicking on various parts of the Save box. All this stuff is explained in Chapter 6.

Quitting Windows 95

Ah! The most pleasant thing you'll do with Windows 95 all day could very well be to stop using it. And you do that the same way you started: by using the Start button, that friendly little helper that popped up the first time you started Windows 95.

Other Windows 95 programs come and go, but the Start button is always on your screen somewhere.

First, make the Start menu pop to the forefront by clicking on the Start button. Keyboard buffs can hold down the Ctrl key and press the Esc key at the same time. Next, click on the Shut down the computer command from the Start button's menu. Windows 95, tearful that you're leaving, sends out one last plea, as shown in Figure 5-8.

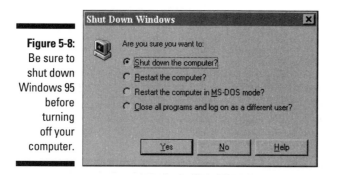

Figure 5-8:
Be sure to shut down Windows 95 before turning off your computer.

If you mean business, click on the Yes button or press Enter. Windows 95 starts to put all of its parts away, preparing to leave the screen of your computer. If, by some odd mistake, you've clicked on the Shut Down button in error, click on the No button, and Windows 95 ignores your faux pas. (Keyboard users must press Tab to highlight the No button and then press Enter.)

Finally, if you want to run a cranky DOS program that doesn't like to run with Windows 95, choose the last option, Restart the computer in MS-DOS mode. (To return to Windows 95 from DOS, type **EXIT** at the C : \> prompt thing.)

    ✔ Be sure to shut down Windows 95 through its official Shut Down program before turning off your computer. Otherwise, Windows 95 can't properly prepare your computer for the event, leading to future troubles.

✔ Holding down Alt and pressing F4 tells Windows 95 you want to stop working in your current program and close it down. If you press Alt+F4 while no programs are running, Windows 95 will figure you've had enough for one day, and it will act as though you clicked on its Sh<u>u</u>t Down button.

✔ When you tell Windows 95 you want to quit, it searches through all your open windows to see whether you've saved all your work. If it finds any work you've forgotten to save, it tosses a box your way, letting you click on the OK button to save it. Whew!

✔ If you happen to have any DOS programs running, Windows 95 stops and tells you to quit your DOS programs first. See, Windows 95 knows how to shut down Windows 95 programs because they all use the same command. But all DOS programs are different. You have to shut the program down manually, using whatever exit sequence you normally use in that program.

✔ If you have a sound card, you hear a pleasant wind-chimes sound telling you that it's time to go home and relax. (Or time to *buy* a sound card if you haven't yet succumbed to the urge.)

✔ You don't *have* to shut down Windows 95. In fact, some people leave their computers on all the time. Just be sure to turn off your monitor; those things like to cool down when they're not being used.

Chapter 6

Field Guide to Windows 95 Buttons, Bars, Boxes, Folders, and Files

As children, just about all of us played with elevator buttons until our parents told us to knock it off. An elevator gave such an awesome feeling of power: Push a little button, watch the mammoth doors slide shut, and feel the responsive push as the spaceship floor begins to surge upward. . . . What fun!

Part of an elevator's attraction still comes from its simplicity. To stop at the third floor, you merely press the button marked 3. No problems there. OK, the parking levels sometimes get a little weird — especially when they're named after fruits or vegetables. Still, the push-and-stand-back-while-the-door-closes concept is classic in its simplicity.

Windows 95 takes the elevator button concept to an extreme, unfortunately, and it loses something in the process. First, some of the Windows 95 buttons don't even *look* like buttons (unless you're heading down to the parking garage). Most of the Windows 95 buttons have ambiguous little pictures rather than clearly marked labels. And the worst of it comes with their terminology:

The phrase *push the button* becomes *click the scroll bar above or below the scroll box on the vertical scroll bars.* Yuck!

When braving your way through Windows 95, don't bother learning all these dorky terms. Instead, treat this chapter as a field guide, something you can grab when you stumble across a confusing new button or box that you've never encountered before. Just page through until you find its picture. Read the description to find out whether that particular creature is deadly or just mildly poisonous. Then read to find out where you're supposed to poke it with the mouse pointer.

You'll get used to the critter after you've clicked on it a few times. Just don't bother remembering the scientific name *vertical scroll bar,* and you'll be fine.

A Typical Window

Nobody wants a field guide without pictures, so Figure 6-1 shows a typical window with its parts labeled.

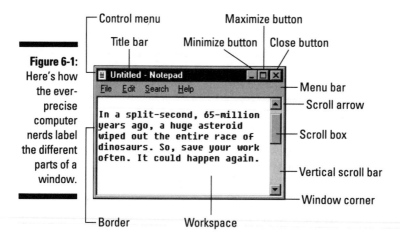

Figure 6-1: Here's how the ever-precise computer nerds label the different parts of a window.

Just as boxers grimace differently depending on where they've been punched, windows behave differently depending on where they've been clicked. The following sections describe the correct places to click and, if that doesn't work, the best places to punch.

✔ Windows 95 is full of little weird-shaped buttons, borders, and boxes. You don't have to remember their Latin or Greek etymologies. The important part is just learning what part you're supposed to click. Then you can start worrying about whether you're supposed to single-click or double-click. (And that little dilemma is explained near the end of this chapter.)

✔ After you've clicked on a few windows a few times, you'll realize how easy it really is to boss them around. The hard part is learning everything for the first time, just like when you stalled the car while learning how to use the stick shift.

Bars

Windows 95 is filled with bars; perhaps that's why some of its programs seem a bit groggy and hung over. Bars simply are thick stripes along the edges of a window. You'll find several different types of bars in Windows 95.

The title bar

The title bar is that topmost strip in any window (see Figure 6-2). It lists the name of the program, as well as the name of any open file. For example, the title bar in Figure 6-2 comes from the Windows 95 Notepad. It contains an untitled file because you haven't had a chance to save the file yet. (For example, the file may be full of notes you've jotted down from an energetic phone conversation with Ed McMahon.)

Figure 6-2:
A title bar lists the program's name along the top of a window.

You choose a name for that file when you save it for the first time. That new filename then replaces the admittedly vague (Untitled) in the title bar.

✔ The title bar merely shows the name of the current program and file. If you've just started to create a file, the title bar refers to that file's name as (Untitled).

✔ The title bar can serve as a *handle* for moving a window around on-screen. Point at the title bar, hold down the mouse button, and move the mouse around. An outline of the window moves as you move the mouse. When you've placed the outline in a new spot, let go of the mouse button. The window leaps to that new spot and sets up camp.

✔ When you're working on a window, its title bar is *highlighted*, meaning that it's a different color from the title bar of any other open window. By glancing at all the title bars on-screen, you can quickly tell which window is currently being used.

To enlarge a window so that it completely fills the screen, double-click on its title bar. It expands to full size, making it easier to read and covering up everything else. No mouse? Then press Alt, the spacebar, and then X.

The menu bar

Windows 95 has menus *everywhere*. But if menus appeared all at once, everybody would think about deep-fried appetizers rather than computer commands. So Windows 95 hides its menus in something called a *menu bar* (see Figure 6-3).

Figure 6-3:
A menu bar
provides a
handy place
for Windows
95 to hide its
cluttersome
menus.

File   Edit   Search   Appetizers   Help

Lying beneath the title bar, the menu bar keeps those little menus hidden behind little words. To reveal secret options associated with those words, click on one of those words.

If you think mice are for milksops, then use the brawny Alt key instead. A quick tap of the Alt key activates the menu words across the top of the window. Press the arrow keys to the right or left until you've selected the word you're after and then press the down-arrow key to expose the hidden menu. (You can also press a word's underlined letter to bring it to life, but that tip is explained later in more detail.)

For example, to see the entrees under Edit, click your mouse button on Edit (or press Alt and then E). A secret menu tumbles down from a trap door, as shown in Figure 6-4, presenting all sorts of *edit-related* options.

Figure 6-4:
Select any
word in the
menu bar to
reveal its
secret
hidden
menu.

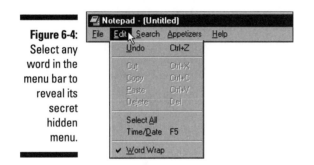

- ✔ When you select a key word in a menu bar, a menu comes tumbling down. The menu contains options related to that particular key word.

- ✔ Just as restaurants sometimes run out of specials, a window sometimes isn't capable of offering all its menu items. Any unavailable options are *grayed out,* as the Cut, Copy, Paste, and Delete options are in Figure 6-4.

- ✔ If you've accidentally selected the wrong word, causing the wrong menu to jump down, just sigh complacently. (S-i-i-i-i-igh.) Then select the word you *really* wanted. The first menu disappears, and the new one appears below the new word.

- ✔ If you want out of Menu Land completely, click the mouse pointer back down on your work in the window's *workspace* — usually the area where you've been typing stuff. (Or press your Alt key, whichever method comes to mind sooner.)

- ✔ Some menu items have *shortcut keys* listed next to them, such as the Ctrl+Z key combination next to the Undo option in Figure 6-4. Just hold down the Ctrl key and press the letter Z to undo your last effort. The Undo option takes place immediately, and you don't have to wait for the menu to tumble down.

If you find yourself performing the same task on a menu over and over, check to see whether there's a shortcut key next to it. By pressing the shortcut key, you can bypass the menu altogether, performing that task instantly.

The scroll bar

The scroll bar, which looks like an elevator shaft, is along the edge of a window (see Figure 6-5). Inside the shaft, a little freight elevator (the *scroll box*) travels up and down as you page through your work. In fact, by glancing at the little elevator, you can tell whether you're near the top of a document, the middle, or the bottom.

Figure 6-5:
Scroll bars
enable you
to page
through
everything
that's in the
window.

For example, if you're looking at stuff near the *top* of a document, the elevator box is near the top of its little shaft. If you're working on the bottom portion of your work, the elevator box dangles near the bottom. You can watch the little box travel up or down as you press the PgUp or PgDn key. (Yes, it's easy to get distracted in Windows 95.)

Here's where the little box in the scroll bar comes into play: By clicking in various places on that scroll bar, you can quickly move around in a document without pressing the PgUp or PgDn key.

✔ Instead of pressing the PgUp key, click in the elevator shaft *above* the little elevator (the *scroll box*). The box jumps up the shaft a little bit, and the document moves up one page, too. Click *below* the scroll box, and your view moves down, just as with the PgDn key.

✔ To move your view up line by line, click on the boxed-in arrow (*scroll arrow*) at the top of the scroll bar. If you hold down the mouse button while the mouse pointer is over that arrow, more and more of your document appears, line by line, as it moves you closer to its top. (Holding down the mouse button while the pointer is on the bottom arrow moves you closer to the bottom, line by line.)

✔ Scroll bars that run along the *bottom* of a window can move your view from side to side rather than up and down. They're handy for viewing spreadsheets that extend off the right side of your screen.

✔ If the scroll bars don't have a little scroll box inside them, you have to use the little arrows to move around. There's no little elevator to play with. Sniff. Sniff.

✔ Want to move around in a hurry? Then put the mouse pointer on the little elevator box, hold down the mouse button, and *drag* the little elevator box up or down inside the shaft. For example, if you drag the box up toward the top of its shaft and release it, you can view the top of the document. Dragging it and releasing it down low takes you near the end.

✔ Windows 95 adds another dimension to some scroll bars: the little elevator's *size*. If the elevator is swollen up so big that it's practically filling the scroll bar, then the window is currently displaying practically all the information the file has to offer. But if the elevator is a tiny box in a huge scroll bar, then you're only viewing a tiny amount of the information contained in the file. Don't be surprised to see the scroll box change size when you add or remove information from a file.

✔ Clicking or double-clicking on the little elevator box itself doesn't do anything, but that doesn't stop most people from trying it anyway.

✔ If you don't have a mouse, you can't play on the elevator. To view the top of your document, hold down Ctrl and press Home. To see the bottom, hold down Ctrl and press End. Or press the PgUp or PgDn key to move one page at a time.

Undoing what you've just done

Windows 95 offers a zillion different ways for you to do the same thing. Here are three ways to access the Undo option, which unspills the milk you've just spilled:

✔ Click on Edit and then click on Undo from the menu that falls down. (This approach is known as *wading through the menus*.) The last command you made is undone, saving you from any damage.

✔ Press and release the Alt key, then press the letter E (from Edit), and then press the letter U (from Undo). (This *Alt key method* is handy when you don't have a mouse.) Your last

bungle is unbungled, reversing any grievous penalties.

✔ Hold down the Ctrl key and press the Z key. (This little quickie is known as the *shortcut key method*.) The last mistake you made is reversed, sparing you from further shame.

Don't feel like you have to learn all three methods. For example, if you can remember the Ctrl+Z key combination, you can forget about the menu method or the Alt key method.

Or, if you don't want to remember *anything*, then stick with the menu method. Just pluck the Undo command as it appears on the menu.

Finally, if you don't have a mouse, you'll have to remember the Alt key or Ctrl key business until you remember to buy a mouse.

The taskbar

Windows 95 converts your computer monitor's screen into a desktop. But because your newly computerized desktop is probably only 14 inches wide, all your programs and windows cover each other up like memos tossed onto a spike.

To keep track of the action, Windows 95 introduces the taskbar. It lies along the bottom of your screen and simply lists what windows are currently open. If you've found the Start button, you've found the taskbar — the Start button lives on the taskbar's left end.

✔ Whenever you open a window, Windows 95 tosses that window's name onto a button on the taskbar. Opening a lot of windows? Then the taskbar automatically shrinks all its buttons so they'll fit.

✔ To switch from one window to another, just click on the desired window's name from its button on the taskbar. Wham! That window shoots to the top of the pile.

✔ All those open windows looking too crowded? Then click on the taskbar with your right mouse button and choose the <u>M</u>inimize All Windows option. All your currently open windows turn into buttons on the taskbar.

✔ In Windows 3.1, double-clicking on the desktop in the background brought up the Task List, a taskbar-like program that listed open windows, let you choose between them, and "tiled" them across your screen for easy access. In Windows 95, clicking on the taskbar with the right mouse button brings up the Task List's equivalent — a menu for organizing your open windows.

✔ Can't find your taskbar? Then try pointing off the edge of your screen, slowly, trying each of the four sides. If you hit the right side, some specially configured taskbars will stop goofing around and come back to the screen.

✔ You can find more information about the taskbar in Chapter 11.

Borders

A *border* is that thin edge enclosing a window. Compared with a bar, it's really tiny.

 ✔ You use borders to change a window's size. You can learn how to do that in Chapter 7.

 ✔ You can't use a mouse to change a window's size if the window doesn't have a border.

 ✔ If you like to trifle in details, you can make a border thicker or thinner through the Windows 95 Control Panel, which is discussed in Chapter 10. In fact, laptop owners often thicken their windows' borders to make them a little easier to grab with those awkward trackballs.

 ✔ Other than that, you won't be using borders much.

The Button Family

Three basic species of buttons flourish throughout the Windows 95 environment: command buttons, option buttons, and minimize/maximize buttons. All three species are closely related, and yet they look and act quite differently.

Command buttons

Command buttons may be the simplest to figure out — Microsoft labeled them! Command buttons are most commonly found in *dialog boxes,* which are little pop-up forms that Windows 95 makes you fill out before it will work for you.

For example, when you ask Windows 95 to open a file, it sends out a form in a dialog box. You have to fill out the form, telling Windows 95 what file you're after, where it's located, and equally cumbersome details.

Table 6-1 identifies some of the more common command buttons that you encounter in Windows 95.

Table 6-1   Common Windows 95 Command Buttons

Command Button	Habitat	Description
OK	Found in nearly every pop-up dialog box	A click on this button says, "I'm done filling out the form, and I'm ready to move on." Windows 95 then reads what you've typed into the form and processes your request. (Pressing the Enter key does the same thing as clicking on the OK button.)
Cancel	Found in nearly every pop-up dialog box	If you've somehow loused things up when filling out a form, click on the Cancel button. The pop-up box disappears, and everything returns to normal. Whew! (The Esc key does the same thing.)
Help	Found in nearly every pop-up dialog box	Stumped? Click on this button. Yet another box pops up, this time offering help on your current situation. (The F1 function key does the same thing.)
Setup... Pizza... Settings...	Found less often in pop-up dialog boxes	If you encounter a button with ellipsis dots (...) after the word, brace yourself: Selecting that button brings yet *another* box to the screen. From there, you must choose even *more* settings, options, or toppings.

✔ By selecting a command button, you're telling Windows 95 to carry out the command that's written on the button. (Luckily, no command buttons are labeled Explode.)

✔ See how the OK button in Table 6-1 has a slightly darker border than the others? That darker border means that the button is highlighted. Anything in Windows 95 that's highlighted takes effect as soon as you press the Enter key; you don't *have* to select it.

✔ Some command buttons have underlined letters that you don't really notice until you stare at them. An underlined letter tells you that you can press that command button by holding down the Alt key while pressing the underlined letter. (That way you don't have to click or double-click if your mouse is goofing up.)

✔ Instead of scooting your mouse to the Cancel button when you've goofed in a dialog box, just press your Esc key. It does the same thing.

If you've clicked on the wrong command button but *haven't yet lifted your finger from the mouse button,* stop! There's still hope. Command buttons take effect only *after* you've lifted your finger from the mouse button. So keep your finger pressed on the button and scoot the mouse pointer away from the button. When the pointer no longer rests on the button, gently lift your finger. Whew! Try *that* trick on any elevator.

Option buttons

Sometimes Windows 95 gets ornery and forces you to choose just a single option. For example, you can elect to *eat* your brussels sprouts or *not* eat your brussels sprouts. You can't choose both, so Windows 95 doesn't let you select both of the options.

Windows 95 handles this situation with an *option button.* When you choose one option, the little dot hops over to it. If you choose the other option, the little dot hops over to it instead. You find option buttons in many dialog boxes. Figure 6-6 shows an example.

Figure 6-6:
When you
choose an
option, the
black dot
hops to it.

Brussels Sprouts Quandary

Should you

○ Eat brussels sprouts

◉ Let brussels sprouts rot

OK   Cancel

✔ Although Windows 95 tempts you with several choices in an option box, it lets you select only one of them. It moves the dot (and little dotted border line) back and forth between the options as your decision wavers. Click on the OK button when you've reached a decision. The *dotted* option then takes effect.

✔ If you *can* choose more than one option, Windows 95 doesn't present you with option buttons. Instead, it offers the more liberal *check boxes,* which are described in the "Check boxes" section later in this chapter.

✔ Option buttons are round. Command buttons, described earlier, are rectangular.

Some old-time computer engineers refer to option buttons as radio buttons, after those push buttons on car radios that switch from station to station, one station at a time.

Minimize/maximize buttons

All the little windows in Windows 95 often cover each other up like teenage fans in the front row of a Guns 'n' Roses concert. In order to restore order, you need to separate the windows by using their minimize/maximize buttons.

These buttons enable you to enlarge the window you want to play with or shrink all the others so they're out of the way. Here's the scoop.

The minimize button is one of three buttons in the upper-right corner of every window. It looks like this:

A click on the *minimize button* makes its window disappear and then reappear as a tiny button on the taskbar along the bottom of your screen. (Click on the button to return the window to its normal size.) Keyboard users can press Alt, the spacebar, and then N to minimize a window.

✔ Minimizing a window doesn't destroy its contents; it just transforms the window into a little button on the bar that runs along the bottom of the screen.

✔ To make the button turn back into an on-screen window, click on it. It reverts to a window in the same size and location as before you shrank it. (Keyboard users can press Alt, the spacebar, and then R.)

✔ Closing a window and minimizing a window are two different things. Closing a window purges it from the computer's memory. In order to reopen it, you need to load it off your hard drive again. Turning a window into an icon keeps it handy, loaded into memory, and ready to be used at an instant's notice.

The maximize button is in the upper-right corner of every window, too. It looks like this:

A click on the *maximize button* makes the window swell up something fierce, taking up as much space on-screen as possible. Keyboard users can press Alt, the spacebar, and then X to maximize their windows.

> ✔ If you're frustrated with all those windows that are overlapping each other, click on your current window's maximize button. The window muscles its way to the top, filling the screen like a *real* program.

> ✔ Immediately after you maximize a window, its little maximize button turns into a *restore button* (described momentarily). The restore button lets you shrink the window back down when you're through giving it the whole playing field.

You don't *have* to click on the maximize button to maximize a window. Just double-click on its *title bar,* the thick strip along the window's top bearing its name. That double-click does the same thing as clicking on the maximize button, and the title bar is a lot easier to aim for.

In the upper right-hand corner of every *maximized* window is the restore button, which looks like this:

When a window is maximized, a click on this button returns the window to the size it was before you maximized it. (Keyboard users can press Alt, the spacebar, and then R.)

> ✔ Restore buttons appear only in windows that fill the entire screen (which is no great loss because you need a restore button only when the window is maximized).

> ✔ DOS programs can run in a window. But when they're in a window, they can't fill the entire screen, even if you click the maximize button. DOS windows just can't grow as large as normal windows. Perhaps they smoked cigarettes in their youth. (Or maybe they didn't read the "Changing Fonts in a DOS Window" trick, described in Chapter 16.)

> ✔ When DOS programs *aren't* running in a window, they can fill the entire screen. Windows 95 hides in the background, tapping its toes until the programs finish and it can grab the screen again. For more information on this confusing DOS stuff, troop to Chapter 16.

Don't bother with this Control-menu button stuff

The Control-menu button provides a quick exit from any window: Just give the little ornament a quick double-click. Other than that feature, however, the Control-menu button is pretty useless, redundant, and repetitive.

For example, by clicking once on the Control-menu button, you get a pull-down menu with a bunch of options. Choose the Move option, and you can move around the window with the keyboard's arrow keys. (But it's much easier to move a window by using the mouse, as you'll find out in Chapter 7.)

Choosing the Size option lets you change a window's size. (But that's much easier with a mouse, too, as you'll find out in Chapter 7.)

Don't bother with the menu's Minimize and Maximize options, either. Those two options have their own dedicated buttons, right in the window's other top corner. Click on the minimize button (the button with the little line on it) to minimize the window; click on the maximize button (the button with the big square on it) to maximize the window. Simple. There's no need to bumble through a menu for the Minimize and Maximize options when minimize and maximize buttons are already staring you in the face.

The Close option is redundant. You could have closed the window by double-clicking on the Control-menu button in the first place and avoided the hassle of going through a menu. Or, click once on the dedicated Close button — the button with the X on it in the window's far, upper-right corner.

So don't bother messing with the Control-menu button because it's just a waste of time.

(You may need to play with it if you're using a laptop and don't have a mouse, however. But even then, you should invest in a trackball, as described in Chapter 2. Until then, press Alt and the spacebar to bring up the Control menu and then press any of the underlined letters to access the function.)

The Dopey Control-Menu Button

Just as all houses have circuit breakers, all windows have *Control-menu buttons.* These buttons hide in the top-left corner of almost every window, where they look like an inconspicuous hood ornament. (Sharp-eyed readers will notice that the button is actually a miniature icon representing the program.)

That little hood ornament hides a menu full of functions, but they're all pretty dopey, so ignore them all except for this one here: Double-click on the Control-menu button whenever you want to leave a window.

  ✔ You can get by without using the Control-menu button at all. Just hold down the Alt key and press the F4 key to close an application and exit the window. Or click on the Close button, that button with the X on it in the window's far, upper-right corner.

> ✔ If you click on the Control-menu button, a secret hidden menu appears, but it's pretty useless. So ignore it, skip the technical chatter in the sidebar about the Control-menu button, and move along to the more stimulating dialog boxes that follow.

Dialog Box Stuff (Lots of Gibberish)

Sooner or later, you'll have to sit down and tell Windows 95 something personal. You'll want to tell Windows 95 the name of a file to open, for example, or the name of a file to print. To handle this personal chatter, Windows 95 sends out a dialog box.

A *dialog box* is merely another little window. But instead of containing a program, it contains a little form or checklist for you to fill out. These forms can have bunches of different parts, which are discussed in the following sections. Don't bother trying to remember the names of the parts, however. It's more important to figure out how they work.

Text boxes

A *text box* works just like a fill-in-the-blanks test in history class. You can type anything you want into a text box — even numbers. For example, Figure 6-7 shows a dialog box that pops up when you want to search for some words or characters in WordPad.

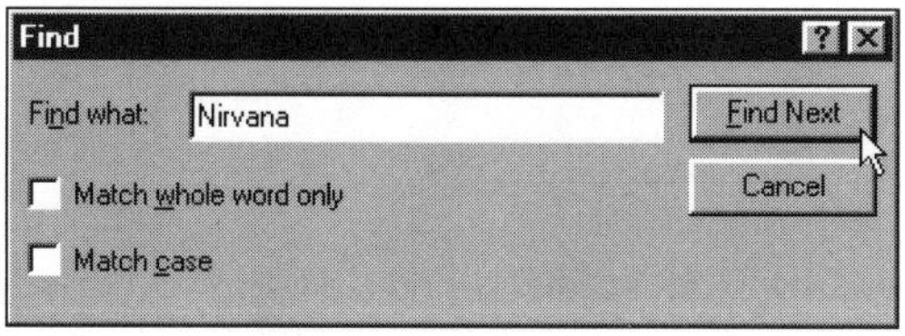

Figure 6-7: This dialog box from WordPad contains a text box.

Find		? ☒
Find what:	Nirvana	Find Next
☐ Match whole word only		Cancel
☐ Match case		

When you type words or characters into this box and press the Enter key, WordPad searches for them. If it finds them, WordPad shows them to you on the page. If it doesn't find them, WordPad sends out a robotic dialog box saying it's finished searching.

✔ Two clues let you know whether a text box is *active,* that is, ready for you to start typing stuff into it: The box's current information is highlighted, or a cursor is blinking inside it. In either case, just start typing the new stuff. (The older, highlighted information disappears as the new stuff replaces it.)

✔ If the text box *isn't* highlighted or there *isn't* a blinking cursor inside it, then it's not ready for you to start typing. To announce your presence, click inside it. Then start typing. Or press Tab until the box becomes highlighted or has a cursor.

✔ If you click inside a text box that already contains words, you must delete the information with the Delete or Backspace key before you can start typing in new information. (Or you can double-click on the old information; that way the incoming text will automatically replace the old text.)

Regular list boxes

Some boxes don't let you type stuff into them. They already contain information. Boxes containing lists of information are called, appropriately enough, *list boxes.* For example, WordPad brings up a list box if you're bored enough to want to change its font (see Figure 6-8).

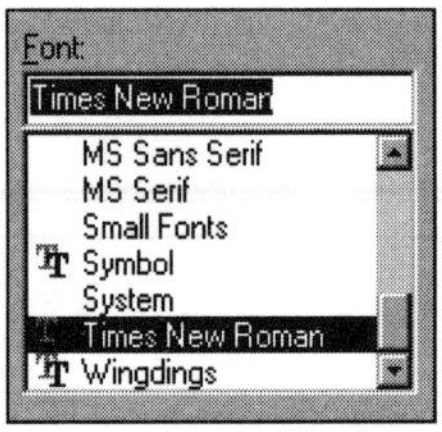

Figure 6-8:
By selecting
a font from
the list box,
you change
the way
letters look
in WordPad.

Font:
Times New Roman

| MS Sans Serif |
| MS Serif |
| Small Fonts |
| 'T' Symbol |
| System |
| Times New Roman |
| 'T' Wingdings |

✔ See how the Times New Roman font is highlighted? It's the currently selected font. Press Enter (or click on the OK command button), and WordPad will use that font in your current paragraph.

✔ See the scroll bars along the side of the list box? They work just as they do anywhere else: Click on the little scroll arrows (or press the up or down arrow) to move the list up or down, and you'll be able to see any names that don't fit in the box.

✔ Many list boxes have a text box above them. When you click on a name in the list box, that name hops into the text box. Sure, you could type the name into the text box yourself, but it wouldn't be nearly as much fun.

When one just isn't enough

Because Windows 95 can display only one pattern on your desktop at a time, you can select only one pattern from the desktop's list box. Other list boxes, like those in Explorer, let you choose a bunch of names simultaneously. Here's how:

✔ To select more than one item, hold down the Ctrl key and click on each item you want. Each item stays highlighted.

✔ To select a bunch of adjacent items from a list box, click on the first item you want. Then hold down Shift and click on the last item you

want. Windows 95 immediately highlights the first item, last item, and every item in between. Pretty sneaky, huh?

✔ Finally, when grabbing bunches of icons, try using the "rubber band" trick: Point at an area of the screen next to one icon, and, while holding down the mouse button, move the mouse until you've drawn a lasso around all the icons. When you've highlighted the icons you want, let go of the mouse button, and they'll remain highlighted. Fun!

✔ When confronted with a bunch of names in a list box, type the first letter of the name you're after. Windows 95 immediately scrolls down the list to the first name beginning with that letter.

Drop-down list boxes

List boxes are convenient, but they take up a lot of room. So Windows 95 sometimes hides list boxes, just as it hides pull-down menus. Then, if you click in the right place, the list box appears, ready for your perusal.

So, where's the right place? It's that downward-pointing arrow button, just like the one shown next to the box beside the Font option in Figure 6-9.

Figure 6-10 shows the drop-down list.

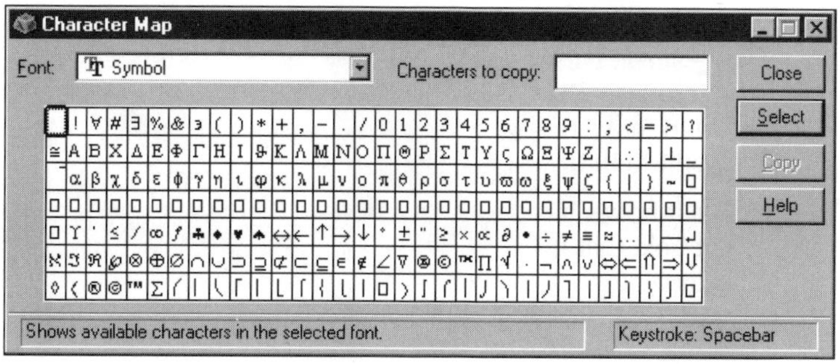

Figure 6-9: Click on the downward-pointing arrow next to the Font box to see a drop-down list box.

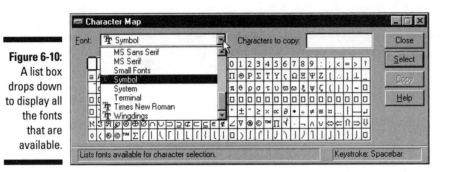

Figure 6-10:
A list box
drops down
to display all
the fonts
that are
available.

To make a drop-down list box drop down without using a mouse, press the Tab key until you've highlighted the box next to the little arrow. Hold down the Alt key and press the down-arrow key, and the drop-down list starts to dangle.

✔ Unlike regular list boxes, drop-down list boxes don't have a text box above them. That thing that *looks* like a text box just shows the currently selected item from the list; you can't type anything in there.

✔ To scoot around quickly in a drop-down list box, press the first letter of the item you're after. The first item beginning with that letter is instantly highlighted. You can press the up- or down-arrow key to see the ones nearby.

✔ Another way to scoot around quickly in a drop-down list box is to click on the scroll bar to its right. (Scroll bars are discussed earlier in this chapter, if you need a refresher.)

✔ You can choose only *one* item from the list of a drop-down list box.

Check boxes

Sometimes you can choose from a whopping number of options in a dialog box. A check box is next to each option, and if you want that option, you click in the box. If you don't want it, you leave the box blank. (Keyboard users can press the up- or down-arrow key until a check box is highlighted and then press the space bar.) For example, with the check boxes in the dialog box shown in Figure 6-11, you pick and choose how the Windows 95 taskbar behaves.

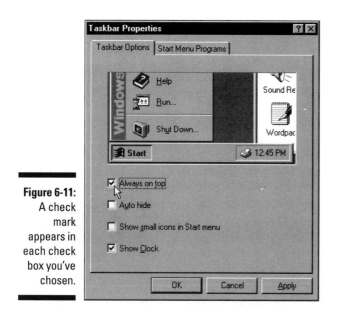

Figure 6-11:
A check
mark
appears in
each check
box you've
chosen.

✔ By clicking in a check box, you change its setting. Clicking in an empty square turns on that option. If the square already has a check mark in it, a click turns off that option, removing the check mark.

✔ You can click next to as many check boxes as you want. With *option buttons,* those things that look the same but are round, you can select only *one* option.

Sliding controls

Rich Microsoft programmers, impressed by track lights and sliding light switches in luxurious model homes, have started to add sliding controls to Windows 95, as well. These "virtual" light switches are easy to use and don't wear out nearly as quickly as the real ones do. To slide a control in Windows 95 — to adjust the volume level, for example — just drag and drop the sliding lever, like the one shown in Figure 6-12.

Figure 6-12:
To slide a lever, point at it, hold down the mouse button, and move your mouse.

Point at the lever with the mouse and, while holding down the mouse button, move the mouse in the direction you'd like the sliding lever to move. As you move the mouse, the lever moves, too. When you've moved the lever to a comfortable spot, let go of the mouse button, and Windows 95 leaves the lever at its new position. That's it.

✔ Some levers slide to the left and right, others move up and down. None of them move diagonally.

✔ To change the volume in Windows 95, click on the little speaker near the clock in the bottom-right corner. A sliding volume control appears, ready to be dragged up or down.

✔ No mouse? Then go buy one. In the meantime, press Tab until a little box appears over the sliding lever; then press your arrow keys in the direction you'd like the lever to slide.

Just Tell Me How to Open a File!

Enough with the labels and terms. Forget the buttons and bars. How do you load a file into a program? This section gives you the scoop. You follow these steps every time you load a file into a program.

Opening a file is a *file-related* activity, so start by finding the word File in the window's menu bar (see Figure 6-13).

Figure 6-13:
To open a file, you first select the word File in the window's menu bar.

Then simply do the following:

1. **Click on File (or press Alt and then F) to knock down that word's hidden little menu.**

   Figure 6-14 shows the File pull-down menu.

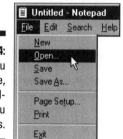

Figure 6-14:
When you select File, the File pull-down menu appears.

2. **Click on Open (or press O) to bring up the Open dialog box.**

   You can predict that Open will call up a dialog box because of the trailing ... things beside Open on-screen. (Those ... things are called an *ellipsis,* or *three dots,* depending on the tightness of your English teacher's hair bun.)

   Figure 6-15 shows the Open dialog box that leaps to the front of the screen. In fact, a similar dialog box appears almost any time you mess with the File pull-down menu in any program.

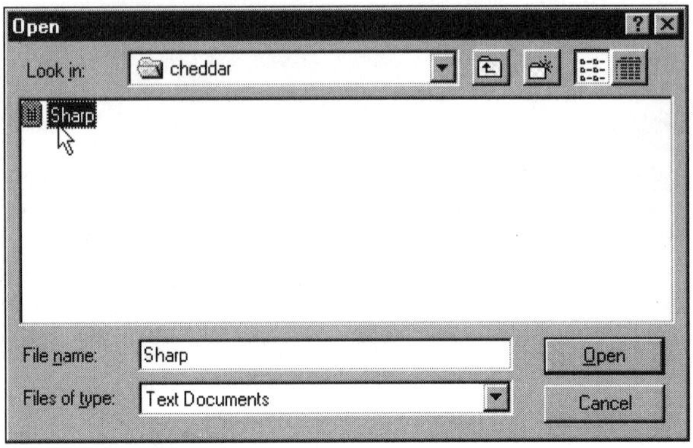

Figure 6-15:
This Open
dialog box
appears
whenever
you open a
file in any
Windows
program.

Open	? ✕
Look in: 📁 cheddar ▼ 🔼 📁 ▦ ▦	
▦ Sharp	
File name: Sharp	Open
Files of type: Text Documents ▼	Cancel

✔ If you find your filename listed in the first list box, in this case, the one listing the SHARP.TXT file, you're in luck. Double-click on the file's name, and it automatically jumps into the program. Or hold down Alt and press N, type in the file's name, and press Enter. Or click on the file's name once and press Enter. Or curse Windows 95 for giving you so many options for such a simple procedure.

✔ If you don't find the file's name, it's probably in a different folder, also known as a *directory.* Click on the little box along the top that is labeled, Look in, and Windows 95 displays a bunch of other folders to rummage through. Each time you click on a different folder, that folder's contents appear in the first list box.

✔ Can't find the right folder or directory? Then perhaps that file is on a different drive. Click on one of the other drive icons listed in the Look in box to search in a different drive. Drive icons are those little gray box things; folder icons, well, look like folders.

✔ Could the file be named something strange? Then click on the Files of type drop-down list box (or hold down Alt and press T) to choose a different file type. To see *all* the files in a directory, choose the All Files (*.*) option. Then all the files in that directory show up.

✔ Don't know what those little icons along the top are supposed to do? Then rest your mouse pointer over the one that has you stumped. After a second or so, the increasingly polite Windows 95 brings a box of explanatory information to the screen. For example, rest the mouse pointer over the folder with the explosion in its corner, and Windows 95 tells you that clicking on that icon creates a new folder.

✔ Still using Windows 3.1 programs? Then you'll still run across the older, Windows 3.1–style boxes for opening files.

✔ This stuff is incredibly mind-numbing, of course, if you've never been exposed to directories, drives, folders, wild cards, or other equally painful carryovers from Windows 95's DOS days. For a more rigorous explanation of this scary file-management stuff, troop to Chapter 12.

Hey! When Do I Click, and When Do I Double-Click?

That's certainly a legitimate question, but Microsoft only coughs up a vague answer. Microsoft says that you should *click* when you're *selecting* something in Windows 95 and you should *double-click* when you're *choosing* something.

Huh?

Well, you're *selecting* something when you're *highlighting* it. For example, you may select a check box, an option button, or a filename. You click on it to *select* it, and then you look at it to make sure that it looks OK. If you're satisfied with your selection, you click on the OK button to complete the job.

To *select* something is to set it up for later use.

When you *choose* something, however, the response is more immediate. For example, if you double-click on a filename, that file immediately loads itself into your program. The double-click says, "I'm choosing this file, and I want it now, buster." The double-click alleviates the need to confirm your selection by clicking on the OK button.

You *choose* something you want to have carried out immediately.

✔ All right, this is still vague. So always start off by trying a single-click. If that doesn't do the job, then try a double-click. It's usually a lot safer than double-clicking first and asking questions later.

✔ If you accidentally double-click rather than single-click, it usually doesn't matter. But, if something terrible happens, hold down the Ctrl key and press the letter Z. You can usually undo any damage.

✔ If Windows 95 keeps mistaking your purposeful double-click as two disjointed single-clicks, then head for the section in Chapter 10 on tinkering with the Control Panel. Adjusting Windows 95 so that it recognizes a double-click when you make one is pretty easy.

When Do I Use the Left Mouse Button, and When Do I Use the Right Mouse Button?

When somebody tells you to "click" something in Windows 95, it almost always means that you should "click with your left mouse button." That's because most Windows 95 users are right-handed, and their index finger hovers over the mouse's left button, making it an easy target.

Windows 95, however, also lets you click your *right* mouse button, and it regards the two actions as completely different.

Pointing at something and clicking the right button often brings up a secret hidden menu with some extra options. Right-click on a blank portion of your desktop, for example, and a menu pops up allowing you to organize your desktop's icons or change the way your display looks. Right-clicking on an icon often brings up a hidden menu, as well.

Or hold down your right mouse button while dragging a folder across the desktop. Windows 95 brings up a menu, asking whether you're sure you want to move the folder over there. If you'd dragged the folder while holding down your left mouse button, Windows 95 wouldn't have asked; it would have simply moved the folder there.

✔ The right mouse button is designed more for advanced users, who like to feel that they're doing something sneaky. That's why clicking the right mouse button often brings up a hidden menu of extra options.

✔ You'll rarely, if ever, need to use the right mouse button. Just about every option it offers can be accomplished in other ways.

Chapter 7
Moving the Windows Around

• •

In This Chapter

▶ Moving a window to the top of the pile

▶ Moving a window from here to there

▶ Making windows bigger or smaller

▶ Shrinking windows onto the taskbar

▶ Turning taskbar icons back into windows

▶ Switching from window to window

▶ Fiddling with the taskbar

• •

*A*h, the power of Windows 95. Using separate windows, you can put a spreadsheet, a drawing program, and a word processor on-screen *at the same time.*

You can copy a hot-looking graphic from your drawing program and toss it into your memo. Stick a chunk of your spreadsheet into your memo, too. And why not? All three windows can be on-screen *at the same time.*

You have only one problem: With so many windows on-screen at the same time, you can't see anything but a confusing jumble of programs.

This chapter shows how to move those darn windows around on-screen so you can see at least *one* of them.

Moving a Window to the Top of the Pile

Take a good look at the mixture of windows on-screen. Sometimes you can recognize a tiny portion of the window you're after. If so, you're in luck. Move the mouse pointer until it hovers over that tiny portion of the window and click the mouse button. Shazam! Windows 95 immediately brings the clicked-on window to the front of the screen.

That newly enlarged window probably covers up strategic parts of other windows. But at least you'll be able to get some work done, one window at a time.

- Windows 95 places a lot of windows on-screen simultaneously. But unless you have two heads, you'll probably use just one window at a time, leaving the remaining programs to wait patiently in the background. The window that's on top, ready to be used, is called the *active* window.

- The active window is the one with the most lively title bar along its top. The active window's title bar is a brighter color than all the others.

- The last window you've clicked on is the active window. All your subsequent keystrokes and mouse movements will affect that window.

- Some programs can run in the background, even if they're not in the currently active window. Some communications programs can keep talking to other computers in the background, for example, and some spreadsheets can merrily crunch numbers, unconcerned with whether they're the currently active window. Imagine!

Although many windows may be on-screen, you can enter information into only one of them: the active window. To make a window active, click on any part of it. It rises to the top, ready to do your bidding.

Another way to move to a window is by clicking on its name in the Windows 95 taskbar. See "The Way-Cool Taskbar" section later in this chapter.

Moving a Window from Here to There

Sometimes you want to move a window to a different place on-screen (known in Windows 95 parlance as the *desktop*). Maybe part of the window hangs off the edge of the desktop, and you want it centered. Or maybe you want to put two windows on-screen side by side so you can compare their contents.

In either case, you can move a window by grabbing its *title bar,* that thick bar along its top. Put the mouse pointer over the window's title bar and hold down the mouse button. Now use the title bar as the window's handle. When you move the mouse around, you tug the window along with it.

When you've moved the window to where you want it to stay, release the mouse button to release the window. The window stays put and on top of the pile.

- ✓ The process of holding down the mouse button while moving the mouse is called *dragging*. When you let go of the mouse button, you're *dropping* what you've dragged.

- ✓ When placing two windows next to each other on-screen, you usually need to change their sizes as well as their locations. The very next section tells how to change a window's size, but don't forget to read "The Way-Cool Taskbar" later in this chapter. It's full of tips and tricks for resizing windows as well as moving them around.

- ✓ Stuck with a keyboard and no mouse? Then press Alt, the spacebar, and M. Then use the arrow keys to move the window around. Press Enter when it's in the right place.

Making a Window Bigger or Smaller

Sometimes moving the windows around isn't enough. They still cover each other up. Luckily, you don't need any special hardware to make them bigger or smaller. See that thin little border running around the edge of the window? Use the mouse to yank on a window's corner border, and you can change its size.

First, point at the corner with the mouse arrow. When it's positioned over the corner, the arrow turns into a two-headed arrow. Now hold down the mouse button and drag the corner in or out to make the window smaller or bigger. The window's border expands or contracts as you tug on it with the mouse, so you can see what you're doing.

When you're done yanking, and the window's border looks about the right size, let go of the mouse button. The window immediately redraws itself, taking the new position.

Here's the procedure, step by step:

1. Point the mouse pointer at the edge of the corner.

It turns into a two-headed arrow, as shown in Figure 7-1.

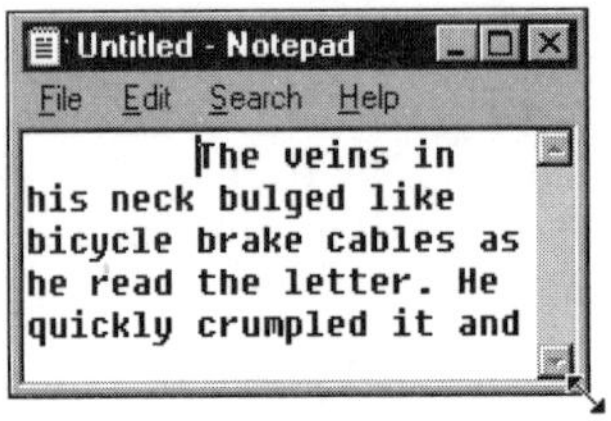

Figure 7-1:
When the mouse points at the window's bottom corner, the arrow grows a second head.

2. Hold down the mouse button and move the two-headed arrow in or out to make the window bigger or smaller.

Figure 7-2 shows how the new outline takes shape when you pull the corner inward to make the window smaller.

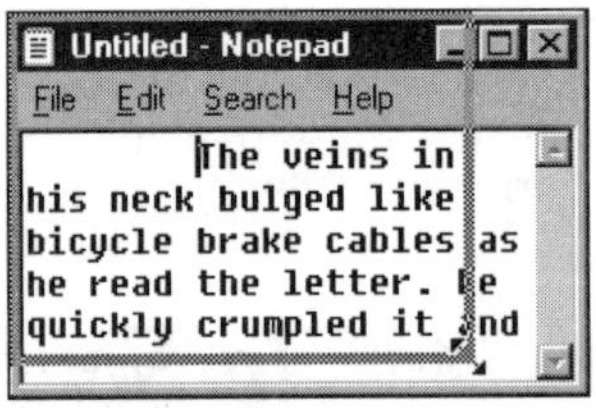

Figure 7-2:
As you move the mouse, the window's border changes to reflect its new shape.

3. Release the mouse button.

The window shapes itself to fit into the border you've just created (see Figure 7-3).

Figure 7-3:
Let go of
the mouse
button, and
the window
fills its
newly
adjusted
border.

That's it!

- ✔ This procedure may seem vaguely familiar because it is. You're just *dragging and dropping* the window's corner to a new size. That *drag and drop* concept works throughout Windows 95. For example, you can *drag and drop* a title bar to move an entire window to a new location on-screen.

- ✔ You can grab the side border of a window and move it in or out to make it fatter or skinnier. You can grab the top or bottom of a window and move it up or down to make it taller or shorter. But grabbing for a corner is always easiest because then you can make a window fatter, skinnier, taller, or shorter, all with one quick flick of the wrist.

If a window is hanging off the edge of the screen, and you can't seem to position it so that all of it fits on screen, try shrinking it first. Grab a visible corner and drag it toward the window's center. Release the mouse button, and the window shrinks itself to fit in its now smaller border. Then grab the window's title bar and hold down the mouse button. When you drag the title bar back toward the center of the screen, you can see the whole window once again.

Making a Window Fill the Whole Screen

Sooner or later you get tired of all this New Age, multiwindow mumbo jumbo. Why can't you just put *one* huge window on-screen? Well, you can.

To make any window grow as big as it gets, double-click on its *title bar,* that topmost bar along the top of the window. The window leaps up to fill the screen, covering up all the other windows.

To bring the pumped-up window back to normal size, double-click on its title bar once again. The window shrinks to its former size, and you can see everything that it was covering up.

- ✔ When a window fills the entire screen, it loses its borders. That means you can no longer change its size by tugging on its title bar or dragging its borders. Those borders just aren't there anymore.

- ✔ If you're morally opposed to double-clicking on a window's title bar to expand it, you can expand it another way. Click on the window's *maximize button,* the middle-most of the three little boxes in its top right corner. The window hastily fills the entire screen. At the same time, the maximize button turns into a *restore* button; click on the restore button when you want the window to return to its previous size.

- ✔ Refer to Chapter 6 for more information on the maximize, minimize, and restore buttons.

- ✔ If you don't have a mouse, you can make the window bigger by holding down the Alt key, pressing the spacebar, and pressing X. But for goodness sake, buy a mouse so you don't have to try to remember these complicated commands!

- ✔ DOS programs running in on-screen windows don't usually fill the screen. When you double-click on their title bars, they get bigger, but Windows 95 still keeps 'em relatively small. If you take them out of the window, however, they fill the screen completely and shove Windows 95 completely into the background. To take a DOS program out of a window, click on the DOS window to make it active and then hold down the Alt key and press Enter. The DOS program suddenly lunges for the entire screen, and Windows 95 disappears. To bring it back, hold the Alt key and press Enter again. (For more of this DOS stuff, see Chapter 14.)

Shrinking Windows to the Taskbar

Windows spawn windows. You start with one window to write a letter to Mother. You open another window to check her address, for example, and then yet another to see whether you've forgotten any recent birthdays. Before you know it, four more windows are crowded across the desktop.

To combat the clutter, Windows 95 provides a simple means of window control: You can transform a window from a screen-cluttering square into a tiny button at the bottom of the screen.

See the three buttons lurking in just about every window's top-right corner?
Click on the *minimize button* — the button with the little line in it. Whoosh! The
window disappears, and a little button appears on the bar running along the
bottom of your screen. Click on that new button on the bar, and your window
hops back onto the screen, ready for action.

The difference can be dramatic. Figure 7-4 shows a desktop with a bunch of
open windows.

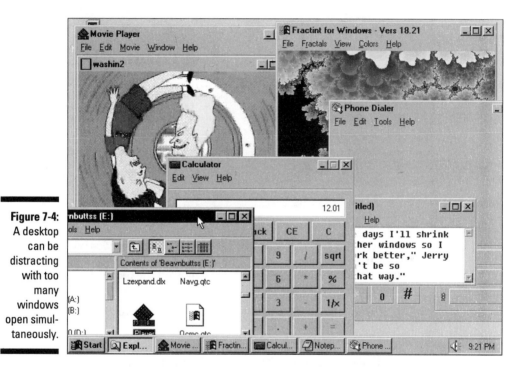

Figure 7-4:
A desktop
can be
distracting
with too
many
windows
open simul-
taneously.

Figure 7-5 shows that same desktop after all windows but one have been turned
into buttons along the taskbar. Those other windows are still readily available,
mind you. Just click on a window's button from the taskbar along the bottom of
the screen, and that window will instantly leap back to its former place on-screen.

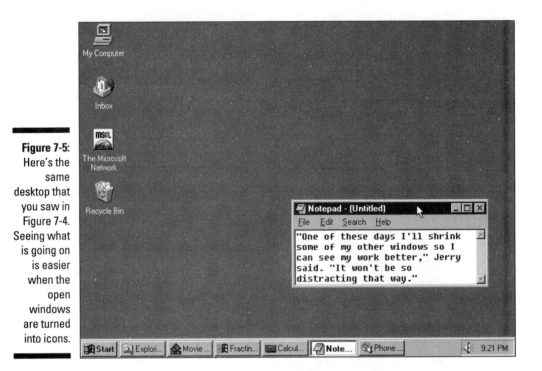

Figure 7-5:
Here's the same desktop that you saw in Figure 7-4. Seeing what is going on is easier when the open windows are turned into icons.

✔ To shrink an open window so that it's out of the way, click on the left-most of the three buttons in the window's top-right corner. The window *minimizes* itself into a button and lines itself up on the bar along the bottom of the screen.

✔ The buttons on the taskbar all have a label so that you can tell which program each button represents.

✔ When you minimize a window, you neither destroy its contents nor close it. You merely change its shape. It is still loaded into memory, waiting for you to play with it again.

✔ To put the window back where it was, click on its button on the taskbar. It hops back up to the same place it was before.

✔ Whenever you load a program by using the Start button or Explorer, that program's name automatically appears on the taskbar. If one of your open windows ever gets lost on your desktop, click on its name on the taskbar. The window will immediately jump to the forefront.

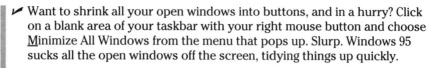

✔ Want to shrink all your open windows into buttons, and in a hurry? Click on a blank area of your taskbar with your right mouse button and choose Minimize All Windows from the menu that pops up. Slurp. Windows 95 sucks all the open windows off the screen, tidying things up quickly.

✔ Keyboard users can press Alt, the spacebar, and N to minimize a window. Holding down Alt and pressing the Tab key to restore the window to its former glory. (That fun little tip gets its own section, titled "The Alt+Tab trick", later in this chapter.)

Turning Taskbar Buttons Back into Windows

To turn a minimized window at the bottom of the screen back into a useful program in the middle of the screen, just click on its name on the taskbar. Pretty simple, huh?

✔ If you prefer wading through menus, then just click on the shrunken window's button with your *right* mouse button. A Control menu shoots out the top of its head. Click on the menu's Restore option, and the program leaps back to its former window position.

✔ In addition to using a click, you can use a few other methods to turn icons back into program windows. The very next section describes one way, and "The Way-Cool Taskbar" section later in this chapter describes another.

Keeping your icons straight

Don't be confused by a program's icon on your desktop and a program's button on the taskbar along the bottom of your screen. They're two different things. The button at the bottom of the screen stands for a program that has already been loaded into the computer's memory. It's ready for immediate action. The icon on your desktop or in Windows 95 Explorer stands for a program that is sitting on the computer's hard disk waiting to be loaded.

If you mistakenly click on the icon in the Explorer or desktop rather than the button on the taskbar at the bottom of the screen, you load a *second* copy of that program. Two versions of the program are loaded: one running as a window and the other running as an taskbar button waiting to be turned back into a window.

Running two versions can cause confusion — especially if you start entering stuff into both versions of the same program. You won't know which window has the *right* version!

Switching from Window to Window

Sometimes switching from window to window is easy. If you can see any part of the window you want — a corner, a bar, or a piece of dust — just click on it. That's all it takes to bring that window to the front of the screen, ready for action.

You can also just click on that window's button on the taskbar along the bottom of your screen. The following sections give a few extra tricks for switching from window to window to window.

The Alt+Tab trick

This trick is so fun that Microsoft should have plastered it across the front of the Windows 95 box instead of hiding it in the middle of the manual.

Hold down the Alt key and press the Tab key. A most welcome box pops up in the center of the screen, naming the last program you've touched (see Figure 7-6).

Figure 7-6:
When you hold down the Alt key and press Tab, Windows 95 displays the name of the last program you used.

Hydrator Inspection - WordPad

If the program you're after is named, rejoice! And remove your finger from the Alt key. The window named in that box leaps to the screen.

If you're looking for a *different* program, keep your finger on the Alt key and press the Tab key once again. At each press of Tab, Windows 95 displays the name of another open program. When you see the one you want, release the Alt key, and then hoot and holler. The program leaps to the screen, ready for your working pleasure.

- ✔ The Alt+Tab trick works even if you're running a DOS program with Windows 95 lurking in the background. The DOS program disappears while the pop-up box has its moment in the sun. (And the DOS program returns when you're done playing around, too.)

- ✔ The Alt+Tab trick cycles through all the currently open programs, whether the programs are in on-screen windows or living their lives as buttons on the taskbar. When you release the Alt key, the program currently listed in the pop-up window leaps to life.

- ✔ The first time you press the Tab key, the little pop-up window lists the name of the program you last accessed. If you prefer to cycle through the program names in the opposite direction, then hold down the Shift key *and* the Alt key while pressing the Tab key. If you agree that this is a pretty frivolous option, then rub your stomach and pat your head at the same time.

The Alt+Esc trick

The concept is getting kind of stale with this one, but here goes: If you hold down the Alt key and press the Esc key, Windows 95 cycles through all the open programs but in a slightly less efficient way.

Instead of bringing its name to a big box in the middle of the screen, Windows 95 simply highlights the program, whether it's in a window or sitting as a button on the taskbar. Sometimes this method can be handy, but usually it's a little slower.

If Windows 95 is currently cycling through a program on the taskbar, the Alt+Esc trick simply highlights the button at the bottom of the screen. That's not much of a visual indicator, and most of the time it won't even catch your eye.

When you see the window you want, release the Alt key. If it's an open window, it becomes the active window. But if you release the Alt key while a button's name is highlighted, you need to take one more step: You need to click on the button to get the window on-screen.

The Alt+Esc trick is a little slower and a little less handy than the Alt+Tab trick described in the preceding section.

The Way-Cool Taskbar

This section introduces one of the handiest tricks in Windows 95, so pull your chair in a little closer. Windows 95 comes with a special program that keeps track of all the open programs. Called the *taskbar*, it always knows what programs are running and where they are. Seen in Figure 7-7, the taskbar normally lives along the bottom of your screen, although Chapter 11 shows how to move it to any edge you want.

Figure 7-7:
Always handy, the taskbar lists your currently running programs and lets you bring them to the forefront by clicking on their names.

From the taskbar, you can perform powerful magic on your open windows, as shown in the next few sections.

 ✔ See how the button for Calculator looks "pushed in" in Figure 7-7? That's because Calculator is the currently active window on the desktop. One of your taskbar's buttons will always look "pushed in" unless you've closed or minimized all the windows on your desktop.

 ✔ Don't see the taskbar? Then hold down Ctrl and press Esc. Windows 95 instantly brings the taskbar to the surface, ready to do your bidding.

Switching to another window

See a window you'd like to play with listed on the taskbar? Just click on its name, and it will rise to the surface. Simple. (Especially if you've ever labored under earlier versions of Windows 3.1.) If the taskbar isn't showing for some reason, pressing Ctrl+Esc calls it to the forefront.

Ending a task

Mad at a program? Then kill it. Click on the program's name on the taskbar with your *right* mouse button and then click on the word Close from the menu that pops up (or press C). The highlighted program quits, just as if you'd chosen its Exit command from within its own window.

The departing program gives you a chance to save any work before it quits and disappears from the screen.

Cascading and tiling windows

Sometimes those windows are scattered *everywhere.* How can you clean up in a hurry? By using the Cascade and Tile commands. Click on a blank spot on the taskbar with the *right* mouse button — the spot on or near the clock is usually good — and the cascade and tile commands appear.

The two commands organize your open windows in drastically different ways. Figure 7-8 shows what your screen looks like when you choose the Cascade command.

Figure 7-8:
The taskbar's Cascade command piles all the open windows neatly across the screen. It's a favorite command of blackjack players.

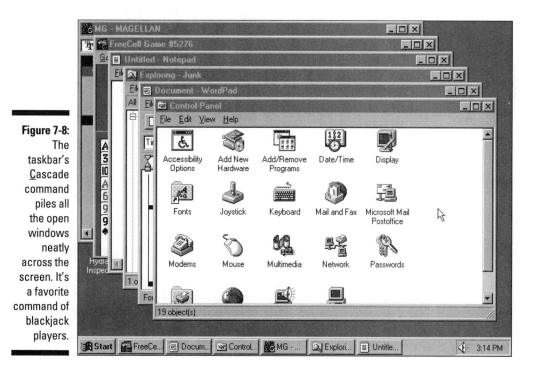

Talk about neat and orderly! The taskbar grabs all the windows and deals them out like cards across the desktop. When you choose the taskbar's Cascade command, all the open windows are lined up neatly on-screen with their title bars showing.

The Tile Horizontally and Tile Vertically commands rearrange the windows, too, but in a slightly different way (see Figure 7-9).

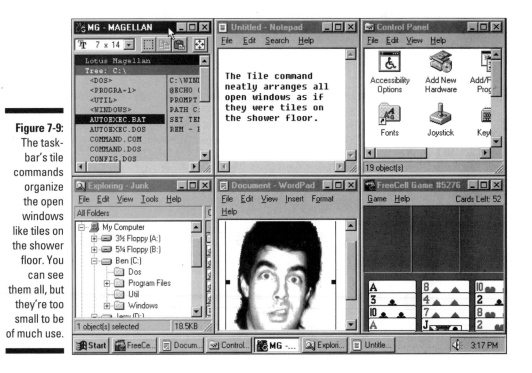

Figure 7-9:
The task-
bar's tile
commands
organize
the open
windows
like tiles on
the shower
floor. You
can see
them all, but
they're too
small to be
of much use.

The tile commands arrange all the currently open windows across the screen, giving each one the same amount of space. This arrangement helps you find a window that has been missing for a few hours.

Note: Both the tile and cascade commands arrange only open windows. They don't open up any windows currently shrunken into buttons on the taskbar.

If you have only two open windows, the tile commands arrange them side by side, making it easy for you to compare their contents. The Tile Vertically command places them side by side *vertically,* which makes them useless for comparing text: You can only see the first few words of each sentence. Choose the Tile Horizontally command if you want to see complete sentences.

Arranging icons on the desktop

The taskbar can be considered a housekeeper of sorts, but it *only* does windows. It arranges the open windows neatly across the screen, but it doesn't touch any icons living on your desktop.

If the open windows look fine, but the desktop's icons look a little shabby, click on a blank area of your desktop with your right mouse button. When the menu pops up from nowhere, click the Arrange Icons command and choose the way you'd like Windows 95 to line up your icons: by Name, Type, Size, or Date.

Or, simply choose the Auto Arrange option from the same menu. Then your desktop's icons will always stay in neat, orderly rows.

The taskbar is an easily accessible helper. Take advantage of it often when you're having difficulty finding windows or when you want to clean up the desktop so you can find things.

Finding the taskbar

Taskbar not along the bottom of your screen? Then hold down Ctrl and press Esc, and the taskbar will instantly appear. If you'd prefer that the taskbar not disappear sometimes, head for Chapter 11. It explains how to customize your taskbar so it doesn't bail on you.

The 5th Wave   By Rich Tennant

"Shoot, that's nothing! Watch me spin him!"

Chapter 8

I Can't Find It!

· ·

· ·

Sooner or later, Windows 95 gives you that head-scratching feeling. "Golly," you say, as you frantically tug on your mouse cord, "that window was *right there* a second ago. Where did it go?"

When Windows 95 starts playing hide-and-seek with your programs, files, windows, or other information, this chapter tells you where to search and how to make it stop playing foolish games. Then when you find your Solitaire window, you can get back to work.

Plucking a Lost Window from the Taskbar

Forget about that huge, 1940s roll-top mahogany desk in the resale shop window. The Windows 95 peewee desktop can't be any bigger than the size of your monitor.

In a way, Windows 95 works more like those spike memo holders than like an actual desktop. Every time you open a new window, you're tossing another piece of information onto the spike. The window on top is relatively easy to see, but what's lying directly underneath it?

If you can see a window's ragged edge protruding from any part of the pile, click on it. The window magically rushes to the top of the pile. But what if you can't see *any* part of the window at all? How do you know it's even on the desktop?

You can solve this mystery by calling up your helpful Windows 95 detective: the taskbar. The taskbar keeps a master list of everything that's happening on your screen (even the invisible stuff).

If the taskbar isn't squatting along one edge of your screen, then just hold down your Ctrl key and press the Esc key. The taskbar pops into action (see Figure 8-1).

Figure 8-1:
The mighty taskbar always contains an up-to-date list of all open windows.

🏁 Start	📄 Hydrator Inspection - Word...	📞 Phone Dialer	🎴 FreeCell	🔊 12:47 PM

See the list of programs stamped onto buttons on the taskbar? Your missing window is *somewhere* on the list. When you spot it, click on its name, and the taskbar instantly tosses your newfound window to the top of the pile.

✔ Most of the time, the taskbar performs admirably in tracking down lost windows. If your window isn't on the list, then you've probably closed it. Closing a window, also known as *exiting* a window, takes it off your desktop and out of your computer's memory. To get that window back, you need to open it again, using the services of the Start button (see Chapter 11), the Explorer (see Chapter 12), or the My Computer program (also in Chapter 12).

✔ I lied. Sometimes a window can be running and yet *not* listed on the taskbar. Some utility programmers figure that people don't *need* to see their programs or their icons. Berkeley Systems' After Dark screen saver, for example, can be running on your screen and yet not show up on the taskbar. It simply runs in the background.

✔ Sometimes you see your missing program listed on the taskbar, and you click on its name to dredge it from the depths. But even though the taskbar brings the missing program to the top, you *still* can't find it on your desktop. The program may be hanging off the edge of your desktop, so check out the very next section.

Finding a Window That's off the Edge of the Screen

Even a window at the top of the pile can be nearly invisible. A window can be moved anywhere on the Windows 95 desktop, including off the screen. In fact, you can inadvertently move 99 percent of a window off the screen, leaving just a tiny corner showing (see Figure 8-2). Clicking on the window's name in the taskbar won't be much help in this case, unfortunately. The window's already on top, but it's still too far off the screen to be of any use.

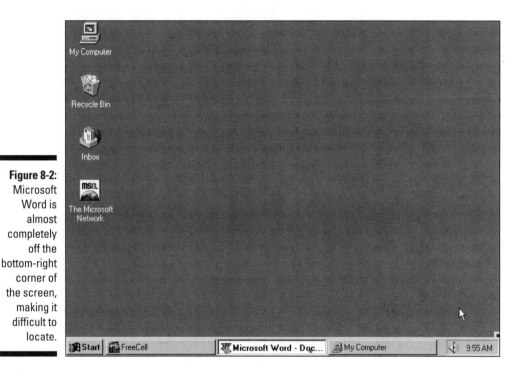

Figure 8-2: Microsoft Word is almost completely off the bottom-right corner of the screen, making it difficult to locate.

- ✔ If you can see any part of the rogue window's *title bar,* that thick strip along its top, hold the mouse button down and *drag* the traveler back to the center of the screen.

- ✔ Sometimes a window's title bar can be completely off the top of the screen. How can you drag it back into view? Start by clicking on any part of the window that shows. Then hold down your Alt key and press the spacebar. A menu appears from nowhere. Select the word Move, and a mysterious four-headed arrow appears. Press your arrow keys until the window's border moves to a more manageable location and then press Enter. Whew! Don't let it stray that far again!

✔ For an easier way to make Windows 95 not only track down all your criminally hidden windows but also line them up on the screen in *mug shot* fashion, check out the next two sections.

Cascading Windows (The "Deal All the Windows in Front of Me" Approach)

Are you ready to turn Windows 95 into a personal card dealer who gathers up all your haphazardly tossed windows and deals them out neatly on the desktop in front of you?

Then turn the taskbar into a card dealer. Click on a blank area of your taskbar — near the clock is good — with your *right* mouse button, and a menu pops up. Click on the <u>C</u>ascade option, and the taskbar gathers all your open windows and deals them out in front of you, just like in a game of blackjack.

Each window's title bar is neatly exposed, ready to be grabbed and repri- manded with a quick click of the mouse.

✔ If the missing window doesn't appear in the stack of neatly dealt windows, then perhaps it's been minimized. The <u>C</u>ascade command gathers and deals only the open windows; it leaves the minimized windows resting as buttons along the taskbar. The solution? Click on the missing window's button on the taskbar *before* cascading the windows across the screen.

✔ For more about the <u>C</u>ascade command, check out Chapter 7.

Tiling Windows (The "Stick Everything on the Screen at Once" Approach)

Windows 95 can stick all your open windows onto the screen at the same time. You'll finally be able to see all of them. No overlapping corners, edges, or menu flaps. Sound too good to be true? It is. Windows 95 *shrinks* all the windows so they fit on the screen. And some of the weird-shaped windows still overlap. But, hey, at least you can see most of them.

Click on a blank area of the taskbar with your right mouse button and choose Tile <u>V</u>ertically or Tile <u>H</u>orizontally from the pop-up menu.

✔ The Tile command pulls all the open windows onto the screen at the same time. If you have two open windows, each of them takes up half the screen. With three windows, each window gets a third of the screen. If you have 12 windows, each window takes up one-twelfth of the available space. (They're *very* small.)

✔ The Tile Vertically command arranges the windows vertically, like socks hanging from a clothesline. Tile Horizontally arranges the windows horizontally, like a stack of folded sweatshirts. The difference is the most pronounced when you're tiling only a few windows, however.

✔ You can find more information about the Tile command in Chapter 7. The minimize button is covered in Chapter 6.

DOS without Getting Lost

Windows 95 gets tricky when you start running DOS programs. Unlike Windows programs, hoggy DOS programs expect to have the entire computer to themselves. Windows 95 has to trick them into thinking everything is normal.

As part of one trick, Windows 95 enables you to run a DOS program so that it takes up the whole screen, just as if you weren't using Windows 95 at all. All you see on the screen is the DOS program. Windows 95 gives no clue that it is lurking somewhere in the background.

This trick makes the DOS program happier, but it can cause headaches for you. You can have a hard time remembering exactly what's happening. Are you running a DOS program under Windows? Did some nasty person boot up an old version of DOS on your computer? Sometimes Windows 95 waits in the background while a DOS prompt sits on the screen with no program showing at all. With all these options, getting lost is easy.

✔ If you think that you may be lost at the DOS prompt, type the following command and then press Enter:

```
C:\> EXIT
```

That is, type **exit** and then press the Enter key. If Windows 95 is waiting in the background, it lurches back to life, banishing the DOS prompt in the process. If you want to return to the DOS prompt for some bizarre reason, click on the Start button and then click on MS-DOS Prompt from the Programs menu.

    ✔ If you're stuck in a DOS program and want to get back to another window, hold down the Alt key and press Esc. If Windows 95 is lurking in the background, it leaps back to the screen, turning your DOS program into a button along the taskbar. Then, because you're back to Windows 95, you can grab the window you *really* want.

    ✔ For more soothing salves to treat DOS-program confusion, check out Chapter 16.

Finding Lost Files, Folders, or Computers (but Not Misplaced Laptops)

Windows 95 has gotten much better at finding lost files and folders. And it should; after all, it's the one who's hiding the darn things. When one of your files, folders, or programs (or computers, if you're on a network) has disappeared into the depths of your computer, make Windows 95 do the work in getting the darn thing back.

Click on the Start button, click on the Find option, and choose either On The Microsoft Network or Files or Folders from the pop-up menu, as seen in Figure 8-3.

Figure 8-3: Windows 95 can search your computer for lost files, folders, and, if you're on a network, lost computers.

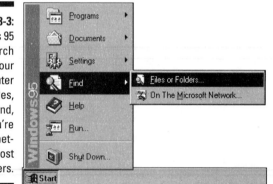

An incredibly detailed program pops up, letting you search for files meeting the most minute criteria. Best yet, it can simply search for missing files by their names. For example, suppose that your file called HYDRATOR INSPECTION disappeared over the weekend. To make matters worse, you're not even sure you spelled *Hydrator* correctly when saving the file.

The solution? Type in any part of the filename you can remember. In this case, type **drat** into the Named box, and click on the Find Now button. The Find program lists any file or folder with a name that contains *drat*, as seen in Figure 8-4. Quick and simple.

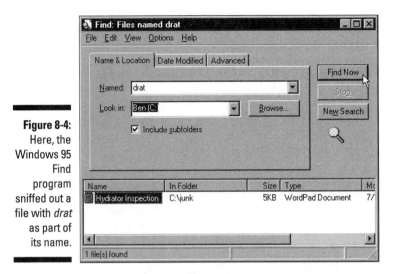

Figure 8-4:
Here, the
Windows 95
Find
program
sniffed out a
file with *drat*
as part of
its name.

✓ Of course, you don't *have* to keep things quick and simple. For example,
the Find program normally searches drive C — your computer's hard
drive. If you'd prefer that it search every nook and cranny — all your hard
drives and even any floppy disks or CD-ROM drives — then click on the
little downward-pointing arrow near the Look in box. When a menu drops
down, click on the My Computer setting. That tells the Find program to
look *everywhere* on your computer.

✓ Make sure a check mark appears in the Include subfolders box, seen in
both Figures 8-3 and 8-4. If that option's not checked, the Find program
searches through only your first layer of folders — it doesn't look inside
any folders living inside of other folders.

✓ Can't remember what you called a file but know the time and date you
created it? Then click on the Date Modified tab along the program's top. That
lets you narrow down the search to files created only during certain times.
(It's especially handy for finding files you know you created yesterday.)

✓ For a quick peek inside some of the files the Find program turned up, click
on the file's name with your right mouse button and choose Quick View
from the menu that pops up. Windows 95 shows you the file's contents
without making you load the program that created the file.

✓ The Advanced option lets people search for specific types of files: Bitmap
files, Faxes, Configuration settings, and other more complicated options.
To be on the safe side, leave it set for All Files and Folders, so you know
the Find command is searching through *everything*.

✓ If you're searching for a computer on a network, click on the Start button and
choose Computer from the Find menu. Type in two backslashes followed by the
computer's name, and Windows 95 ferrets out that computer on the network.
For example, you'd type **\\yachtclub** to find the computer named YachtClub.

Finding Snippets of Stored Information

Help! You remember how much Mr. Jennings *loved* that wine during lunch, so you stealthily typed the wine's name into your computer. Now, at Christmas time, you don't remember the name of the file where you saved the wine's name. You don't remember the date you created the file, either, or even the folder where you stashed the file. In fact, the only thing you remember is how you described the wine's bouquet when typing it into your computer: "Like an alligator snap from behind a barge."

Luckily, that's all Windows 95 needs in order to find your file. Click on the Start button and choose Files and Folders from the F̲ind menu, as seen in Figure 8-3. When the Find program pops up, click on the tab marked Advanced, click in the box marked C̲ontaining text, and type **barge**, as seen in Figure 8-5.

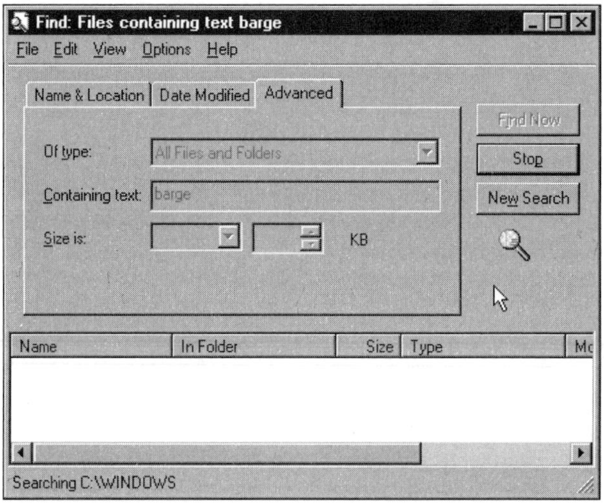

Figure 8-5:
The
Windows 95
Find
program will
search the
entire
computer
for a file
containing
the word
barge.

> **Find: Files containing text barge**
>
> File Edit View Options Help
>
> | Name & Location | Date Modified | Advanced |
>
> Of type: All Files and Folders
>
> Containing text: barge
>
> Size is: KB
>
> Find Now
> Stop
> New Search
>
> | Name | In Folder | Size | Type | Mo |
>
> Searching C:\WINDOWS

Just like in the previous section, the Find program searches the computer, looking for files meeting your specifications. This time, however, it searches inside the files themselves, looking for the information you're after.

✔ Feel free to limit your search, using any of the tips and examples discussed in the previous section; they apply here as well.

✔ CD-ROM discs take a *long* time to search. You can speed things up by telling the Find program to limit its search to hard disks. (Just popping the CD out of the drive is one way to keep the Find program from searching it.)

✔ When searching for files containing certain words, type in the words *least* likely to turn up in other files. For example, the word *barge* is more unique than *like, an, snap,* or *behind;* therefore, it's more likely to bring up the file you're searching for. And if *barge* doesn't work, try *alligator.*

Peeking into Icons with Quick View

When you open a *real* manila folder, it's easy to separate the food coupons from the letters to a congressperson; the pieces of paper look completely different. But although Windows 95 sticks titles beneath all the icons in its folders, the icons often look like one big blur, as seen in Figure 8-6. Which icon stands for what? And where is that letter to the congressperson, anyway?

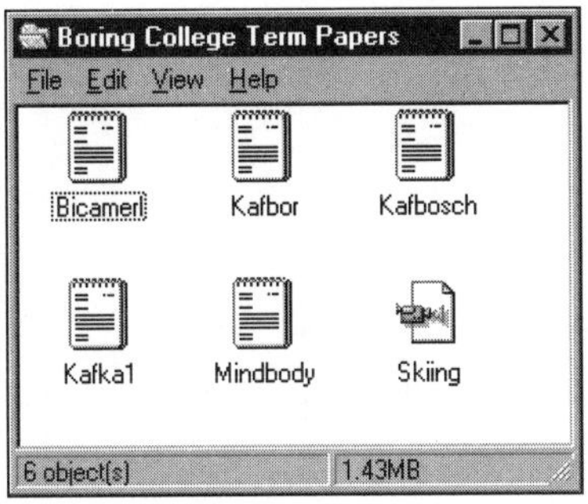

Figure 8-6:
Even with their labels, the icons in Windows 95 are sometimes hard to tell apart from each other.

You can double-click on an icon to see what file it stands for — a double-click tells Windows 95 to load the file into the program that created it and bring them both to the screen. But there's a faster way to get a sneak peek of what's inside many Windows 95 icons. Here's how the Quick View feature works:

1. **While pointing at an icon, click your right mouse button.**

   A menu will pop up, as seen in Figure 8-7. If Windows 95 recognizes the type of file, you'll see the option Quick View on the menu.

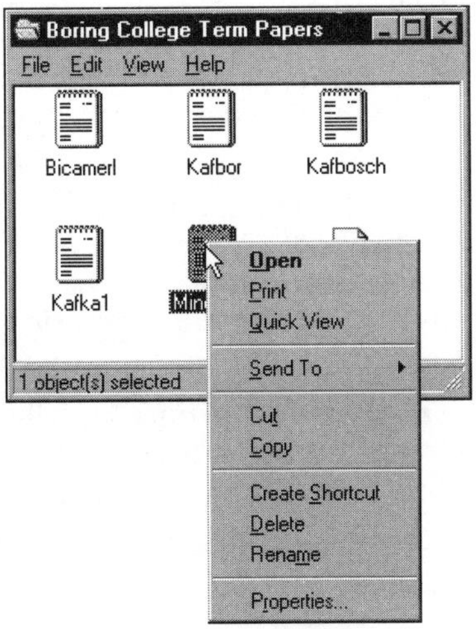

Figure 8-7:
Click on an icon with your right mouse button to see if Windows 95 offers the Quick View option.

2. Choose Quick View from the menu.

As seen in Figure 8-8, the Quick View option shows you what's inside the file without taking the time to load the program that created it. It's a quick way to sort through files with similar-looking icons.

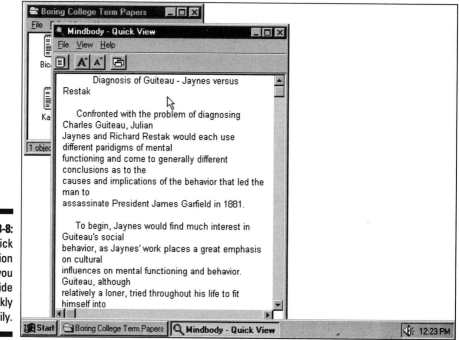

Figure 8-8:
The Quick View option lets you peek inside files quickly and easily.

✔ Windows 95 lets you use up to 255 characters when naming files. When you first install Windows 95, however, all your old files will still have their eight-character filenames. By using Quick View, you can peek into your old files and give them better names. First, peek into the file to see what's in there. When you've decided on a longer, more descriptive name, choose the Rename command. (It's on the same menu as the Quick View command.)

✔ The Quick View command works with a few dozen of the most popular formats, including Lotus 1-2-3, bitmap, WordPad, Microsoft Word for Windows, and WordPerfect. A company called Inso Corporation (800-333-1395) sells a special "add-on" Quick View utility that lets you peek inside more than 100 types of files.

✔ Once you've found the file you're after, you can open it easily from within Quick View: Click on the little icon in the upper-left corner — the icon beneath the word File. Quick View immediately opens the file for editing.

Chapter 9
Sharing Information (Moving Around Words, Pictures, and Sounds)

● ●

In This Chapter

▶ Understanding cutting, copying, and pasting

▶ Highlighting what you need

▶ Cutting, copying, deleting, and pasting what you've highlighted

▶ Making the best use of the Clipboard

▶ Putting scraps on the Desktop

▶ Object Linking and Embedding

▶ Controlling the Print Manager

● ●

*U*ntil Windows came along, IBM-compatible computers had a terrible time sharing anything. Their programs were rigid, egotistical things, with no sense of community. Information created by one program couldn't always be shared with another program. Older versions of programs passed down this selfish system to newer versions, enforcing the segregation with *proprietary file formats* and *compatibility tests*.

To counter this bad trip, the Windows programmers created a communal workplace where all the programs could groove together peacefully. In the harmonious tribal village of Windows, programs share their information openly in order to make a more beautiful environment for all.

In the Window's co-op, all the windows can beam their vibes to each other freely, without fear of rejection. Work created by one Windows program is accepted totally and lovingly by any other Windows program. Windows programs treat each other equally, even if one program is wearing some pretty freaky threads or, in some gatherings, *no threads at all.*

This chapter shows you how easily you can move those good vibes from one window to another.

Examining the Cut and Paste Concept (and Copy, Too)

Windows 95 took a tip from the kindergartners and made *cut and paste* an integral part of all its programs. Information can be electronically *cut* from one window and *pasted* into another window with little fuss and even less mess.

Just about any part of a window is up for grabs. You can highlight an exceptionally well-written paragraph in your word processor, for example, or a spreadsheet chart that tracks the value of your Indian-head pennies. After *highlighting* the desired information, you press a button to *copy* or *cut* it from its window.

At the press of the button, the information heads for a special place in Windows 95 called the *Clipboard.* From there you can paste it into any other open window.

The beauty of Windows 95 is that with all those windows on-screen at the same time, you can easily grab bits and pieces from any of them and paste all the parts into a new window.

- Unlike DOS programs, Windows programs are designed to work together, so taking information from one window and putting it into another window is easy. Sticking a map onto your party fliers, for example, is *really* easy.

- Cutting and pasting works well for the big stuff, like sticking big charts into memos. But don't overlook it for the small stuff, too. For example, copying someone's name and address from your address book program is quicker than typing it by hand at the top of your letter. Or, to avoid typographical errors, you can copy an answer from the Windows 95 Calculator and paste it into another program.

- Cutting and pasting is different from that new *Object Linking and Embedding* stuff you may have heard people raving about. That more powerful (and, naturally, more confusing) *OLE* stuff gets its own section later in this chapter.

- When you cut or copy some information, it immediately appears in a special Windows program called the *Clipboard Viewer.* From the Clipboard, it can be pasted into other windows. The Clipboard has its own bag of tricks, so it gets its own section later in this chapter.

✔ Although the Clipboard Viewer comes installed with Windows 3.1, Microsoft doesn't automatically install the Clipboard Viewer program with Windows 95. That means you'll need to head for the Control Panel's Add/Remove Programs icon and tell Windows 95 to copy the Clipboard Viewer to your hard drive, a process described in Chapter 10. (If you installed Windows 95 over Windows 3.1, your faithful old Clipboard Viewer will still be on your hard drive.)

Highlighting the Important Stuff

Before you can grab information from a window, you have to tell the window exactly what parts you want to grab. The easiest way to tell it is to *highlight* the information with a mouse.

You can highlight a single letter, an entire novel, or anything in between. You can highlight pictures of water lilies. You can even highlight sounds so that you can paste belches into other files (see the OLE section later in this chapter).

In most cases, highlighting involves one swift trick with the mouse: Put the mouse arrow or cursor at the beginning of the information you want and hold down the mouse button. Then move the mouse to the end of the information and release the button. That's it! All the stuff lying between your mouse moves is highlighted. The information usually turns a different color so that you can see what you've grabbed. An example of highlighted text is shown in Figure 9-1.

Figure 9-1: Highlighted text turns a different color for easy visibility.

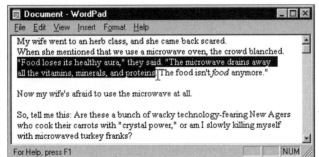

If you're mouseless, use the arrow keys to put the cursor at the beginning of the stuff you want to grab. Then hold down the Shift key and press the arrow keys until the cursor is at the end of what you want to grab. You see the stuff on-screen become highlighted as you move the arrow keys. This trick works with almost every Windows 95 program. (If you're after text, hold down the Ctrl key, too, and the text is highlighted word by word.)

Some programs have a few shortcuts for highlighting parts of their information:

✔ To highlight a single *word* in Notepad, WordPad, or most text boxes, point at it with the mouse and double-click. The word turns black, meaning that it's highlighted. (In WordPad you can hold down the button on its second click, and then, by moving the mouse around, you can quickly highlight additional text word by word.)

✔ To highlight a single *line* in WordPad, click next to it in the left margin. Keep holding down the mouse button and move the mouse up or down to highlight additional text line by line.

✔ To highlight a *paragraph* in WordPad, double-click next to it in the left margin. Keep holding down the mouse button on the second click and move the mouse to highlight additional text paragraph by paragraph.

✔ To highlight an entire *document* in WordPad, hold down the Ctrl key and click anywhere in the left margin. (To highlight the entire document in Notepad, press and release the Alt key and then press E and then A. So much for consistency between Windows 95 programs. . . .)

✔ To highlight a portion of text in just about any Windows 95 program, click at the text's beginning, hold down the Shift key, and click at the end of the desired text. Everything between those two points becomes highlighted.

✔ To highlight part of a picture or drawing while in Paint, click on the little tool button with the dotted lines in a square. (It's called the Select tool, as Windows 95 informs you if you rest your mouse pointer over the tool for a second.) After clicking on the Select tool, hold down the mouse button and slide the mouse over the desired part of the picture.

After you've highlighted text, you must either cut it or copy it *immediately.* If you do anything else, like absentmindedly click the mouse someplace else in your document, all your highlighted text reverts to normal, just like Cinderella after midnight.

Be careful after you highlight a bunch of text. If you press any key — the spacebar, for example — Windows 95 immediately replaces your highlighted text with the character that you type — in this case, a space. To reverse that calamity and bring your highlighted text back to life, hold down Alt and press the Backspace key.

DOS windows have their own methods of highlighting information. Check out the section "Using Copy and Paste with a DOS Program," later in this chapter, for the real dirt.

Deleting, Cutting, or Copying What You Highlighted

After you've highlighted some information (which is described in the preceding section, in case you just entered the classroom), you're ready to start playing with it. You can delete it, cut it, or copy it. All three options differ drastically.

Deleting the information

Deleting the information just wipes it out. Zap! It just disappears from the window. To delete highlighted information, just press the Delete or Backspace key.

- ✔ If you've accidentally deleted the wrong thing, panic. Then hold·down the Ctrl key and press the letter Z. Your deletion is graciously undone. Any deleted information pops back up on-screen. Whew!

- ✔ Holding down the Alt key and pressing the Backspace key also undoes your last mistake. (Unless you've just said something dumb at a party. Then use Ctrl+Z.)

Cutting the information

Cutting the highlighted information wipes it off the screen, just as the Delete command does, but with a big difference: When the information is removed from the window, it is copied to a special Windows 95 storage tank called the *Clipboard*.

When you're looking at the screen, cutting and deleting look identical. In fact, the first few times you try to cut something, you feel panicky, thinking that you may have accidentally deleted it instead. (This feeling never really goes away, either.)

To cut highlighted stuff, hold down the Shift key and press the Delete key. Whoosh! The highlighted text disappears from the window, scoots through the underground tubes of Windows 95, and waits on the Clipboard for further action.

- ✔ One way to tell whether your Cut command actually worked is to paste the information back into your document. If it appears, you know that the command worked, and you can cut it out again right away. If it doesn't appear, you know that something has gone dreadfully wrong. (For the Paste command, discussed a little later, hold down the Shift key and press the Insert key, that 0 on the numeric keypad.)

✓ Microsoft's lawyers kicked butt in the Apple lawsuit, so Windows 95 uses the same cut keys as the Macintosh. You can hold down the Ctrl key and press the letter X to cut. (Get it? That's an *X*, as in *you're crossing,* or *X-ing, something out.*)

Copying the information

Compared with cutting or deleting, *copying* information is quite anticlimactic. When you cut or delete, the information disappears from the screen. But, when you copy information to the Clipboard, the highlighted information just sits there in the window. In fact, it looks as if nothing has happened, so you repeat the Copy command a few times before giving up and just hoping it worked.

To copy highlighted information, hold down the Ctrl key and press the Insert key (the 0 on the numeric keypad or Ins on some keyboards). Although nothing seems to happen, that information really will head for the Clipboard.

✓ Windows 95 uses the same Copy keys as the Macintosh does. If you don't like the Ctrl+Insert combination, you can hold down the Ctrl key and press C to copy. That combination is a little easier to remember, actually, because C is the first letter of *copy.*

✓ To copy an image of your entire Windows 95 desktop (the *whole screen*) to the Clipboard, press the Print Screen key, which is sometimes labeled PrtSc or something similar. (Some older keyboards make you hold down the Shift key simultaneously.) A snapshot of your screen heads for the Clipboard, ready to be pasted someplace else. Computer nerds call this snapshot a *screen shot.* All the pictures of windows in this book are screen shots. (And, no, the information doesn't also head for your printer.)

✓ To copy an image of your currently active window (just one window — nothing surrounding it), hold down the Alt key while you press your Print Screen key. The window's picture appears on the Clipboard. (You usually don't have to hold down the Shift key with this one, even for wacky keyboards. But if Alt+Print Screen doesn't work, hey, try holding down the Shift key anyway.)

Finding out more about cutting, copying, and deleting

Want to know more about cutting, copying, and deleting? Read on (you really should read this stuff):

✔ Windows 95 often puts "toolbars" across the tops of its programs. Figure 9-2 shows the toolbar buttons that stand for cutting, copying, and pasting things.

✔ The cut, copy, and paste process works differently in DOS windows. See "Using Copy and Paste with a DOS Program" in this chapter for a dose of DOS details.

✔ If you prefer to use menus, the Cut, Copy, and Paste commands tumble down when you select the word <u>E</u>dit on any menu bar.

✔ When you're using the Print Screen key trick to copy a window or the entire screen to the Clipboard (see the preceding section), one important component is left out: The mouse arrow is *not* included in the picture, even if it was in plain sight when you took the picture. (Are you asking yourself how all the little arrows got in this book's pictures? Well, I drew most of 'em in by hand!)

✔ Sometimes figuring out whether the Cut or Copy commands are really working is difficult. To know for sure, keep the Windows Clipboard Viewer showing at the bottom of the screen. Then you can watch the images appear on it when you press the buttons. (The Clipboard Viewer is listed on the Start menu under Accessories, which is listed in the Programs section. Not listed? Head for Chapter 10; you'll have to tell Windows 95 to install the Clipboard Viewer program.)

✔ Don't keep screen shots or large graphics on the Clipboard any longer than necessary. They consume a lot of memory that your other programs could be using. To clear off any memory-hogging detritus, copy a single word to the Clipboard or call up the Clipboard Viewer and press Delete.

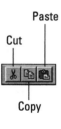

Figure 9-2:
From left to right, clicking on these toolbar buttons will cut, copy, or paste.

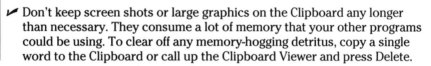

Paste

Cut

Copy

Pasting Information into Another Window

After you've cut or copied information to the special Windows 95 Clipboard storage tank, it's ready for travel. You can *paste* that information into just about any other window.

Pasting is relatively straightforward compared with highlighting, copying, or cutting: Click the mouse anywhere in the destination window and click in the spot where you want the stuff to appear. Then hold down the Shift key and press the Insert key (the 0 key on the numeric keypad). Presto! Anything that's sitting on the Clipboard immediately leaps into that window.

> ✔ Another way to paste stuff is to hold down the Ctrl key and press V. That combination does the same thing as Shift+Insert. (It also is the command those funny-looking Macintosh computers use to paste stuff.)
>
> ✔ You also can choose the Paste command from a window's menu bar. Select the word Edit and then select the word P̲aste. But don't select the words Paste S̲pecial. That command is for the Object Linking and Embedding stuff, which gets its own section later in this chapter.
>
> ✔ Some programs have toolbars along their top. Clicking on the Paste button, seen in Figure 9-2, will paste the Clipboard's current contents into your document.
>
> ✔ The Paste command inserts a *copy* of the information that's sitting on the Clipboard. The information stays on the Clipboard, so you can keep pasting it into other windows if you want. In fact, the Clipboard's contents stay the same until a new Cut or Copy command replaces them with new information.

Using Copy and Paste with a DOS Program

DOS programs all behave a little strangely under Windows 95. Likewise, the Copy and Paste commands work a little differently. It gets kind of complicated, so you should really think about ditching your DOS programs and switching to Windows programs if you're serious about copying and pasting.

You must remember certain rules when you use the Copy and Paste commands with DOS programs:

Rule 1: You can't cut text or anything else from a DOS program in Windows 95. You can only *copy* stuff. The original information always remains in your DOS program.

Rule 2: You can't paste anything but text into most DOS programs.

Rule 3: You can't paste text into a DOS program when it's running in *full-screen mode,* meaning that it's taking up the entire screen.

Rule 4: When you copy information from a DOS program, you need to decide beforehand whether you want to copy a *picture* from the DOS window or copy *text* — actual words. You can't copy a picture out of a DOS program unless the DOS program is running in a window. The upcoming two sections explain the procedures for copying pictures and text from a DOS program.

Rule 5: Copying and pasting from DOS programs is decidedly complicated and tedious, as evidenced by rules 1 through 4.

Copying a picture from a DOS program

To copy a picture from a DOS program, run the program in its own window on-screen. Then hold down the Alt key while pressing the Print Screen key.

The Alt+Print Screen key trick copies a *graphic image* of the DOS window to the Windows 95 Clipboard. From there you can paste the picture into the Windows 95 graphics program, Paint, and clean it up a little before copying it to its final destination.

  ✔ This method gives you a snapshot of the DOS program that is running in the window. It is surrounded by typical window dressing, like menu bars, title bars, scroll bars, and the like. You can erase these extraneous elements in Paint to make the picture look better.

  ✔ If you use this trick to copy a DOS program that's showing only text, you get just a *picture* of that text. You can't copy the text into a word processor or arrange it into paragraphs. It's just a picture, like a Polaroid snapshot of an open book.

Copying text from a DOS program

If the DOS program is running full-screen, press your Print Screen key. (Some keyboards make you hold down the Shift key simultaneously.) Even though Windows 95 is running invisibly in the background, it dredges all the text showing in the DOS program and copies it onto the Clipboard. (Not to the printer, though. Print Screen doesn't do that in Windows 95.)

If the DOS program is running in a *window* on-screen, here's how to grab that text using a mouse:

  1. **Click on the DOS program's Mark button — the button with a little square made of dotted lines along the window's top.**

A tiny flashing square appears in the upper-left corner of the screen, as barely visible in Figure 9-3.

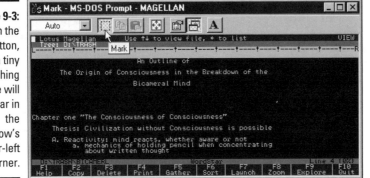

Figure 9-3:
Click on the Mark button, and a tiny flashing square will appear in the window's upper-left corner.

2. **Hold down the mouse button when you're at the beginning of what you want to grab, move the mouse to the end of the text, and then release the mouse button.**

   Your screen looks similar to the one shown in Figure 9-4.

3. **When the information you're after changes color, press Enter.**

   Wham! Windows 95 copies that highlighted text to the Clipboard.

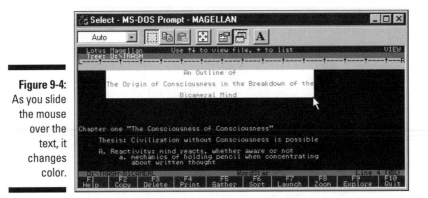

Figure 9-4:
As you slide the mouse over the text, it changes color.

✔ When you grab text from a DOS application in a window, you can grab it only in square- or rectangular-shaped chunks. That limitation is not as bad as it seems, though, because Windows 95 tosses out any extraneous spaces at the ends of lines.

✔ You can't retain any of the special formatting the DOS text may have had, such as boldface or underline. Any adjacent graphics are also left out. In addition, if the text itself is in graphics form, like fancy letters or something, you can't grab it as text.

✔ This *Select mode* stuff can be confusing: Your DOS application is frozen on-screen and doesn't respond. It's frozen because you're picking chunks out of it. And you can tell that you're picking chunks out of it by looking at the title bar: The word *Select* is in front of the program's name.

✔ If you change your mind and don't want to grab information out of there, press Esc, and everything goes back to normal. As normal as a computer can be, anyway.

✔ Trying to do all this with a keyboard instead of a mouse? Then you'll have to do all of this: Press Alt+Spacebar, and choose Mark from the Edit menu. The DOS window will go into Select mode. Tap the arrow keys until the cursor rests at the beginning of the text you want to grab; then, while holding down Shift, press the arrow keys until the cursor rests at the end of the text you want to grab. When the text you're after is highlighted, press Enter. Whew! Windows 95 then copies it to the Clipboard.

Pasting text into a DOS program

Most DOS programs are text-based critters. You can't copy any graphics into most of them. You can dump some words into them, however, by doing this: With the program running in a window, move the cursor to the spot where you'd like the text to appear. Next, click on the little Paste icon from the DOS window's toolbar. (The Paste icon, shown in Figure 9-2, has a little Clipboard on it.)

Any text on the Clipboard is instantly poured into the DOS program, starting where you left the cursor sitting.

Note: You'll probably have to reformat the text after you pour it into the DOS program. The sentences usually break in all the wrong places. Plus you lose any special formatting, such as boldface or underline. Hey, that's what you get for still clinging to your stubborn old DOS programs!

Stuck with a DOS program that refuses to run in a window? Windows 95 can still paste some text into it. When the program is running full-screen, click where you want the text to appear. Then hold down the Alt key and press the Esc key. The DOS program turns into a button on the taskbar at the bottom of your screen. Click on the DOS program's button with your right mouse button and watch as its Control menu rises eerily from the top of its head. Click on the word Edit and then on the word Paste. Presto! The text on the Clipboard jumps into your DOS program, right where you left the cursor sitting.

Using the Clipboard Viewer

Windows 95 employs a special program to let you see all the stuff that's being slung around by cutting and copying. Called the *Clipboard Viewer,* it's merely a window that displays anything that has been cut or copied to the Clipboard.

To see the Clipboard Viewer, click on the Start button and click on Clipboard Viewer from the Accessories menu (which pops up when you rest the mouse pointer over the Programs area). Inside the Clipboard Viewer, you see any information you've cut or copied recently. Figures 9-5, 9-6, and 9-7 show some examples.

Figure 9-5:
This Clipboard contains a recently copied picture of a chip.

Figure 9-6:
This Clipboard contains text recently copied from a DOS program.

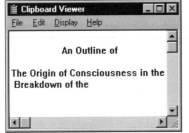

Figure 9-7:
This Clipboard contains a sound copied from the Windows 95 Sound Recorder.

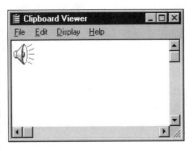

Keeping the Clipboard clear

Whenever you cut or copy something, that information heads for the Clipboard. And it stays there, too, until you cut or copy something else to replace it. But while that information sits there on the Clipboard, it uses up memory.

Windows 95 needs all the memory it can get, or it begins running slowly or balking at opening more windows. Big chunks of text, pictures, and sounds can consume a lot of memory, so clear off the Clipboard when you're through

cutting and pasting to return the memory for general Windows use.

To clear off the Clipboard quickly, just copy a single word to the Clipboard: Double-click on a word in a text file, hold down the Ctrl key, and press C.

Or, if the Clipboard Viewer is up on-screen, click on it to bring it to the forefront and then press the Delete key. You clear the Clipboard off, enabling Windows 95 to use the memory for more pressing matters.

✔ Sometimes the Clipboard Viewer can't show you exactly what you've copied. For example, if you copy a sound from the Windows 95 Sound Recorder, you just see a picture of the Sound Recorder's icon. And, at the risk of getting metaphysical, what does a sound look like anyway?

✔ The Clipboard functions automatically and transparently. Unless you make a special effort, you don't even know it's there. (That's why the Clipboard Viewer is handy — it lets you see what the Clipboard is up to.)

The *Clipboard* is a special area inside memory where Windows 95 keeps track of information that's been cut or copied. The *Clipboard Viewer* is a program that lets you see the information that's currently on the Clipboard.

✔ To better track what's being cut and pasted, some people leave the Clipboard Viewer sitting open at the bottom of the screen. Then they can actually *see* what they've cut or copied.

✔ Most of the time, the Clipboard is used just for temporary operations — a quick cut here, a quick paste there, and then on to the next job. But the Clipboard Viewer lets you save the Clipboard's contents for later use. Choose File from the menu bar and then choose Save As from the pull-down menu. Type in a filename and click on the OK command button (or just press Enter).

✔ The Clipboard can hold only one thing at a time. Each time you cut or copy something else, you replace the Clipboard's contents with something new. If you want to collect a bunch of *clips* for later pasting, use the Save As option described in the preceding paragraph. The Clipboard also starts up empty each time you start Windows 95.

> ✔ No Clipboard Viewer on your Start menu? Windows 95 doesn't always install it automatically. Head for the Add/Remove Programs section in Chapter 10 for ways to add the Windows accessories that Windows 95 left out.

Looking at Cool Object Linking and Embedding Stuff

Because the concepts of cutting and pasting are so refreshingly simple, Microsoft complicated them considerably with something called *Object Linking and Embedding,* known as *OLE.* It sounds complicated, so I'll start with the simple part: the object.

The *object* is merely the information you want to paste into a window. It can be a sentence, a road map, a sneeze sound, or anything else that you can cut or copy from a window.

Normally, when you paste an object into a window, you're pasting the same kind of information. For example, you paste text into a word processor and pictures into the Windows 95 Paint program. But what if you want to paste a sound into Write, the Windows 95 word processor?

That's where Object Linking and Embedding comes in, offering subtle changes to the paste concept. You'll probably never use them, but they can be fun to fiddle around with on cloudy days. Beware, however: OLE awareness is the first step down those ever-spiraling stairs toward computer-nerd certification.

Embedding

On the surface, *embedding* an object looks just like pasting it. The object shows up in the window. Big deal. But, when you embed an object, you're also embedding the name of the program that created that object. When you double-click on the object, poof! The program that created it jumps to the top of the screen, ready to edit it.

For example, you can embed a spreadsheet chart showing your current net worth in a letter you're writing to an old high-school friend. Then, if the stock market changes before you mail the letter, you can easily update the letter's chart. Just call up the letter in your word processor and double-click on the chart. The spreadsheet that created the chart pops up, ready for you to make the changes. When you're done, you close the spreadsheet. The spreadsheet disappears, leaving the updated chart in your letter.

Embedding is really pretty handy. You don't have to remember the chart's filename. You don't even have to call up your spreadsheet. Windows 95 does all that grunt work automatically. Just double-click on the chart, make the changes when your spreadsheet appears, and then quit the spreadsheet to return to the letter.

As with most things in Windows 95, the OLE concept is easier to use than its name implies.

Linking

Linking looks just like embedding or pasting. Your chart appears in your letter, just as before. But here's where things get weird: You're not really pasting the chart. You're pasting the chart's *filename*.

The word processor runs over to the file containing the chart, sees what the chart looks like, and then puts a copy of it in the letter.

What's the point? Well, unlike with pasting or embedding, you're keeping only one copy of the chart around. When you call up the chart in your spreadsheet and change it, those changes are automatically reflected in your word processor the next time you load that letter. With only one *real* version of the object lying around, every copy is always the right version.

> ✔ Not all Windows 95 programs can handle Object Linking and Embedding. In fact, of the programs that come in the Windows 95 box, only WordPad and the obtuse Object Packager are really OLE savvy.

> ✔ *Dynamic Data Exchange* was an earlier method for sharing information between Windows-based programs. It never really worked all that well, and OLE pretty much replaces it. So don't bother trying to learn what it was or, actually, used to be.

> ✔ Object Linking and Embedding can get pretty complex, so the vast majority of Windows 95 users simply acknowledge that their computer can do that stuff and let the technicians play with it.

Should you paste, embed, or link your important objects? Here's what to do:

> ✔ Use *Paste* for objects you'll never want to change.

> ✔ *Embed* objects if you want to be able to edit them easily at a later date.

> ✔ Choose the *Link* option if you want several programs to share the same version of a single object.

Leaving Scraps on the Desktop Deliberately

The Clipboard's a handy way to copy information from one place to another, but it has a major limitation: Every time you copy something new to the Clipboard, it replaces what was copied there before. What if you want to copy a *bunch* of things from a document?

If you were cutting and pasting over a real desktop, you could leave little scraps lying everywhere, ready for later use. The same *scraps* concept works with Windows 95: You can move information from window to window, using the desktop as a temporary storage area for your scraps of information.

For example, let's say you have some paragraphs in a WordPad document you want to copy to some other places. Highlight the first paragraph, drag it out of the WordPad window, and drop it onto the desktop. Poof! A small Scrap icon will appear on your desktop. See another interesting paragraph? Drag it onto the desktop, as well: Another Scrap icon appears.

Eventually, you'll have copies of your report's best paragraphs sitting in little scraps on your desktop. To move any of the scraps into another document, just drag them into that other document's window and let go.

Any remaining, unused scraps can be dumped into the Recycling Bin, or simply left on the desktop, adding a nice, comfortable layer of clutter.

To make a scrap, highlight the information you want to move, usually by running the mouse pointer over it while holding down the mouse button. Then, point at the highlighted information and, while holding down the mouse button, point at the Desktop. Let go of the mouse button, and a scrap containing that information appears on the Desktop.

Note: Not all Windows 95 applications support Scraps. In fact, WordPad is the only program in the Windows 95 box that can use Scraps.

Controlling the Printer

Many of the Windows 95 features work in the background. You know that they're there *only* when something is wrong and weird messages start flying around. The Windows 95 print program is one of those programs.

When you choose the Print command in a program, you may see the little Windows 95 printer icon appear at the bottom corner of your screen. When your printer stops spitting out pages, the little printer icon disappears.

When everything is running smoothly, the printer icon looks like this in the corner of your taskbar:

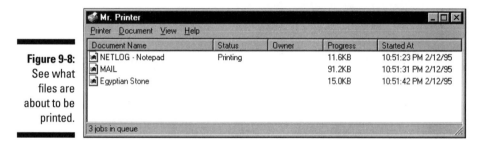

Your printer can print only one thing at a time. If you try to print a second memo before the first one is finished, Windows 95 jumps in to help. It intercepts all the requests and lines them up in order, just like a harried diner cook.

To check up on what is being sent to the printer, double-click on the taskbar's little printer icon, and you see the print program in all its glory, as shown in Figure 9-8.

Figure 9-8:
See what
files are
about to be
printed.

Document Name	Status	Owner	Progress	Started At
NETLOG - Notepad	Printing		11.6KB	10:51:23 PM 2/12/95
MAIL			91.2KB	10:51:31 PM 2/12/95
Egyptian Stone			15.0KB	10:51:42 PM 2/12/95

Mr. Printer
Printer   Document   View   Help

3 jobs in queue

✔ When the printer is through with NETLOG, it moves to the second file in the lineup, which, in this case, is MAIL.

✔ Changing the order of the files as they're about to be printed is easy. For example, to scoot EGYPTIAN STONE ahead of MAIL, click on its name and hold down the mouse button. Then *drag* the file up so it cuts in front of MAIL. Release the button, and the Print Manager changes the printing order. (The printing order is called a *queue,* pronounced *Q.)*

✔ To cancel a print job, click on the filename you don't like with your right mouse button and then choose Cancel Printing from the menu that pops up.

✔ If the boss is walking by the printer while you're printing your party flier, choose Document from the menu and select Pause Printing from the menu that drops down. The printer will stop. When the boss is out of sight, click on Pause Printing again to continue.

✔ If you're on a network (shudder), you may not be able to change the order in which files are being printed. You may not even be able to pause a file.

✔ If your printer is not hooked up, Windows 95 will probably try to send your file to the printer anyway. When it doesn't get a response, it sends you a message that your printer isn't ready. Plug the printer in, turn it on, and try again. Or hit Chapter 17 for more printer troubleshooting tips.

Chapter 10

Customizing Windows 95 (Fiddling with the Control Panel)

• •

In This Chapter

▶ Exploring the Control Panel

▶ Customizing the display

▶ Changing colors

▶ Changing video modes

▶ Understanding TrueType fonts

▶ Making Windows 95 recognize your double-click

▶ Setting the computer's time and date

▶ Changing to a different printer

▶ Making cool barf sounds with multimedia

▶ Installing new computer parts

▶ Installing or removing programs

▶ Avoiding dangerous icons

• •

*I*n a way, working with Windows 95 is like remodeling a bathroom. You can spend time on the practical things, like calculating the optimum dimensions for piping or choosing the proper brand of caulking to seal the sink and tub. Or you can spend your time on the more aesthetic options, like adding an oak toilet-paper holder, a marble countertop, or a rattan cover for the Kleenex box.

You can remodel Windows 95, too, and in just as many ways. On the eminently practical side, head for the Windows 95 Control Panel, call up the System icon, and spend hours optimizing the Virtual Memory settings.

Or check out the Control Panel's more refined options: Change the color of the title bars to teal, for example, or cover the Windows 95 desktop with daisy patterns or argyle wallpaper.

This chapter shows you how to turn Windows 95 into that program you've always dreamed of owning someday. (Although you *still* can't have *bay* windows. . . .)

Finding the Control Panel

The Control Panel is the cupboard that holds most of the Windows 95 switches. Flip open the Control Panel, and you can while away an entire workday adjusting all the various Windows 95 options.

To find it, click on the Start button, choose Settings, and click on Control Panel. The Control Panel window pops up, as shown in Figure 10-1. Each icon in the window represents a switch that controls part of the computer.

Figure 10-1:
Double-click on an icon in the Control Panel to reveal hidden switches controlling that particular area.

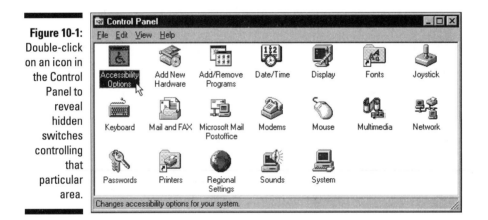

Everybody's Control Panel looks different because everybody can afford different computer toys. For example, some modem hounds have special icons that control the way their modems collect mail from all their electronic mailboxes. Others have icons that help them agonize over settings for their networks or sound cards. Table 10-1 takes a look at some of the icons you might come across in your copy of Windows 95.

Each of these options is discussed in more glowing detail later in this chapter.

For a quick way to access your Control Panel, double-click on the My Computer icon on the corner of your desktop. You'll find a Control Panel folder inside, waiting to be opened with a double-click.

Table 10-1	Deciphering the Control Panel Icons
This Icon	*Does This*
Accessibility Options	Windows 95 can be customized to work more easily for people with physical limitations. The screen can be made more readable, for example, or the numeric keypad can be converted into a makeshift mouse (which is also handy for laptop users).
Add New Hardware	Installed that new (insert name of expensive computer gadget here)? Head for this area to summon the "Hardware Installation Wizard." The Wizard handles the messy chores of introducing Windows 95 to new computer parts.
Add/Remove Programs	Installed that new (insert name of expensive software here)? Double-click here to make Windows 95 automatically install your new software. Use this icon to tell Windows 95 to add on any optional components, too, like the FreeCell card game or Backup program. (You still have to insert the disks, though.)
Date/Time	This area lets you change your computer's date, time, and time zone settings.
Display	Double-click the Display icon to change your screen's wallpaper, color scheme, number of available colors, resolution, screen-saver, and other display-oriented settings.
Fonts	Windows 95 comes with fonts like Arial and Courier. If you head back to the software store and buy more, like Lucida-Blackletter and Lucida Handwriting, install them by double-clicking on this icon. (**Nerdly Note:** This is actually a *shortcut* to the real Fonts setting area. Shortcuts are covered in Chapters 4 and 11.)
Joystick	Finally! Windows games can now use a joystick. Here's where you can calibrate and test your joystick if you're losing.
Keyboard	Here you can change how long the keyboard takes to repeat a letter when you hold down a key. Yawn. Rarely used. Or, if you pack up the computer and move to Sweden, double-click here to switch to the Swedish language format. (Or Belgian, Finnish, Icelandic, and a bunch of other countries' formats.) Finally, here's where you tell Windows 95 whether you've upgraded from an older 83- or 84-key keyboard to a newer 101- or 102-key keyboard — the ones with the numeric keypads.

(continued)

Table 10-1 *(continued)*

This Icon	Does This
Microsoft Exchange Profiles	E-mail junkies with pen pals from several different sources — Office networks, CompuServe, The Microsoft Network, or even a fax program — can stick all their mail into one big "Inbox" through this program. You'll need a computer nerd to set this one up, however.
Microsoft Mail Postoffice	Save this one for the office Network guru. You aren't missing much, just the mechanics of linking computers so that people can swap information.
Modems	Before you can talk to other computers over the phone lines, you'll need a modem. Double-click here, and Windows 95 will try to figure out what sort of modem you have so that it can start bossing it around.
Mouse	Make that mouse scoot faster across the screen, change it from right-handed to left-handed, fine-tune your double-click, choose between brands, and change all sorts of mouse-related behaviors.
Multimedia	Sound-card owners can drop by here to tweak their gear settings, adjust playback/record volumes, fiddle with MIDI instruments, and play with other goodies like video capture cards and laser disc players.
Network	Yech. Let your network folks mess with this one. They're getting paid extra for it.
Passwords	More network stuff for the weary. This setting is where your office network guru makes an agonizing decision: Should different users of a single PC be allowed to set up their own wallpaper, or should everybody in the office be stuck with the same boring picture?
Printers	Come here to tell Windows 95 about your new printer, adjust the settings on your old printer, or choose which printer (or fax card) you'd like Windows 95 to use. **Technical Note:** This isn't really an icon; it's a shortcut that leads to the Printer setup program.
Regional Settings	Used mostly by laptoppers with Frequent Flyer cards, this area changes the way Windows 95 displays and sorts numbers, currency, the date, and the time. It's worth checking out just for the fun "global" animation, though. (If you've simply changed time zones, just click on the date/time display on the bottom right corner of the taskbar, a process described in Chapter 11.)

This Icon	Does This
 Sounds	The most fun! Make Windows 95 play different sounds for different events. For example, hear a cool Pink Floyd riff whenever a Windows 95 error message pops up on-screen. (Windows 95 comes with a few sounds, but you'll have to record Pink Floyd yourself, unfortunately.)
 System	Like race-car mechanics, computer gurus can fiddle around in here for hours. Don't play in here unless a nearby computer guru can serve as Safety Patrol. This is scary stuff.

Customizing the Display

The most-often-used part of the Control Panel is probably the Display icon, which looks like this:

Display

When you open this door, you can change the wallpaper, screen saver, and other visual aspects of the Windows 95 desktop (see Figure 10-2).

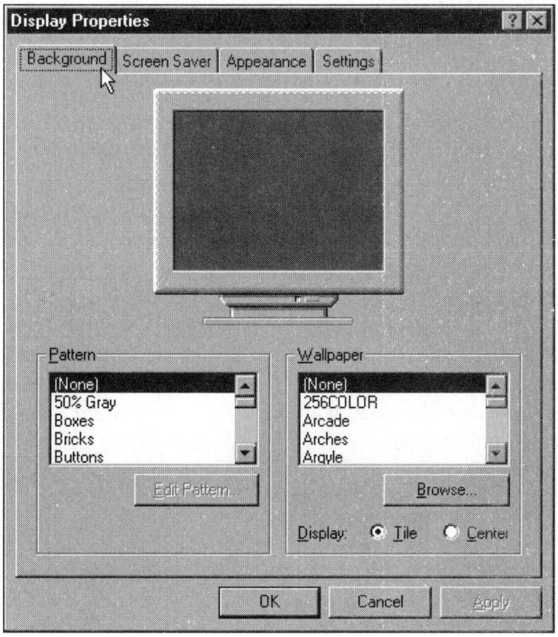

Figure 10-2:
The Display icon lets you change your desktop's colors, resolution, wallpaper, screen saver, and other display-oriented options.

Unlike several other switches in the Control Panel, the Display icon doesn't control anything too dangerous. Feel free to fiddle around with all the settings. You can't cause any major harm. If you do want to play, however, be sure to write down any original settings. Then you can always return to normal if something looks odd.

You don't have to root through the Start button and the Control Panel to get to the Display icon's contents. Instead, just click on a blank part of your desktop by using your right mouse button. When the menu pops up out of nowhere, click on Properties. That bypasses the Control Panel and takes you straight to the Display settings area.

The display's background (hanging new wallpaper)

When Windows 95 first installs itself, it paints a dull green background across the screen and then starts sprinkling windows and icons over it. Windows 95 *has* to choose that dull green in the beginning, or nobody would think it's a *serious business application.*

However, Microsoft snuck other backgrounds, known as *wallpaper,* into the Windows 95 box. Those pieces of wallpaper are hiding on the hard drive, just waiting to be installed. Different wallpaper can reflect different personalities (see Figure 10-3). For example, you can turn the window's background into a pile of fallen autumn leaves. You can choose an argyle pattern that matches your socks. Or you can create your own wallpaper in Paint, the Windows 95 graphics program, and hang your new wallpaper yourself.

To change the wallpaper, double-click on the Display icon from the Control Panel. (Or click on a blank spot of your desktop with your right mouse button and choose Properties from the menu that appears from nowhere.)

A rather large dialog box appears (refer to Figure 10-2). Look for the word Wallpaper hovering over a list of names and click on one of the names. Wham! Windows 95 displays a small preview of how your selection would look as wallpaper (see Figure 10-4).

To see more names on the list, click on the little arrows on the bar next to the names. If you aren't using a mouse, you can select a listed item by using the arrow keys to highlight the item you want and then pressing Enter. In a long list, you can find a certain name more quickly by pressing the name's first letter.

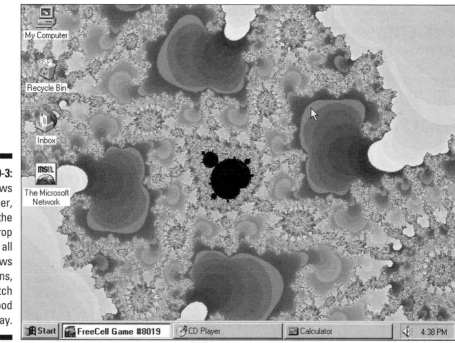

Figure 10-3:
Windows
wallpaper,
the
backdrop
beneath all
the windows
and icons,
can match
your mood
for the day.

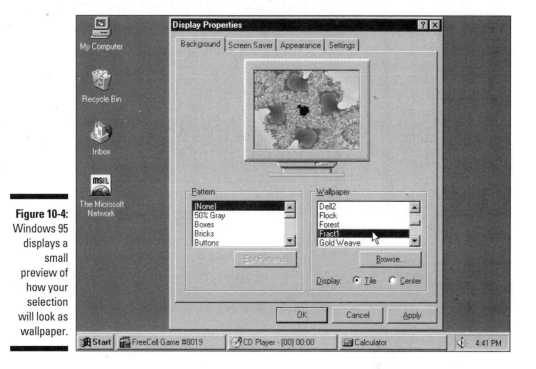

Figure 10-4:
Windows 95
displays a
small
preview of
how your
selection
will look as
wallpaper.

When you see the name of the wallpaper you want, select it. Then choose the Apply button to make Windows 95 install it. Like the way your new wallpaper looks on-screen? Then choose the OK command button. The dialog box disappears, and you are back at your desktop (with the new wallpaper displayed proudly in the background).

✔ Wallpaper can be *tiled* across the screen or *centered.* Small pictures should be *tiled,* or painted repeatedly across the screen. Larger pictures look best when they're centered. Select the option button next to your preference; the buttons lurk beneath the list of wallpaper names. Or try them both and then choose the one you like best.

✔ Wallpaper files are merely *bitmaps,* or files created in Windows 95 Paint. (Bitmap files end with the letters BMP.) Anything you create in Windows 95 Paint can be used as wallpaper. In fact, you can even use Paint to alter the wallpaper Microsoft provided with Windows 95.

✔ Windows 95 only lists wallpaper that's stored directly in the Windows directory. If you create a potential wallpaper in Paint, you have to move the file to the Windows directory before it shows up in the Desktop dialog box's master list; or you have to choose the file by clicking on the Browse button. If this concept seems strange, foreign, confusing, or all three, check out Chapter 12 for more information about directories and moving files between them.

Wallpaper looks like a lot of fun, but it may be *too much* fun if your computer doesn't have at least 4MB of RAM. Wallpaper can use up a great deal of the computer's memory, consistently slowing Windows 95 down. If you find yourself running out of memory, change the wallpaper to the (None) option. The screen won't look as pretty, but at least Windows 95 will work.

Small files that are *tiled* across the screen take up much less memory than large files that are *centered* on-screen. If Windows 95 seems slow or it sends you furtive messages saying it's running out of memory, try tiling some smaller bits of wallpaper. Also, try black-and-white wallpaper; it doesn't slow down Windows 95 as much.

✔ The Pattern option sprinkles tiny lines and dots across the screen, providing a low-budget alternative to wallpaper. To add or change those sprinkles, click on one of the names listed in the Pattern section, right next to the list of wallpaper names (refer to Figure 10-2). Choose from the patterns Microsoft provided; or if you're desperate for something to do, click on the Edit Pattern button to create your own little patterns.

✔ Patterns are a poor-man's wallpaper. They're only one color, and they don't vary much. If Windows 95 keeps complaining about needing more memory, however, dump your wallpaper and switch to patterns. They don't eat up nearly as much memory.

✔ In order to see patterns across the back of the desktop, you need to change the wallpaper option to (None); otherwise, the patterns won't show up.

The display's screen saver

In the dinosaur days of computing, computer monitors were permanently damaged when an oft-used program burned its image onto the screen. The program's faint outlines showed up even when the monitor was turned off.

To prevent this *burn-in,* people installed a *screen saver* to jump in when a computer hadn't been used for a while. The screen saver would either blank the screen or fill it with wavy lines to keep the program's display from etching itself into the screen.

Today's monitors don't really have this problem, but people use screen savers anyway — mainly because they look cool.

✔ Windows comes with several screen savers built in, although none of them is activated at first. To set one up, click on the Screen Saver tab along the top of the Display properties dialog box (refer to Figure 10-2). Then click on the downward-pointing arrow in the Screen Saver box. Finally, select the screen saver you want.

✔ Immediately after choosing a screen saver, click on the Preview command button to see what the screen saver looks like. Wiggle the mouse or press the spacebar to come back to Windows 95.

✔ Fiddlers can click on Settings for more options. For example, you can control the colors and animation speed.

✔ Click in the Password protected box to set a password; then when the screen saver kicks in, you won't be able to see the screen again until you type in the password. If you forget your password, turn to Chapter 18 for help.

✔ Click on the up or down arrows next to Wait to tell the screen saver when to kick in. If you set the option to 5, for example, Windows 95 waits until you haven't touched the mouse or keyboard for five minutes before letting the screen saver out of its cage.

✔ Windows 95 comes with more screen savers than it initially installs. To make Windows 95 install all its screen savers, use the Control Panel's Add/ Remove Programs icon, described later in this chapter. (**Hint:** The Flying through Space screen saver looks cool.)

The display's appearance (getting better colors)

If you paid extra for a fancy color monitor and video card, the time has come to put them to use. You can make Windows 95 appear in any color you want by clicking on the tab marked Appearance, found along the top of the Display menu.

The Appearance dialog box opens, enabling you to choose between several Microsoft-designed color schemes or to create your own. (Tell your boss that a more pleasant color scheme will enhance your productivity.) Figure 10-5 shows the Appearance dialog box.

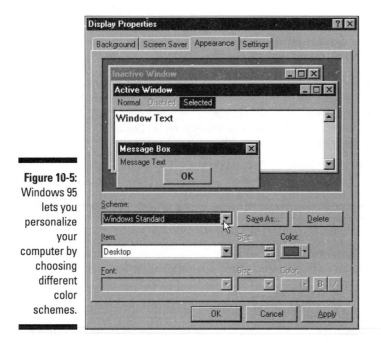

Figure 10-5: Windows 95 lets you personalize your computer by choosing different color schemes.

To choose among previously designed color schemes, click on the arrow next to the box beneath Scheme. After the list drops down, click on the name of the scheme you want to try out. Each time you select a new color scheme, the sample window shows you how the colors will look.

If you want to change one of the color schemes slightly, go for it: Click on the box beneath Item to see a list of areas you can fiddle with. For example, to change the font Windows 95 uses for icon titles, choose Icon Title from the list and select a different font from the ones listed in the Font box.

And, if you want even more choices, you can mix your own colors by choosing Other from the Color menu and choosing the Define Custom Colors command button.

Feel free to play around with the colors by trying out different schemes or designing your own combinations. Playing with the colors is an easy way to see what names Windows 95 uses for its different components. It's also a fun way to work with dialog boxes. But if you goof something awful, and all the letters suddenly disappear, click the Cancel button. (It's the middle of the three buttons along the bottom.) Letters disappear when they've been changed to white on a white background.

- ✔ Color schemes don't refer to color alone; they can change the appearance of Windows 95 in other ways. For example, the Horizontal Icon Spacing setting determines how closely your icons sit next to each other. The Scrollbar setting determines the width of the scroll bars and their elevator-like buttons you click on to move around in a document.

- ✔ Created an outstanding new color scheme? Then click on the Save As button and type in a new name for your creation. If you ever grow weary of your creative new color scheme, you can always return to the Windows 95 original colors by selecting Windows Standard.

- ✔ Windows 95 continues to display your newly chosen colors until you head back to the Appearance icon and change them again.

- ✔ All this talk of "dialog boxes," "command buttons," and "funny arrow things" got you down? Then head to Chapter 6 for a field guide to figuring out Windows 95 menus.

Display settings (playing with new video modes)

Just as Windows 95 can print to hundreds of different brands of printers, it can accommodate zillions of different monitors, too. It can even display different *video modes* on the same monitor.

For example, Windows 95 can display different amounts of color on-screen, or it can shrink the size of everything, packing more information onto the screen. The number of colors and the size of the information on-screen comprise a *video mode*, or *video resolution*.

Some Windows 95 programs only work in a specific video mode, and those programs casually ask you to switch to that mode. Huh?

Here's what's happening: Monitors plug into a special place on the back of the computer. That special place is an outlet on a *video card* — the gizmo that translates your computer's language into something you can *see* on the monitor. That card handles all the video-mode switches. By making the card switch between modes, you can send more or fewer colors to your monitor or pack more or less information onto the screen.

To make a video card switch to a different video mode, click on the Settings tab, one of the four tabs along the top of the Control Panel's Display menu, shown in Figure 10-2. (Can't find the Display menu? Click on a blank part of your desktop by using the right mouse button and choose Properties from the menu that springs up.)

As shown in Figure 10-6, the Settings menu lets you select the video mode you want Windows 95 to display on-screen. (Click on the arrow next to the Color palette box to change the number of colors Windows 95 is currently displaying; click in the Desktop area box to change the current resolution.) Windows 95 gives you a chance to back out if you choose a video mode your computer can't handle, thank goodness.

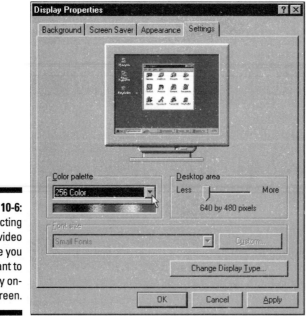

Figure 10-6:
Selecting
the video
mode you
want to
display on-
screen.

✔ When Windows 95 switches to the new resolution, it gives you 15 seconds to click on a button saying that you approve of the change. If your card or monitor can't handle the new resolution, you won't be able to see the button on-screen. Then, because you didn't click on the button, Windows 95 automatically changes back to the original resolution. Whew!

✔ Monitors and cards can display Windows 95 in different *resolutions*. The higher the resolution, the more information Windows 95 can pack onto the screen. (And the smaller the windows become, too.) Windows 95 refers to resolution as *Desktop area*. For more information about this monitor/card/resolution stuff, troop over to Chapter 2 and read the section about computer parts that I told you to ignore.

✔ To switch to a higher resolution, use your mouse to slide the little bar in the Desktop area box. Then watch how the screen changes. The more you slide the bar to the right, the more information Windows 95 can pack onto the screen. Unfortunately, the information also gets smaller. Click on the Apply button after you choose a new resolution to see it in action.

✔ Earlier versions of Windows made users shut down Windows when changing resolution. Windows 95 isn't nearly as rude. You can change resolution while all your programs are still running. (Make sure that you've saved your work anyway, however. Who *really* trusts their computer to be polite these days?) Also, Windows 95 still needs to shut down and restart when switching the amount of colors it can display.

✔ Want to change the amount of colors Windows 95 can throw onto the screen? Then click on the little arrow in the Color palette box. When the list drops down, choose the amount of colors you're after.

✔ New video cards usually come with a disk that contains special information called a *driver*. If Windows 95 doesn't recognize your breed of video card, it might ask you to insert this disk when you're changing video modes.

✔ The more colors you ask Windows 95 to display, the slower it runs. Usually, it's best to stick with 256 colors unless you have a fancy video card, a fancy monitor to go with it, and want to look at ultra-realistic photos on-screen.

✔ If you'll be looking at pictures stored through Kodak's PhotoCD technology, you'll probably want Windows 95 to display as many colors as possible — often 65,000 (16-bit) or 1.6 million (24-bit). Switch back to fewer colors when you're done, however, if Windows 95 starts running too slowly.

✔ If Windows 95 acts goofy with your video card or monitor — or you've recently installed new ones — head for the "Installing New Hardware" section later in this chapter. Windows 95 probably needs to be formally introduced to your new equipment before it will talk to it.

Understanding the Fuss about TrueType Fonts

In the first few versions of Windows, the *fonts,* or sets of letters, numbers, and other characters, produced individual letters and numbers that looked kind of jagged. A capital A, for example, didn't have smooth, diagonal lines. Instead, the sides had rough ridges that stuck out. They usually looked fine on the printer but pretty awful on-screen, especially when the headlines were in large letters.

Windows 3.1 introduced a new font technology called TrueType fonts to eliminate the jaggies and make the screen match more closely what comes out of the printer. The technology is still around in Windows 95.

Double-click on the Control Panel's Fonts icon to see what fonts come with Windows 95, to install additional fonts, or to delete the ugly ones you don't like anymore:

Fonts

Double-click on any of the font icons, and you'll see what that particular font looks like. For example, a double-click on the icon marked Courier New Italic brings up an eye chart displaying how that font would look on the printed page, as shown in Figure 10-7.

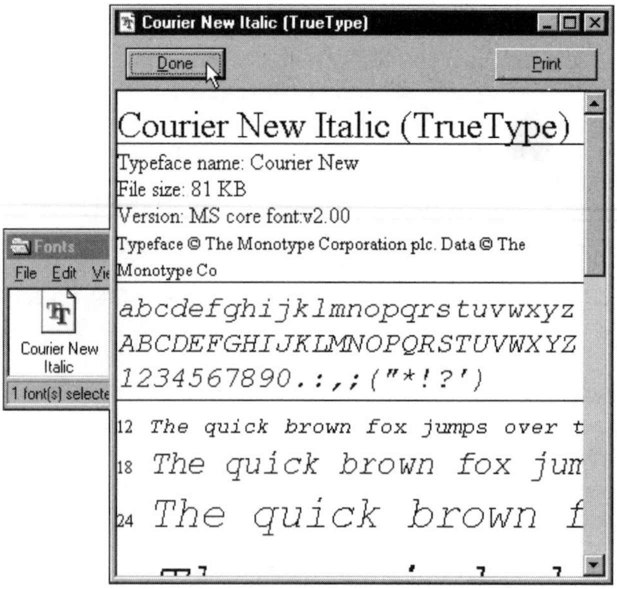

Figure 10-7:
Double-click
on a font
icon to see
what it
looks like.

Courier New Italic (TrueType)

Done   Print

Courier New Italic (TrueType)

Typeface name: Courier New
File size: 81 KB
Version: MS core font:v2.00
Typeface © The Monotype Corporation plc. Data © The Monotype Co

Fonts

File Edit Vie

Courier New
Italic

1 font(s) selecte

abcdefghijklmnopqrstuvwxyz
ABCDEFGHIJKLMNOPQRSTUVWXYZ
1234567890.:,;("*!?')

12 *The quick brown fox jumps over t*

18 *The quick brown fox jum*

24 *The quick brown f*

✔ Icons marked with the letters "TT" are TrueType fonts, so they'll always look better than the fonts marked with the letter A.

✔ *Note:* You'll probably never need to fiddle with the Fonts icon. Just know that it's there in case you ever want to get fancy and install more fonts on your computer. So pretend the technical sidebar about TrueType stuff doesn't even exist.

Fonts can eat up a lot of hard drive space. If you've installed some fonts that you no longer use, delete them. Double-click on the Control Panel's Fonts icon, click with your right mouse button on the name of the font you no longer use, and then choose <u>D</u>elete from the pop-up menu. A box appears, asking whether you're sure that you want to remove that font; click the <u>Y</u>es button if you *really* want to give it the purge.

To be on the safe side, don't delete any fonts that come with Windows 95; only delete fonts that you've installed yourself. Windows programs often borrow Windows 95 fonts for menus; if you delete those fonts, your menus will mysteriously vanish.

Just what is this TrueType stuff, anyway?

In early versions of Windows, people with fancy fonts had a problem. They could create some fine-looking documents that would have raised a smile from Gutenberg himself. But when they copied a document to a disk and gave it to somebody else, that person couldn't see those same fancy fonts. Only people who had those same fancy fonts already *installed* on their computer could see the document the way it was supposed to look.

TrueType fixes that problem handily by *embedding* the font in the document itself. You can create a letter in Write by using fancy TrueType fonts; when you give a disk with the letter on it to a friend, that person can see the same fonts in the letter, even if those fonts aren't installed on their computer.

At least, the TrueType fonts included with Windows 95 will work that way; some other TrueType fonts don't embed themselves.

Also, TrueType fonts are *scaleable.* You can make them bigger or smaller, and they still look nice. Earlier font technology required a different set of fonts for each size. The files were pretty hoggy compared with TrueType technology.

Most people get along fine with the fonts that are included with Windows 95, so they never have to worry about TrueType or how it works.

Making Windows 95 Recognize Your Double-Click

Clicking twice on a mouse button is called a double-click; you do a lot of double-clicking in Windows 95. But sometimes you can't click fast enough to suit Windows 95. It thinks your double-clicks are just two single clicks. If you have this problem, head for the Control Panel's Mouse icon:

Mouse

When you double-click on the Mouse icon, the Mouse dialog box pops up (see Figure 10-8). If your mouse dialog box doesn't look like the one in Figure 10-8, the company that made your mouse slipped its own software into the Control Panel. The following instructions may not work for you, but you can generally access the same types of options for any mouse. If your menu looks weird, try pressing F1 for help.

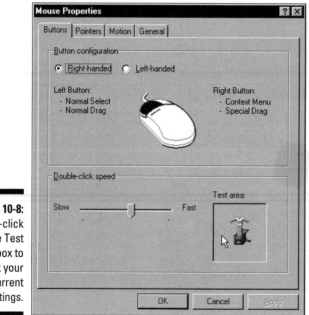

Figure 10-8:
Double-click
in the Test
area box to
check your
current
settings.

To check the double-click speed, double-click in the box marked Test area. Each time Windows 95 recognizes your double-click, a little puppet with water-buffalo horns pops out of the Jack in the Box. Double-click again, and the puppet disappears.

Slide the scroll box toward the words Fast or Slow until Windows 95 successfully recognizes your double-click efforts. Click on the OK command button when you're through, and you're back in business.

✔ Can't double-click on the Mouse icon quickly enough for Windows 95 to open the darn thing up? Then just click once, and poke the Enter key with your finger. Or, click once with the right button and choose Open from the menu that shoots out of the mouse icon's head. Yep, there are a lot of ways to do the same thing in Windows 95.

✔ If you're left-handed, click in the little circle marked Left-handed, shown along the top of Figure 10-8, and click on the Apply button. Then you can hold the mouse in your left hand and yet still click with your index finger.

✔ For a psychedelic experience, click on the tab marked Motion along the window's top and then click in the box marked Show pointer trails. Windows 95 will make *ghost arrows* follow the mouse pointer. Laptop users can spot the arrow more easily when it is followed by ghosts. The more you slide the little box toward the long side of the bar, the longer your trail of mouse ghosts will grow.

✔ The mouse arrow doesn't have to move at the same speed as the mouse. To make the arrow *zip* across the screen with just a tiny push, click on the Motion tab along the top. Then, in the Pointer speed box, slide the little box toward the side of the scroll bar marked Fast. To slow down the mouse, allowing for more precise pointing, slide the box toward the Slow side.

Setting the Computer's Time and Date

Many computer users don't bother to set the computer's clock. They just look at their wristwatches to see when it's time to stop working. But they're missing out on an important computing feature: Computers stamp new files with the current date and time. If the computer doesn't know the correct date, it stamps files with the *wrong* date. Then how can you find the files you created yesterday? Last week?

Also, Windows 95 sometimes does some funny things to the computer's internal clock, so you may want to reset the date and time if you notice that the computer is living in the past.

To reset the computer's time or date, choose the Control Panel's
Date/Time icon:

Date/Time

A double-click on the Date/Time icon brings a little calendar to the screen,
shown in Figure 10-9. To change the date, just click on the correct date as listed
on the on-screen calendar. If the date's off by a month or more, click on the
little arrow next to the currently listed month. A list drops down, letting you
choose a different month. To change the year or the hour, click on the number
you'd like to change and then click on the up or down arrows to make the
number bigger or smaller. When the number is correct, click on the OK button
for Windows 95 to make the changes.

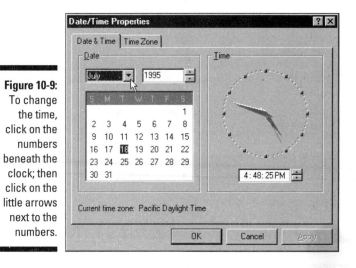

Figure 10-9:
To change
the time,
click on the
numbers
beneath the
clock; then
click on the
little arrows
next to the
numbers.

REMEMBER

✔ Moved to a new time zone? Then click on the Time Zone tab along the
top of the window. When the map of the world appears, click on the
country you've settled down in, and Windows 95 will automatically
choose the new time zone. Or, if you can't find your country on the map,
click on the downward-pointing arrow next to the currently listed time
zone. A *long* list of countries appears; click on the one where you're
currently hanging your hat.

✔ Windows 95 has a Find program, described in Chapter 11, that can locate
files by the time and date they were created — but *only* if you keep your
computer's date and time set correctly.

✔ Most computers have an internal clock that automatically keeps track of the time and date. Nevertheless, those clocks aren't always reliable, especially among laptops with "power-saving" features. Check your $2,000 computer's clock against your $20 wristwatch every few weeks to make sure that the computer is on the mark.

For an even quicker way to change your computer's time or date, double-click on the little clock Windows 95 puts on the taskbar that lives along the edge of the screen. Windows 95 brings up the Date/Time menu, just as if you'd waded through the Control Panel and double-clicked on the Date/Time icon.

Fiddling with the Printer

Most of the time, the printer will work fine. Especially after you turn it *on* and try printing again. In fact, most people will never need to read this section.

Occasionally, however, you may need to tweak some printer settings. You'll need to install a new printer or remove an old one that you've sold (so it won't keep cluttering up the list of printers). Either way, start by choosing the Control Panel's Printers icon:

Printers

The Printers dialog box surfaces, as shown in Figure 10-10.

Figure 10-10:
Double-clicking the Add Printer icon tells Windows 95 about your new printer.

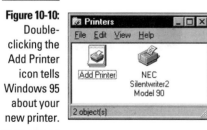

If you're installing a new printer, grab the Windows 95 compact disc or floppy disks that came in the box; you'll need them during the installation.

1. **To add a new printer, double-click on the Add Printer icon.**

   Déjà vu! You see the same list of printers as when you first installed Windows 95.

2. **Just as before, choose the Next button and then use the PgUp and PgDn keys to choose your printer's manufacturer and model number.**

   The Add Printer Wizard box lists the names of printer manufacturers on the left; click on the name of your printer's manufacturer, and the right side of the box lists the models of printers that manufacturer makes.

3. **When you see your printer listed, press Enter or double-click on the printer's name. Windows 95 asks you to stick the appropriate setup disks into a drive, and the drive makes some grinding noises.**

   After a moment, you see the new printer listed in the box.

4. **Click on the new printer's icon and choose the Set As Default Printer option from the window's File menu.**

   That's it. If you're like most people, your printer will work like a charm. If it doesn't, you may have to wade through the technical stuff in the sidebar about printer ports and such.

If you have more than one printer attached to your computer, choose your most-oft-used printer as the *default* printer. That choice tells Windows 95 to assume that it's printing to that oft-used printer.

✔ To remove a printer you no longer use, click on its name and then click on the Delete command button. That printer's name will no longer appear as an option when you try to print from a Windows 95-based program.

✔ You can change most of the printer options in the program you're printing from. Click on Files in the menu bar and then click on Print Setup. From there, you can often access the same box of printer options as you find in the Control Panel.

✔ Some printers offer a variety of options. For example, you can print from different paper trays or print at different resolutions. To play with these options, click on the Printer's icon with the right mouse button and choose Properties from the menu that pops up. Although different models of printers offer different options, most let you change paper size, fonts, and types of graphics.

✔ If your printer isn't listed in the Windows 95 master list, you have to contact the printer's manufacturer for a *driver.* When it comes in the mail, repeat the process for adding a printer, but click on the Have Disk button. Windows 95 asks you to stick in the manufacturer's disk so that it can copy the *driver* onto the hard disk. (For more information, check out the section in on installing new hardware, later in this chapter.)

🖊 Working with printers can be more complicated than trying to retrieve a stray hamster from under the kitchen cupboards. Feel free to use any of the Help buttons in the dialog boxes. Chances are they'll offer some helpful advice, and some are actually customized for your particular brand of printer. Too bad they can't catch hamsters.

Windows 95 is a little better at housekeeping than Windows 3.1, especially when it comes to deleting old files. When you delete a printer from the Control Panel, Windows 95 asks if you'd like to remove the old printer drivers, too. (Click on the <u>Y</u>es button, unless you think you'll be adding that printer back on in the near future.)

Printer ports and configuration nonsense

Windows 95 shoots information to printers through ports (little metal outlets on the computer's rump). Most printers connect to a port called *LPT1:*, or the first *line printer port*.

Always choose this option first. If it works, skip the rest of this technical chatter. You've already found success!

Some people, however, insist on plugging printers into a second printer port, or *LPT2:*. (If you meet one of these people, ask them why.) Still other people buy *serial* printers, which plug into *serial ports* (also known as *COM ports*).

Different brands of printers work with Windows 95 in different ways, but here are a few tips: To connect a printer to a different port, click on the printer's icon with your right mouse button and choose P<u>r</u>operties from the pop-up menu. Click on the tab marked Details,

and you can select the port you want. Look to see what port you're plugging the printer into, and select that port from the menu. (Computer ports are rarely labeled, so you'll probably have to bribe a computer guru to help you out. Start tossing Cheetos around your chair and desk; computer gurus are attracted by the smell.)

If you're connecting a printer to a serial port, you need to do one more little chore: configure the serial port. Click on the P<u>o</u>rt Settings box and make sure that the following numbers and characters appear, in this order: `9600, 8, N, 1, Xon/Xoff.`

The printer should be all set. If not, call over a computer guru. At least you only have to go through all this printer hassle once — unless you buy another printer.

Sound and Multimedia

The term *multimedia* means mixing two or more mediums — usually combining sound and pictures. A plain old television, for example, could be called a *multimedia tool,* especially if you're trying to impress somebody.

Windows 95 can mix sound and pictures if you have a *sound card:* a gizmo costing about $100 that slips inside the computer and hooks up to a pair of speakers or a stereo.

Macintosh computers have had sound for years. And for years, Mac owners have been able to *assign sounds to system events.* In lay language, that means having the computer make a barfing sound when it ejects a floppy disk.

In Windows 95, you can't assign sounds to the floppy drives, but you can assign noises to other *events* by double-clicking on the Control Panel's Sounds icon:

Sounds

The Sounds dialog box appears (see Figure 10-11.) Windows 95 automatically plays sounds for several system events. An event can be anything as simple as when a menu pops up or when Windows 95 first starts up in the morning.

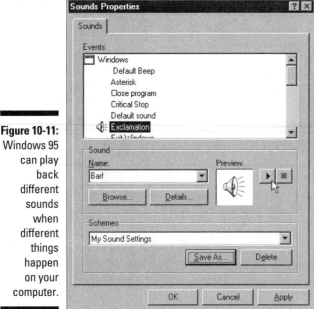

Figure 10-11:
Windows 95
can play
back
different
sounds
when
different
things
happen
on your
computer.

Windows 95 lists the events on the top of the box and lists the possible sounds directly below them in the box called <u>N</u>ame. To assign a sound, click on the event first and then click on the sound you want to hear for that event. In Figure 10-11, for example, Windows 95 is set up to make a barfing sound whenever it sends out an urgent dialog box with an exclamation point in it.

✔ Satisfied with your new choices of sounds? Then click in the box marked <u>S</u>ave As, and change the words Windows Default to something else, like My Sound Settings. That way you can still change back to the more polite Windows Default sounds when you don't want houseguests to hear your computer barf. (You can change back to My Sound Effects after they've left.)

✔ To take advantage of this multimedia feature, you have to buy and install a sound card. Then you have to tell Windows 95 about your new card by clicking on the Control Panel's Add New Hardware icon, described later in this chapter.

✔ To hear a sound before you assign it, click on its name and then click on the Preview button (the little black triangle next to the speaker).

✔ You can record your own sounds through most sound cards. You can probably pick up a cheap microphone at Radio Shack; many sound cards don't include one.

✔ Be forewarned: Sound consumes a *lot* of disk space, so stick with short recordings — short and sweet B. B. King guitar riffs, for example, or the sound of a doorbell ringing.

✔ Sound card not working right? You might have to muddle through the Multimedia icon, described in the dreary technical box that follows.

Multimedia setup problems

Multimedia gadgetry inevitably brings a multitude of setup problems. There are simply too many file formats and program settings for an easy ride. Although Windows 95 does an excellent job of setting up your computer's hardware automatically, the Control Panel's Multimedia icon lets techno-fiddlers change some of the settings. Because different computers use different parts, the settings listed under the Multimedia icon will vary, but here's a general look at what they can do:

Audio: This page controls your sound card's volume settings as well as its recording quality. The better the quality of the recording, the more hard disk space your recordings consume. A quicker way to adjust the volume is to simply click the little speaker in the corner of the taskbar.

MIDI: Musicians can tell Windows 95 about new MIDI instruments on this page.

CD Music: Mostly useful for adjusting the volume of headphones that plug into a CD-ROM's headphone jack.

Joystick: If your computer has a game port (found on most sound cards), come here to calibrate your joystick for Windows 95 games.

Advanced: Here Windows 95 lists all the multimedia devices attached to your computer (as well as a few devices you might want to add to your computer in the future). By clicking on a device and clicking on the Properties button near the bottom, you can turn a device on or off.

Adding New Hardware

When you wolf down a sandwich for lunch, you know what you ate. After all, you picked it out at the deli counter, chewed it, swallowed it, and wiped the bread crumbs away from the corner of your mouth.

But when you add a new part to your computer, it's turned off — Windows 95 is asleep. And when you turn the computer back on and Windows 95 returns to life, it probably won't notice the new part.

Here's the good news, however: If you simply tell Windows 95 to *look* for the new part, it will probably find it. In fact, Windows 95 will not only spot the new part, but it will introduce itself and start a warm and friendly working relationship using the right settings.

The Control Panel's Add New Hardware icon handles the process of introducing Windows 95 to anything you've recently attached to your computer. Here's what it looks like:

Add New
Hardware

Here's how to tell Windows 95 to look for any new computer parts you may have stuffed inside or plugged into your computer:

1. **Double-click on the Control Panel's Add New Hardware icon.**

   The Windows 95 Hardware Installation Wizard pops out of a hat, ready to introduce Windows 95 to whatever part you've stuffed inside your computer.

2. **Click on the Next button.**

   Windows 95 presents a list of computer parts on-screen.

3. **If you know what type of computer part you've installed, click on its name from the list; otherwise, choose Automatically detect installed hardware. Then click on the Next button.**

   Usually you'll have an inkling as to what you've installed: a new video card or modem, for example, or perhaps a sound card or CD-ROM drive. If so, click on the gadget's name from the box; otherwise, leave the program set on automatic.

Here's where things start getting a little different. If you choose Automatically detect installed hardware, Windows 95 looks inside your computer, sniffing out new parts. If it finds anything that looks new, it lists it. Did it guess right? Then click on the Finish button and follow the instructions. If it didn't find anything, though, you need to contact the manufacturer of your new part and ask for a *Windows 95 driver.*

If you didn't choose Automatically detect installed hardware but clicked on the name of your device instead, Windows 95 shows you a list of manufacturers. Click on the manufacturers that made your particular part, and Windows 95 shows you a list of models that manufacturer makes. See yours listed? Then click on the Finish button and follow the instructions. If it's not listed, you need to contact the company that made your new part and ask them for a *Windows 95 driver.*

- ✔ Adding a new modem? Then Windows 95 will want to know your current country and area code, as well as whether you dial a special number (such as a *9*) to reach an outside line. If you want to change this stuff later, double-click on the Control Panel's Modem icon — that brings you to the same page that the Add New Hardware icon does.

- ✔ Windows 95 is pretty good about identifying various gadgets that people have stuffed inside it, especially if your computer is "Plug and Play" compatible and you're installing a "Plug and Play" part. You'll find more information about Plug and Play in Chapter 4.

- ✔ If you're not sure what type of part you've installed, but you know the company that made it, choose "Unknown hardware," the choice at the bottom of the "Install specific hardware" list. Then, when Windows 95 lists a bunch of companies, click on the company that made your part. Windows 95 will list all of that company's parts it can recognize.

- ✔ In Windows 3.1, you had to know where you were going in order to get something done. Windows 95 is much more forgiving, and lots of the icons' functions are overlapping. If you install a new modem, for example, you can use the Add New Hardware icon or the Modem icon to introduce it to Windows 95. Adding a new printer? Use either the Add New Hardware icon or the Printer icon; both take you to the same place — the spot where you tell Windows 95 about your new printer.

Adding and Removing Programs

By adding an Add/Remove Programs icon to the Control Panel, Windows 95 is trying to trick you into thinking it's easier than ever to install a program. Nope. Here's what the icon looks like:

Add/Remove
Programs

Here's how the installation programs work if you're lucky. When you get a new program, look for a disk marked Install or Installation, and stick the disk into any disk drive that it fits. If the program came on a compact disc, put the disc into your compact disc drive.

Next, double-click on the Control Panel's Add/Remove Programs icon, click on the Install button, and click on Next from the next screen. Windows 95 searches all your disk drives for a disk containing an installation program; if it finds an installation program, it runs it, effectively installing the program. If it doesn't find one, it just gives up.

✔ Most programs you buy at software stores come with installation programs, so Windows 95 can install them without too much trouble. Some of the smaller shareware programs found on on-line services don't come with installation programs, unfortunately, so you'll have to install them yourself.

✔ Forced to install a DOS or Windows program yourself? Make a new folder somewhere on your hard drive and copy all the files from the program's disk to the new folder. Then to load the program, double-click on the program's icon from within that folder. Chapter 11 is filled with tips on creating folders, copying files, and sticking new programs on the Start menu.

✔ The Add/Remove Programs icon can *uninstall* programs, but only if those programs have been designed with the *uninstall* feature in mind. That means you won't find very many — if any — of your programs listed on the *uninstall* menu.

✔ Until the built-in uninstall feature of Windows 95 catches on, the easiest way to remove old or unwanted Windows programs is to buy a third-party *uninstaller* program, such as Quarterdeck's Cleansweep or Microhelp's Uninstaller.

✔ The Setup tab at the top of the Add/Remove Programs screen lets you add or remove some of the programs that came with Windows 95: programs for laptop users, extra wallpaper and sounds, network utilities, games, The Microsoft Network on-line service, and a few other goodies. To add one of the programs, click in its check box. To remove one you've installed, click in its check box. (Its check mark disappears, as does the program, when you click on the Apply button.)

✔ For safety's sake, make a Startup Disk — a disk that can still start up your computer if something dreadful happens. Put a blank floppy — or a floppy with destructible information — in drive A and click on the Startup Disk tab from the top of the Add/Remove Programs program. Click the Create Disk button and follow the instructions.

Learning Which Icons to Avoid

Unless you have a very pressing reason, avoid these icons in the Control Panel: Network, Regional Settings, Keyboard, System, Microsoft Exchange Profiles, Microsoft Mail Post Office, and Passwords.

✔ The Network icon controls how Windows 95 talks to other computers through your office's network — those cables meandering from PC to PC. Talk to your network administrator before playing with this icon "just to see what it does."

✔ The Regional Settings icon changes the keyboard layout to the one used by people in other countries. It doesn't make the Windows 95 dialog boxes appear in German (although you can order the German version of Windows 95 from Microsoft). Instead, a foreign keyboard layout makes certain keys produce foreign characters. It also changes the way currency appears and stuff like that. You can easily leave the keyboard set for Taiwan by accident, and then you wonder why the time and date look funny.

✔ The Keyboard icon doesn't do any major damage, but it doesn't do any major good, either. It controls how fast a key repeats if you hold it down. Big deal. If the keyboard isn't mmmaking characters repeat, then don't messsssss with it. In case you're into the Dvorak keyboard layout, it is listed here as well.

✔ The information listed in the System icon turns on network hounds and techno-nerds. It's out of the realm of this book. Ditto for the Mail and FAX and Microsoft Mail Post Office (although you'll find a little on-line stuff covered in Chapter 13).

✔ Finally, the Passwords icon is kind of like the switch in the new Ford Explorer that can remember different seat- and mirror-adjustment settings for up to four different drivers. By assigning different passwords to different computer users, Windows 95 can switch to a customized desktop setting for each person who logs in.

Part III
Using Windows 95 Applications (and Running DOS, Should the Mood Strike)

The 5th Wave   **By Rich Tennant**

US INQUIRER
ELVIS ALIVE!
LIVING WITH OZZIE NELSON

MICHAEL JACKSON TO WED HIMSELF!!

US INQUIRER
GRANDMOTHER GIVES BIRTH TO EGGPLANT SHAPED LIKE RICHARD NIXON!
NIXON DENIES RUMORS OF INVOLVEMENT

US INQUIRER
TALKING DOG REPLACES OPRAH!
DONOHUE WORRIED

US INQUIRER
MAN TRANSPLANTS OWN KIDNEY!!
USED GARDENING TOOLS

US INQUIRER
VANNA SECRETLY MARRIED TO PEE WEE HERMAN
SECRET WORD IS "HONEYMOON"

US INQUIRER
UFO'S LAND IN VENICE BEACH, CA.
! NO ONE NOTICES!

ALIENS OPEN NEW CUISINE RESTAURANT

US INQUIRER
ANCIENT ALIVE

US INQUIRER
REMOTE TRIBE WORSHIPS !! LAVA LAMP !!
COMPANY SEEKS ROYALTIES

JIM BAKER STARTS PTLL CLUB

MANAGING EDITOR

"A STORY ABOUT A SOFTWARE COMPANY THAT SHIPS BUG-FREE PROGRAMS ON TIME, WITH TOLL-FREE SUPPORT, AND FREE UPGRADES? NAAAH – TOO WEIRD."

In this part . . .

Did you know that

- Kleenex were called Celluwipes back in 1924?

- Fred MacMurray's face was the model for comic book hero Captain Marvel?

- Smokey Bear's first name was Hot Foot Teddy?

- Windows 95 comes with a bunch of free programs that aren't even mentioned on the outside of the box?

This part takes a look at all the stuff you're getting for nothing. Well, for the price on your sales receipt, anyway.

Chapter 11

The Windows 95 Desktop, Start Button, and Taskbar

. . . .

In This Chapter

▶ Using the desktop

▶ Making shortcuts

▶ Deleting files, folders, programs, and icons

▶ Retrieving deleted items from the Recycle Bin

▶ The Start button's reason to live

▶ Putting programs on the Start button menu

▶ Using the taskbar

. . . .

*I*n the old days of computing, pale technoweenies typed disgustingly long strings of code words into computers to make the computers do something. *Anything.*

Windows 95 brings computers to the age of modern convenience. To start a program, simply click on a button. There's a slight complication, however: The buttons no longer *look* like buttons. In fact, some of the buttons are hidden, revealed only by the push of yet another button (if you're lucky enough to stumble upon the right place to push).

This chapter covers the three main Windows 95 buttonmongers: the desktop, the taskbar, and that mother of all buttons — the Start button.

Rolling Objects along the Windows 95 Desktop

Normally, nobody would think of mounting a desktop sideways. Keeping the pencils from rolling off a normal desk is hard enough.

But in Windows 95, your computer monitor's screen is known as the Windows *desktop*, and it's the area where all your work takes place. When working with Windows 95, you'll be creating files and folders right on your new electronic desktop and scattering those files and folders across the screen.

For example, need to write a letter asking the neighbor to return the circular saw she borrowed? Here's how to put the desktop's functions to immediate use.

Point at just about any Windows 95 item and click your right mouse button to see a menu listing the things you're allowed to do with that item.

1. **Click on the desktop with your right mouse button.**

    A menu pops up, as shown in Figure 11-1.

2. **Point at the word New and click on WordPad Document from the menu that appears.**

    Since you're creating something new — a new letter — you should point at the word New. Windows 95 lists the new things you can create on the desktop. Choose WordPad Document, as shown in Figure 11-2.

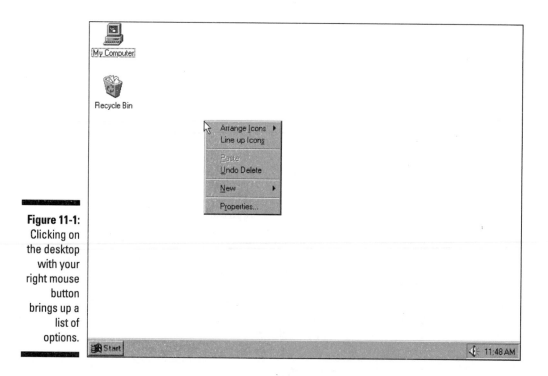

Figure 11-1:
Clicking on the desktop with your right mouse button brings up a list of options.

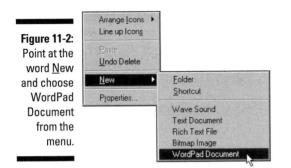

Figure 11-2:
Point at the
word <u>N</u>ew
and choose
WordPad
Document
from the
menu.

3. Type a title for your letter and press Enter.

When an icon for a WordPad document appears on the desktop, Windows
95 doesn't want you to lose it. So the first step is to give it a name of up to
255 characters. As soon as you start typing, your new title replaces the old
name of New WordPad Document, as shown in Figure 11-3.

Figure 11-3:
Start typing
to create
the icon's
new name.

4. Double-click on your new icon, write your letter, save it, and print it.

Double-clicking on the new icon calls up WordPad, the word processor, so
you can write the letter requesting the return of your circular saw. Done
writing? Then move on to Step 5.

5. Click on <u>S</u>ave from WordPad's <u>F</u>ile menu to save the letter.

**6. Head back to WordPad's <u>F</u>ile menu and choose <u>P</u>rint to send the letter
to the printer.**

**7. To store the file, drag the icon to a folder. Or to delete it, drag the file to
the Recycle Bin.**

When you've finished writing and printing the letter, you need to decide
what to do with the file. You can simply leave its icon on your desk, but
that clutters things up. If you'd like to save the letter in a folder, click on
the desktop with your right mouse button and choose <u>F</u>older from the
<u>N</u>ew menu. Windows 95 tosses a new folder onto your desktop, ready for
you to drag your letter into.

Or, if you want to delete the letter, drag the icon to your Recycle Bin
(described in the next section).

- Windows 95 is designed for you to work right on the desktop. From the desktop, you can create new things like files, folders, sounds, and graphics — just about anything. After working with your new file or folder, you can store it or delete it.

- You can store your favorite files and folders right on the desktop. Or, to be more organized, you can drag your files and folders into the folders listed in the My Computer window. (The My Computer program gets a lot more coverage in Chapter 12.)

- Confused about what something is supposed to do? Click on it with your right mouse button. Windows 95 tosses up a menu listing just about everything you can do with that particular object. This trick works on the desktop or just about any icon you'll come across.

- Desktop looking rather cluttered? Make Windows 95 line up the icons in orderly rows: Click on the desktop with the right mouse button, point at the Arrange Icons option, and choose by Name from the menu.

Using the Recycle Bin

The Recycle Bin, that little wastebasket with green arrows in the upper-left corner of the desktop, is supposed to work like a *real* Recycle Bin — something you can fish the Sunday paper out of if somebody pitched the comics section before you had a chance to read it.

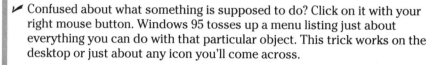

Recycle Bin

Terribly boring desktop trivia

That's right—Windows 95 considers the desktop to be a mammoth folder. That mammoth folder opens across your screen when you start Windows 95, and it closes up when you shut down Windows 95 with the Start button's Sh*u*t Down command.

And because the desktop's a folder, it's actually a subdirectory, too. Windows 95 normally hides it from view, but if you choose Options from the Explorer's *V*iew menu to display *hidden* files, you'll see the Desktop folder resting casually in the Windows 95 directory.

Made any new folders on the desktop? Those folders are really just subdirectories of the Desktop directory.

If you want to get rid of something in Windows 95 — a file or folder, for example — simply drag it to the Recycle Bin. Point at the file or folder's icon with the mouse and, while holding down the left mouse button, point at the Recycle Bin. Let go of the mouse button, and your detritus disappears. Windows 95 stuffs it into the Recycle Bin.

But if you want to bypass that cute metaphor, there's another way to delete stuff: Click on your unwanted file or folder's icon with the right mouse button and choose Delete from the menu that pops up. Whoosh! Windows 95 asks cautiously if you're *sure* you want to delete the icon. If you click on the Yes button, Windows 95 dumps the icon into the Recycle Bin, just as if you'd dragged it there.

So, if you like to "drag and drop," feel free to drag your garbage to the Recycle bin and let go. If you prefer the menus, click with your right mouse button and choose Delete. Or if you like alternative lifestyles, click on the unwanted icon with your left button and push your keyboard's Delete key. All three methods toss the file into the Recycle Bin, where it can be salvaged later or, eventually, purged for good.

- ✔ Want to retrieve something you've deleted? Double-click on the Recycle Bin icon, and a window appears, listing deleted items. See the name of your accidentally deleted icon? Then drag it to the desktop. Point at the icon's name and, while holding down the left mouse button, point at the desktop. Let go of the mouse button, and the Recycle Bin coughs up the deleted item, good as new.

- ✔ Sometimes the Recycle Bin can get pretty full. If you're searching fruitlessly for a file you've recently deleted, tell the Recycle Bin to sort the filenames in the order in which they were deleted. Click on View, point at Arrange Icons, and choose by Delete Date from the menu that pops out. Instead of listing the deleted files in alphabetical order, Recycle Bin now lists the most recently deleted files at the bottom.

- ✔ The Recycle Bin's icon changes from an empty wastepaper basket to a full one as soon as it's holding a deleted file.

- ✔ A full Recycle Bin can eat up 10 percent of your hard disk space. To free up some space, empty it. Click on the Recycle Bin with your right mouse button and choose Empty Recycle Bin from the menu. Then click on the Yes button when Windows 95 asks if you're sure you want to *really* delete those files and folders that you've already deleted once. Cautious program, that Windows 95.

- ✔ You can control how long the Recycle Bin holds on to your deleted files. Click on the Recycle Bin with your right mouse button and choose Properties from its menu. Normally, Recycle Bin waits until your deleted files consume 10 percent of your hard drive before it begins purging your oldest deleted files. If you want the Recycle Bin to hang on to more deleted files, increase the percentage. If you're a sure-fingered clicker who never makes mistakes, decrease the percentage.

Making a shortcut

Some people like to organize their desktop, putting a pencil sharpener on one corner and a box of Kleenex on the other corner. Other people like their Kleenex box in the top desk drawer. Microsoft knew that one desktop design could never please everybody, so Windows 95 lets people customize their desktops to suit individual tastes and needs.

For example, you may find yourself frequently copying files to a floppy disk in drive A. Normally, to perform that operation, you open the My Computer icon and drag your files to the drive A icon living in there. But there's a quicker way, and it's called a Windows 95 *shortcut*. A shortcut is simply a push button — an icon — that stands for something else.

For example, here's how to put a shortcut for drive A on your desktop:

1. **Double-click on the desktop's My Computer icon.**

   The My Computer folder opens up, showing the icons for your disk drives as well as folders for your Control Panel and Printer. (My Computer gets more coverage in Chapter 12.)

2. **With your right mouse button, drag the drive A icon's shortcut to the desktop.**

   Point at the drive A icon and, while holding down your right mouse button, point at the desktop, as shown in Figure 11-4. Let go of your mouse button.

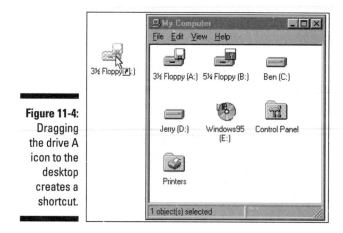

Figure 11-4: Dragging the drive A icon to the desktop creates a shortcut.

3. Choose Create Shortcut(s) Here from the menu.

Windows 95 puts an icon for drive A on your desktop, but it looks a little different from the drive A icon you dragged. Since it's only a shortcut — not the original icon — it has a little arrow in its corner, as shown in Figure 11-5.

Figure 11-5:
The icon on the left is a shortcut that stands for the icon on the right.

Shortcut to 3½   3½ Floppy (A:)
Floppy (A)

That's it. Now you won't need to root through the My Computer or Explorer folders and programs to access drive A. The drive A shortcut on your desktop works just as well as the *real* drive A icon found in My Computer and Explorer.

✔ A shortcut is the equivalent of an icon in Windows 3.1's Program Manager — a push button that starts a program or loads a file. A shortcut for a disk drive is just like the disk drive icons along the top of Windows 3.1's File Manager, too.

✔ Feel free to create desktop shortcuts for your most commonly accessed programs, files, or disk drives. Shortcuts are a quick way to make Windows 95 easier to use.

✔ If your newly dragged icon doesn't have an arrow in its bottom corner, it's not a shortcut. Instead, you've dragged the *real* program to your desktop, and other programs might not be able to find it. Drag the icon back to where it was and try again. (You probably mistakenly held down the *left* mouse button instead of the correct button — the *right* button.)

✔ Grown tired of a shortcut? Feel free to delete it. Deleting a shortcut has no effect on the original file, folder, or program that it represents.

✔ You can make as many shortcuts as you'd like. You can even make several shortcuts for the same thing. For example, you can put a shortcut for drive A in *all* of your folders.

✔ Windows 95's shortcuts aren't very good at keeping track of moving files. If you create a shortcut to a file or program and then move the file or program to a different spot on your hard drive, the shortcut won't be able to find that file or program anymore.

Uh, what's the difference between a shortcut and an icon?

An icon for a file, folder, or program looks pretty much like a shortcut, except the shortcut has an arrow wedged in its lower reaches. And double-clicking on a shortcut and double-clicking on an icon do pretty much the same thing: start a program or load a file or folder.

But a shortcut is only a servant of sorts. When you double-click on the shortcut, it runs over to the program, file, or folder that the shortcut represents and kickstarts that program, file, or folder into action.

You could do the same thing yourself by rummaging through your computer's folders, finding the program, file, or folder you're after, and personally double-clicking on its icon to bring it to life. But it's often more convenient to create a shortcut so you don't have to rummage so much.

  ✔ If you delete a shortcut — the icon with the little arrow — you're not doing any real harm. You're just firing the servant that fetched things for you, probably creating more work for yourself in the process.

  ✔ If you accidentally delete a shortcut, you can pull it out of the Recycle Bin, just like anything else that's deleted in Windows 95.

The Start Button's Reason to Live

The Start button lives on your taskbar, and it's always ready for action. By using the Start button, you can start programs, adjust Windows 95's settings, find help for sticky situations, or, thankfully, shut down Windows 95 and get away from the computer for a while.

The little Start button is so eager to please, in fact, that it starts shooting out menus full of options as soon as you click on it. Just click on the button once, and the first layer of menus pops out, as shown in Figure 11-6.

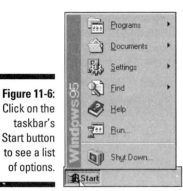

Figure 11-6:
Click on the
taskbar's
Start button
to see a list
of options.

The explosive Table 11-1 shows what the different parts of the Start button do when you point at them.

Table 11-1	The Start Button
This Part	*Does This When You Point at It*
Programs ▶	Probably the most used spot. Point here, and a second menu appears, listing available programs and folders containing related programs.
Documents ▶	Point here to see the names of the last 15 files you've played with. Spot one you want to open again? Click on its name to reopen it.
Settings ▶	Allows access to the Control Panel and Printer settings, as well as ways to customize the Start button menus and taskbar.
Find ▶	Lost a program or file? Head here to make Windows 95 search for it.
Help	Clicking here does the same thing as pressing F1 — it brings up the Windows 95 Help menu.
Run...	Used mostly by old-school, "stick-shift" computer users, it lets you start a program by typing in the program's name and *path*.
Shut Down...	Click here to either shut down and restart Windows, close all programs and log on as a different user, or shut it down for the day.
Start	Clicking on the Start button makes the Start menu shoot out of the button's head.

- ✔ Microsoft boiled down the Windows 3.1 Program Manager and came up with the Start button. The Start button can handle just about everything the Program Manager does. Those folders listed on the Start button's Programs menu would be program groups in the Program Manager. Imagine!

- ✔ The Start button's menu changes as you add programs to your computer. That means that the Start button on your friend's computer will probably have slightly different menus than the ones on your own computer.

- ✔ See the little arrows on the menu next to the words Programs, Documents, Settings, and Find? The arrows mean that when you point at those words, another menu pops up, offering more detailed options.

- ✔ Need to open a file yet another time? Before you spend time clicking your way through folders, see if it's listed under the Start button's Documents area. You'll find your past 15 documents listed there, ready to be opened with a click.

Starting a program from the Start button

This one's easy. Click on the Start button and when the menu pops out of the button's head, point at the word Programs. Yet another menu pops up, this one listing the names of programs or folders full of programs.

If you see your program listed, click on the name. Wham! Windows 95 kicks that program to the screen. If you don't see your program listed, try pointing at the folders listed on the menu. New menus fly out of those folders, listing even more programs.

When you spot your program's name, just click on it. In fact, you don't have to click until you see the program's name: The Start button opens and closes all the menus automatically, depending on where the mouse arrow is pointing at the time.

- ✔ Still don't see your program listed by name? Then head for Chapter 8 and find the "Finding Lost Files and Folders" section. You can tell Windows 95 to find your program for you.

- ✔ There's another way to load a program that's not listed — if you know where the program's living on your hard drive. Choose Run from the Start button menu, type in the program's name, and press Enter. If Windows 95 finds the program, it runs it. If it can't find the program, though, click on the Browse button. Shazam! Yet another box appears, this time listing programs by name. Pick your way through the dialog box until you see your program; then double-click on its name and click on the OK button to load it.

- ✔ If you don't know how to *pick your way through* this particular dialog box, head to the section of Chapter 6 on opening a file. (This particular dialog box rears its head every time you load or save a file or open a program.)

Adding a program to the Start button

The Windows 95 Start button works great — until you're hankering for something that's not listed on the menu. How do you add things to the Start button's menu?

If you're installing a Windows program that comes with its own installation program, breathe a sigh of relief. Those programs automatically put themselves on the Start button's menu. But what if your program comes from a simpler household and doesn't have an installation program? Well, it means more work for you, as described here:

1. **Copy the program to your hard drive.**

   Create a new folder somewhere on your hard drive and copy your new program and its files to that folder. (And turn to Chapter 12 if you're a little sketchy about creating folders and copying files.)

2. **Click on the Start button and then point at <u>S</u>ettings.**

   A menu shoots out from the right side of the Start menu.

3. **Click on <u>T</u>askbar and then click on the Start Menu Programs tab.**

   The tab lurks along the top, on the right side.

4. **Click on the <u>A</u>dd button and then click on B<u>r</u>owse.**

   A new box pops up, as shown in Figure 11-7.

TECHNICAL STUFF

Is <u>R</u>un a *real* DOS command line?

For the most part, Windows 95 treats the Start button's <u>R</u>un command just like a regular ol' DOS command line. When you type in the name of a Windows or DOS program, Windows 95 tries to run it. Windows 95 first searches the current directory and then it looks along the path. If Windows 95 can't find the program, it sends out a message of complaint. (Just click on the OK button and start over.)

If Windows 95 doesn't find the program, you have to type in the path name along with the program's name. For example, to load WordPerfect, you type something like this:

`C:\WORDS\WP\WP`

The Start button's <u>R</u>un command line differs from the DOS command line in one key area: It can't handle DOS commands like DIR and TYPE.

If you're salivating at the thought of a command line, you probably shouldn't be running Windows 95. If you're looking for a quick, menuless way to call up a program, though, you might want to give the <u>R</u>un command an occasional shot.

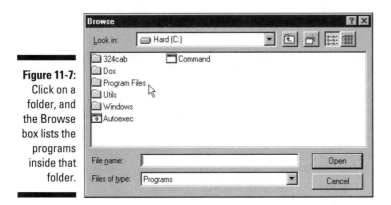

Figure 11-7:
Click on a
folder, and
the Browse
box lists the
programs
inside that
folder.

Click on the folder to which you copied the program and its files.

Hint: If you can't find that folder, click on the icon of the little folder with the arrow inside, up near the top. Doing that tells Windows 95 to work its way up the folder listings, eventually showing you a list of your computer's disk drives.

5. **Double-click on the icon of the program you want to add.**

The program's filename appears in the Command line box. (By double-clicking on the program's name, you were able to avoid typing in the name yourself.)

6. **Click on the Next button and then double-click on the folder where you'd like your program to appear on the Start menu.**

For example, if you want your new program to appear under the Programs heading, simply click on the Programs folder. In fact, Windows 95 automatically highlights the Programs folder, assuming you'll want to install your new program there.

7. **Type the name that you want to see on the menu for that program and then click on the Finish button.**

Most people just type the program's name. (Just as many people have nicknames, most program's filenames are different from their *real* names. For example, you'd probably want to change WP — the filename — to WordPerfect — the program's real name.)

8. **Click on the OK button at the bottom of the box.**

That gets rid of the Taskbar Properties box and *really* finishes the job. Now, when you click on the Start button, you'll see your new program listed on the menu.

A quicker but dirtier way to add programs to the Start menu

There's a quicker way to add a program to the Start menu, but it's not as versatile. The steps listed let you add a program's icon anyplace on the menu. But if you simply want the program's icon on the menu *now,* and you don't care about location, try this:

Open the My Computer or Explorer program and find the folder to which you've copied your pro-

gram. Then drag the program's icon over to the Start button and let go. Point at the program and, while holding down the mouse button, point at the Start button. When the icon hovers over the Start button, let go of the mouse button.

Now, when you click on the Start button, you'll see your newly installed program's icon at the very top.

✔ These steps can put both Windows and DOS programs on your Start menu. (If your DOS program doesn't work, head for Chapter 14, which is full of ways to doctor your DOS programs into health under Windows 95. Plus, it shows how to change the program's icon.)

✔ Windows 95 lets you add programs to the Start menu in several ways. The one I just listed is probably the easiest one to follow step by step.

✔ To get rid of unwanted menu items, follow these steps but choose the Remove button instead of the Add button in Step 4.

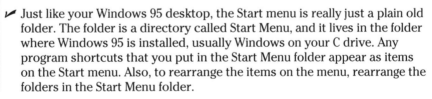

✔ Just like your Windows 95 desktop, the Start menu is really just a plain old folder. The folder is a directory called Start Menu, and it lives in the folder where Windows 95 is installed, usually Windows on your C drive. Any program shortcuts that you put in the Start Menu folder appear as items on the Start menu. Also, to rearrange the items on the menu, rearrange the folders in the Start Menu folder.

Shutting down Windows 95

Although the big argument used to be about whether pasta is fattening, today's generation has found a new source of disagreement: Should a computer be left on all the time or turned off at the end of the day? Both camps have decent arguments, and there's no real answer (except you should always turn off your monitor when you won't be using it for a half hour or so).

However, if you want to turn off your computer, don't just head for the off switch. First, you need to tell Windows 95 about your plans.

To do that, click on the S̲hut Down command from the Start menu and then click on the S̲hut down the computer button from the box that appears. Finally, click on the Y̲es button; that tells Windows 95 to put away all your programs and make sure you've saved all your important files.

After Windows 95 has prepared the computer to be turned off, you'll see a message on the screen saying it's okay to reach for the big red switch.

✔ If Windows 95 is acting weird — or if Windows 95 tells you to shut down and restart your computer — click on the S̲hut Down command from the Start menu. However, choose the R̲estart the computer option from the box. Windows 95 saves all your files, shuts itself down, and comes back to life, ready for more work.

✔ Don't turn off your computer unless you've first used the S̲hut Down command from the Start button. Windows 95 needs to prepare itself for the shutdown, or it might accidentally eat some of your important information.

The Taskbar

Put a second or third window onto the Windows 95 desktop, and you'll immediately see the Big Problem: Windows and programs tend to cover each other up, making them difficult to locate.

The solution is the taskbar. Shown in Figure 11-8, the taskbar is that little bar running along the bottom edge of your screen.

The taskbar keeps track of all the open folders and currently running programs by listing their names. And, luckily, the taskbar is almost always visible, no matter how cluttered your desktop becomes.

✔ When you want to bring a program, file, or folder to the forefront of the screen, click on its name on the taskbar.

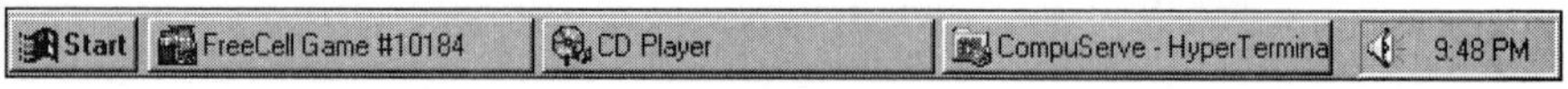

Figure 11-8:
The taskbar
lists the
names of all
your
currently
running
programs
and open
folders.

| 🏁 Start | 🎴 FreeCell Game #10184 | 💿 CD Player | 📞 CompuServe - HyperTermina | 🔊 9:48 PM |

✔ If the taskbar *does* manage to disappear, press Ctrl+Esc; that usually brings it to the surface.

✔ If you can only see part of the taskbar — it's hanging off the edge of the screen, for example — point at the edge you can see. When the mouse pointer turns into a two-headed arrow, hold down your mouse button and move the mouse to drag the taskbar back into view.

✔ If the taskbar looks too bloated, try the same trick. Point at its edge until the mouse pointer turns into a two-headed arrow and then drag the taskbar's edge inward until it's the right size.

The taskbar works somewhat like the minimized icons Windows 3.1 loads along the bottom of your screen. There are a few key differences, however: Windows 3.1 only displays icons of *minimized* programs; the taskbar displays icons for any currently running program. Also, Windows 3.1 lets you drag and drop files onto minimized icons — you can hear a WAV file by dragging and dropping it onto a minimized Media Player icon, for example. But you can't drag and drop anything onto the taskbar's program icons; you can only drag and drop files onto open windows.

Clicking on the taskbar's sensitive areas

Like a crafty card player, the taskbar comes with a few tips and tricks. For one thing, it has the Start button. With a click on the Start button, you can launch programs, change settings, find programs, get help, and order pizza. (Well, you can't order pizza, but you can do all the things mentioned in the Start button section earlier in this chapter.)

But the Start button is only one of the taskbar's tricks; some others are listed in Figure 11-9.

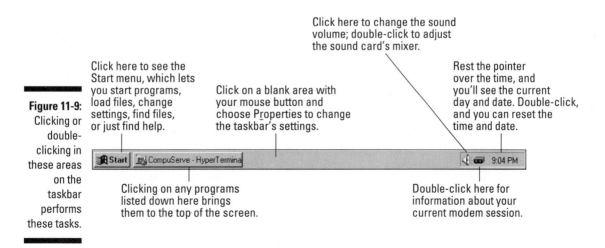

Figure 11-9: Clicking or double-clicking in these areas on the taskbar performs these tasks.

Click here to change the sound volume; double-click to adjust the sound card's mixer.

Click here to see the Start menu, which lets you start programs, load files, change settings, find files, or just find help.

Click on a blank area with your mouse button and choose Properties to change the taskbar's settings.

Rest the pointer over the time, and you'll see the current day and date. Double-click, and you can reset the time and date.

Clicking on any programs listed down here brings them to the top of the screen.

Double-click here for information about your current modem session.

Clicking on the Start button brings up the Start menu, described earlier in this chapter. Also, hold the mouse pointer over the clock, and Windows 95 shows the current day and date. Or if you want to change the time or date, a double-click on the clock summons the Windows 95 time/date change program.

If you have a sound card, a click on the little speaker brings up the volume control, shown in Figure 11-10. Slide the volume knob up for louder sound; slide it down for peace and quiet. (Or click on the Mute box to turn the sound off completely.)

Figure 11-10:
Clicking on the little speaker lets you adjust the sound card's volume.

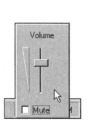

Double-click on the little speaker to bring up a more advanced mixer program, shown in Figure 11-11, if your sound card offers that feature. Mixers let you adjust volume levels for your microphone, line inputs, CD players, and other features.

Figure 11-11:
Double-clicking on the little speaker brings up a mixer program for the sound card.

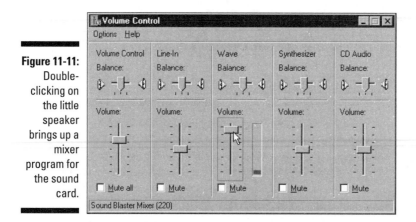

If you're running a modem, a little picture of a modem appears next to the clock, as shown in Figure 11-12. Double-click on the modem to see statistics on the amount of data your modem is pushing and pulling over the phone lines.

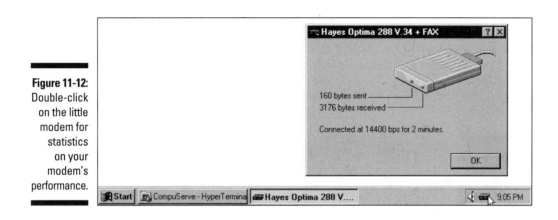

Figure 11-12: Double-click on the little modem for statistics on your modem's performance.

- ✔ Other icons often appear next to the clock, depending on what Windows 95 is up to. If you're printing, for example, you'll see a little printer down there. Laptops sometimes show a battery monitor. As with all the other icons, a double-click on the printer or battery monitor brings up information about the printer's or battery's status.

- ✔ Want to minimize all your desktop's open windows in a hurry? Click on a blank part of the taskbar with your right mouse button and choose the Minimize All Windows option from the pop-up menu. All the programs keep running, but they're now minimized to icons along the taskbar. To bring them back to the screen, just click on their names from the taskbar.

- ✔ To organize your open windows, click on a blank part of the taskbar with your right mouse button and choose one of the tile commands. Windows 95 scoops up all your open windows and lays them back down in neat, orderly squares.

Customizing the taskbar

Although Windows 95 starts the taskbar along the bottom of the screen, it doesn't have to stay there. If you'd prefer that your taskbar hang from the top of your screen like a bat, just drag it there. Point at a blank spot of the taskbar and, while holding down your mouse button, point at the top of the screen. Let go of the mouse button, and the taskbar dangles from the roof, as shown in Figure 11-13.

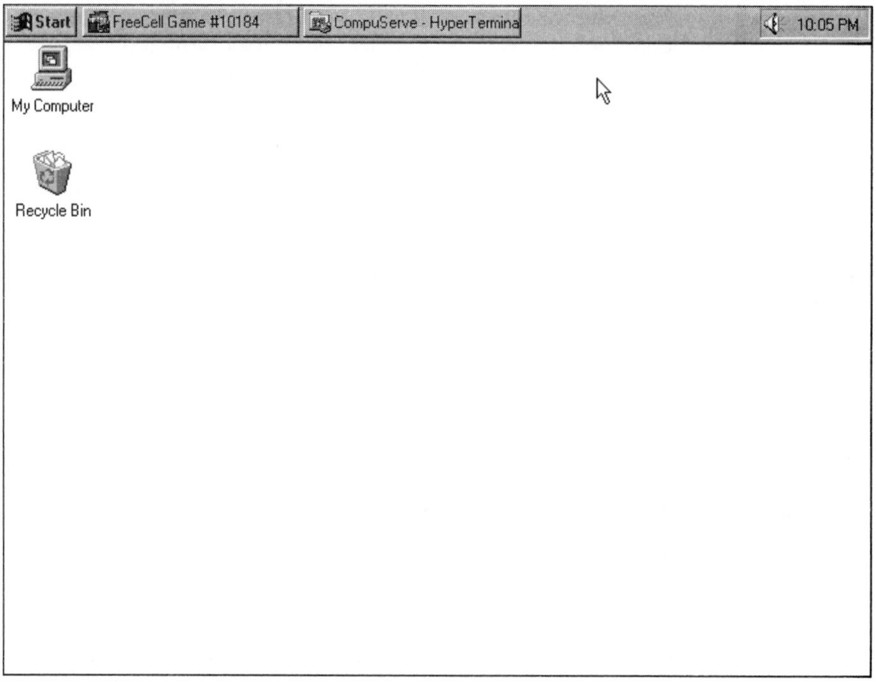

| Start | FreeCell Game #10184 | CompuServe - HyperTerminal | 10:05 PM |

My Computer

Recycle Bin

Figure 11-13:
The taskbar
can be
moved to
any side of
the screen
by dragging
it there.

Prefer it along one side? Then drag it there, as shown in Figure 11-14. (The buttons become more difficult to read, however.)

If the taskbar is starting to look too crowded, you can make it wider by dragging its edges outward, as shown in Figure 11-15.

✔ To change other taskbar options, click on a bare taskbar area with your right mouse button and choose Properties from the pop-up menu. From there, you can make the taskbar always stay on top of the current pile of windows, make the taskbar automatically hide itself, hide the clock, and shrink the Start menu's icons. Whenever you click on an option button, a handy on-screen picture previews the change. If the change looks good, click on the OK button to save it.

✔ Feel free to experiment with the taskbar, changing its size and position until it looks right for you. It won't break.

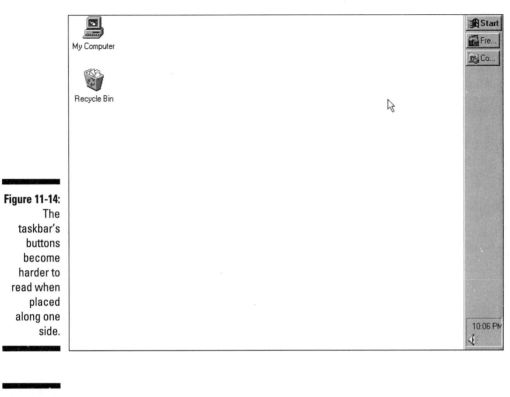

Figure 11-14:
The taskbar's buttons become harder to read when placed along one side.

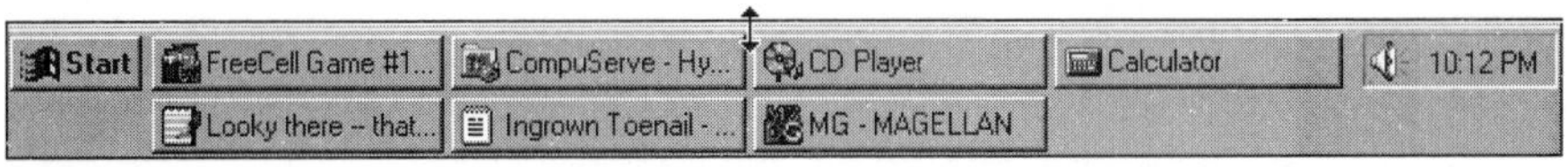

Figure 11-15:
Dragging the taskbar's edge upward gives the icons more room to display their titles.

Chapter 12

Those Scary Explorer and My Computer Programs

*T*he Explorer program is where people wake up from the Windows dream, clutching a pillow in horror. They bought Windows to make their computers easier to use, to lift them from the DOS psychobabble of *folder levels* and *application extensions* and *hidden files.*

But open Explorer, and those ugly DOS terms leer up at you. You not only have to juggle that painfully technical DOS stuff, but you have to do it while bouncing from button to button. The My Computer program isn't quite as painful, but it's still awkward enough to leave a few bruises.

This chapter explains how to use the Explorer and My Computer programs, and along the way it dishes out a big enough dose of DOS for you to get your work done. But, if you're really into file management (heaven knows why), consider picking up this book's forefather, *DOS For Dummies,* published by IDG Books Worldwide. It goes into just enough detail (yet keeps the dirge level gratefully low).

Why Is Explorer So Scary?

Explorer is an awkward mixture of two wildly different computing worlds: DOS and Windows. It's as if somebody tried to combine an automobile with a bathtub. Then everybody's confused when the door opens and water pours out.

To join in the confusion, click on a folder with your right mouse button and, when the little menu pops out, choose the <u>E</u>xplore option.

Everybody organizes his or her computer differently. Some people don't organize their computers at all. So your Explorer window looks a little different from the one shown in Figure 12-1.

Like Explorer, the My Computer program, shown in Figure 12-2, lets you sling files around but in a slightly different way. The My Computer program is a big panel of buttons — sort of an extension of your desktop — and Explorer is a big panel of filenames. In fact, some people like Explorer's *text-based* system of names better than My Computer's *picture-based* system. (It's that right-brained versus left-brained stuff.)

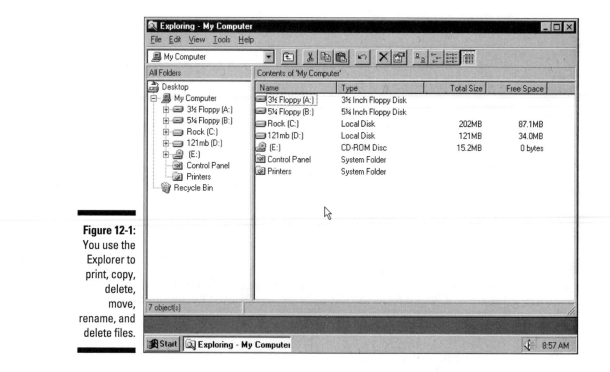

Figure 12-1:
You use the
Explorer to
print, copy,
delete,
move,
rename, and
delete files.

Figure 12-2:
The My
Computer
program
performs
the same
tasks as
Explorer, but
in slightly
different
ways.

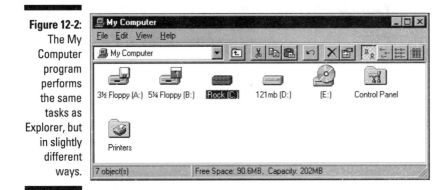

The icons in Windows 3.1 Program Manager are just buttons that stand for your programs. Deleting them doesn't harm the actual program. That's not true with the Windows 95 My Computer program. Unless the icon you're deleting has a little arrow lodged in its lower left side, that icon is an actual program or file. Make sure that you're deleting the icon you want. (And if you goof and delete the wrong one, fish it back out of the Recycle Bin as soon as possible.)

✔ In a way, learning how to deal with files is like learning how to play the piano: Neither is intuitively obvious, and you'll hit some bad notes with both. Don't be frustrated if you don't seem to be getting the hang of it. Liberace would have hated file management at first, too.

✔ Tired of using a menu to load Explorer? Then press the Shift key while double-clicking any folder you want to explore. The Explorer program pops up, showing you the contents of the current folder.

Getting the Lowdown on Folders

This stuff is really boring, but if you don't read it, you'll be just as lost as your files.

A *folder* is a workplace on a disk. Hard drives are divided into many folders to separate your many projects. You can work with the spreadsheet, for example, without having all the word-processing files get in the way.

Any disk can have folders, but hard drives need them the most because they need a way to organize their thousands of files. By dividing a hard drive into little folder compartments, you can more easily see where everything sits.

The Explorer and My Computer programs enable you to move around to different folders and peek at the files you've stuffed inside each one. It's a pretty good organizational scheme, actually. Socks never fall behind a folder and jam the drawer.

Folders used to be called *directories* and *subdirectories*. But some people were getting used to that, so the industry switched to the term *folders*.

✔ Folders can be inside folders to add a deeper level of organization, like adding drawer partitions to sort your socks by color. Each sock color partition is a smaller, organizing folder of the larger sock-drawer folder.

✔ Of course, you can ignore folders and keep all your files right on the Windows 95 desktop. That's like tossing everything into the back seat of the car and pawing around to find your Kleenex box a month later. Stuff you've organized is a lot easier to find.

✔ If you're eager to create a folder or two (and it's pretty easy), page ahead to this chapter's "Creating a Folder" section.

✔ Windows created several folders when it installed itself on your computer. It created a Windows folder to hold most of its programs and a bunch of folders inside that to hold its internal engine parts.

✔ Just as manila folders come from trees, computer folders use a *tree metaphor*, as shown in Figure 12-3, as they branch out from one main folder to several smaller folders.

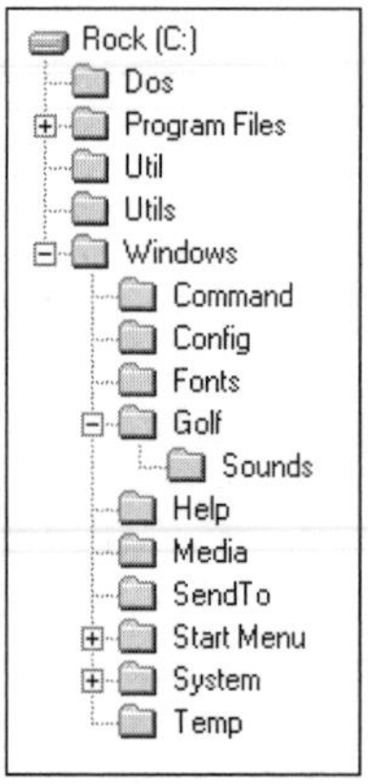

Figure 12-3:
The
structure of
folders
inside your
computer is
tree-like,
with main
folders
branching
out to
smaller
folders.

```
Rock (C:)
   Dos
 + Program Files
   Util
   Utils
 - Windows
      Command
      Config
      Fonts
    - Golf
         Sounds
      Help
      Media
      SendTo
    + Start Menu
    + System
      Temp
```

What's all this path stuff?

Sometimes Windows 95 can't find a file, even if it's sitting right there on the hard disk. You have to tell Windows where the file is sitting — a process it calls *browsing*—and in order to do that, you need to know that file's *path*.

A path is like the file's address. When heading for your house, a letter moves to your country, state, city, street, and finally, hopefully, your apartment or house number. A computer path does the same thing. It starts with the letter of the disk drive and ends with the name of the file. In between, the path lists all the folders the computer must travel through in order to reach the file.

For example, look at the Sounds folder in Figure 12-3. For Windows 95 to find a file stored there, it starts from the C:\ folder, travels through the Windows folder, and then goes through the Golf folder. Only then does it reach the Sounds folder.

Take a deep breath. Exhale. Quack like a duck, if you like. Now, the *C* in C:\ stands for disk drive C.

(In the path, a disk drive letter is always followed by a colon.) The disk drive letter and colon make up the first part of the path. All the other folders are inside the big C: folder, so they're listed after the C: part. DOS separates these nested folders with something called a backslash, or \ . The name of the actual file — let's say GRUNT.WAV — comes last.

C:\WINDOWS\GOLF\SOUNDS\GRUNT.WAV is what you get when you put it all together, and that's the official path of the GRUNT.WAV file in the Sounds folder.

This stuff can be tricky, so here it is again: The letter for the drive comes first, followed by a colon and a backslash. Then come the names of all the folders, separated by backslashes. Last comes the name of the file (with no backslash after it).

When you click on folders, Windows 95 puts together the path for you. Thankfully.

Peering into Your Drives and Folders

Knowing all this folder stuff can impress the people at the computer store. But what counts is knowing how to use the Explorer and My Computer programs to get to a file you want. Never fear. Just read on.

Seeing the files on a disk drive

Like everything else in Windows 95, disk drives are represented by buttons, or icons:

3½ Floppy (A:)   5¼ Floppy (B:)   Rock (C:)   121mb (D:)   (E:)

Those disk drive buttons live in both the Explorer and My Computer programs (although the ones in Explorer are usually smaller). See the little disks above the icons labeled *Floppy*? Those are pictures of the types of floppy disks that fit into those drives. You'll see a compact disc floating above drive E: That means double-clicking on that compact disc icon shows you what's currently in your compact disc drive. Hard drives don't have anything hovering over them except a nagging suspicion that they'll fail horribly at the worst moment.

- ✔ If you're kinda sketchy on those disk drive things, you probably skipped Chapter 2. Trot back there for a refresher course.

- ✔ Double-click on a drive icon in My Computer, and a window comes up to display the drive's contents. For example, put a disk in drive A and double-click on My Computer's drive A icon. A new window leaps up, showing what files and folders live on the disk in drive A.

- ✔ Click on a drive icon in Explorer, and you'll see the drive contents on the right side of the window.

- ✔ A second window comes in handy when you want to move or copy files from one folder or drive to another, as discussed in the "Copying or Moving a File" section.

- ✔ The first two icons stand for the floppy drives, drive A and drive B. If you click on a floppy drive icon when no disk is in the drive, Windows 95 stops you gently, suggesting that you insert a disk before proceeding further.

Seeing what's inside folders

Because folders are really little storage compartments, Windows 95 uses a picture of a little folder to stand for each separate place for storing files.

To see what's inside a folder, in My Computer or on the desktop, just double-click on the picture. A new window pops up, showing that folder's contents.

Folder-opening works differently in Explorer. In Explorer, folders line up along the left side of a window. One folder, the one you're currently exploring, has a little box around its name.

The files living inside that particular folder appear on the right side of the window.

It all looks somewhat like Figure 12-4.

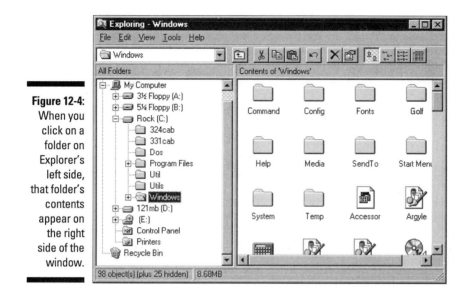

Figure 12-4:
When you
click on a
folder on
Explorer's
left side,
that folder's
contents
appear on
the right
side of the
window.

To peek inside a folder while in Explorer, click on its name on the left side of the window. You see two things: That folder's next level of folders (if it has any) appear beneath it on the left side of the window, and that folder's filenames spill out into the right side of the window.

✔ As you keep climbing farther out on a branch and more folders appear, you're moving toward further levels of organization. If you climb back inward, you reach files and folders that have less in common.

✔ Yeah, this stuff is really confusing, but keep one thing in mind: Don't be afraid to double-click, or even single-click, on a folder just to see what happens. Clicking on folders just changes your viewpoint; nothing dreadful happens, and no tax receipts fall onto the floor. You're just opening and closing file cabinet drawers, peeking into folders along the way.

✔ To climb farther out on the branches of folders, keep double-clicking on new folders as they appear.

✔ To move back up the branches in Explorer, double-click on a folder closer to the left side of the window. Any folders beneath that folder are now hidden from view.

✔ Sometimes a folder contains too many files to fit in the window. To see more files, click on that window's scroll bars. What's a scroll bar? Time to whip out your field guide, Chapter 6.

While in Explorer, move the mouse pointer over the bar separating a folder on the left from its filenames on the right. When the pointer turns into a mutant two-headed arrow, hold down the mouse button. Then move the bar to the left to give the filenames more room, or to the right to give the folders on the right more room. Let go of the mouse when the split is adjusted correctly and the window reshapes itself to the new dimensions.

Can't find a file or folder? Instead of rummaging through folders, check out the Find command described in Chapter 8. It's the fastest way to find files and folders that were "there just a moment ago."

Loading a Program or File

A *file* is a collection of information on a disk. Files come in two basic types: program files and data files.

Program files contain instructions that tell the computer to do something: balance the national budget or ferret out a fax number.

Data files contain information created with a program, as opposed to computer instructions. If you write a letter to the grocer complaining about his soggy apricots, you're creating a data file.

To open either kind of file in Windows 95, double-click on its name. A double-click on a program file's name brings the program to the screen, whether you found the filename listed in My Computer, Explorer, or even the Find program. If you double-click on a data file, Windows 95 loads the file *and* the program that created it. Then it brings both the file and the program to the screen at the same time.

- ✔ Windows 95 sticks little icons next to filenames so you know whether they're program or data files. In fact, even folders get their own icons so that you won't confuse them with files. Chapter 24, at the tail-end of the book, provides a handy reference for figuring out what icon is what. (The tail-end of the book is easier to find than this chapter.)

- ✔ Because of some bizarre New School of Computing mandate, any data file that Windows recognizes is called a *document*. A document doesn't have to contain words; it can have pictures of worms or sounds of hungry animals.

If the program or folder you're after is already highlighted, just give the Enter key a satisfying little pound with your index finger. That not only keeps your computer from getting out of line, but it shows you how many different ways Windows 95 lets you do things (which means that you don't need to worry about knowing them all).

Don't bother reading this hidden technical stuff

Sometimes programs store information in a data file. They may need to store information about the way the computer is set up, for example. To keep people from thinking that those files are trash and deleting them, the program hides those files.

You can view the names of these hidden files and folders, however, if you want to play voyeur. Se-lect View from the menu bar and then choose Options from the pull-down menu. Select the Show all files button and then choose the OK button.

The formerly hidden files appear alongside the other filenames. Be sure not to delete them, how-ever: The programs that created them will gag, possibly damaging other files.

Deleting and Undeleting Files and Folders

Sooner or later, you'll want to delete a file that's not important anymore — yesterday's lottery picks, for example, or something you've stumbled on that's too embarrassing to save any longer. But then, hey, suddenly you realize that you've made a mistake and deleted the wrong file. Not to worry: The Windows 95 Recycle Bin can probably resurrect that deleted file if you're quick enough.

Getting rid of a file or folder

To permanently remove a file from the hard drive, click on its name. Then press the Delete key. This surprisingly simple trick works for files, programs, and even folders.

The Delete key deletes entire folders, as well as any folders inside them. Make sure that you've selected the right file before you press the Delete key.

- ✔ When you press Delete, Windows tosses a box in your face, asking whether you're sure. If you are, choose the Yes button.

- ✔ Be extra sure that you know what you're doing when deleting any file that has an exclamation point in its icon. These files are sometimes hidden files, and the computer wants you to leave them alone. (Other than that, they're not particularly exciting, despite the exclamation point.)

- ✔ As soon as you learn how to delete files, you'll want to read the very next section, "How to undelete a file."

Deleting a shortcut from the desktop, My Computer, or Explorer just deletes a button that loads a program. You can always put the button back on. Deleting an icon that doesn't have the little shortcut arrow removes that *file* from the hard disk and puts it into the Recycle Bin, where it will eventually disappear.

How to undelete a file

Sooner or later, your finger will push the Delete key at the wrong time, and you'll delete the wrong file. A slip of the finger, the wrong nudge of a mouse, or, if you're in Southern California, a small earthquake at the wrong time can make a file disappear. Zap!

Scream! When the tremors subside, double-click on the Recycle Bin, and the Recycle Bin box drops down from the heavens, as shown in Figure 12-5.

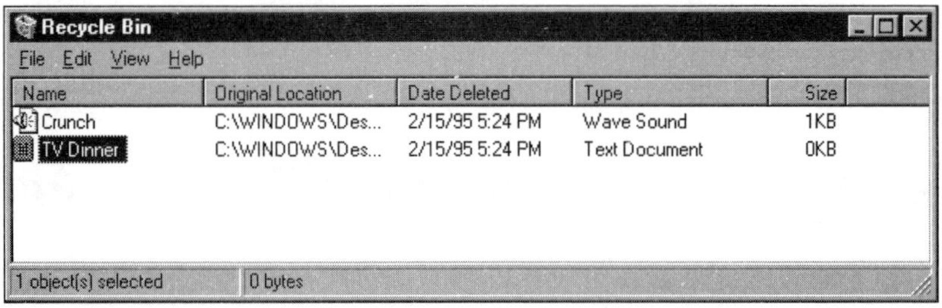

Figure 12-5:
The Recycle
Bin drops
down from
the heavens
to save the
day.

Name	Original Location	Date Deleted	Type	Size
Crunch	C:\WINDOWS\Des...	2/15/95 5:24 PM	Wave Sound	1KB
TV Dinner	C:\WINDOWS\Des...	2/15/95 5:24 PM	Text Document	0KB

Recycle Bin — File Edit View Help — 1 object(s) selected   0 bytes

The files listed in the Recycle Bin can be brought back to life simply by dragging them out of the Recycle Bin box: Use the mouse to point at the name of the file you want to retrieve and, while holding down the mouse button, point at the desktop. Then let go of the mouse. Windows 95 moves the once-deleted file out of the Recycle Bin and places the newly revived file onto your desktop.

> ✔ Once the file's on your desktop, it's as good as new. Feel free to store it in any other file for safekeeping.

> ✔ Unfortunately, the Recycle Bin only holds Windows 95 programs. Don't expect to find any deleted DOS or Windows 3.1 programs in the Recycle Bin.

> ✔ The Recycle Bin normally holds about ten percent of your hard disk's space. For example, if your hard drive is 200MB, the Recycle Bin will hold on to 20MB of deleted files. When it reaches that limit, it starts deleting the oldest files to make room for the incoming deleted files. (And the old ones will be gone for good, too.)

Copying or Moving a File

To copy or move files to different folders on your hard drive, use your mouse to *drag* them there. For example, here's how to move a file to a different folder on your hard drive:

1. **Move the mouse pointer until it hovers over the file you want to move and then press and hold down the mouse button.**

2. **While holding down the mouse button, use the mouse to point at the folder to which you'd like to move the file.**

   The trick is to hold down the mouse button the whole time. When you move the mouse, its arrow drags the file along with it. For example, Figure 12-6 shows how Explorer looks when I drag the ZIGZAG.BMP file from my Windows folder on the right to my Junk folder on the left.

Figure 12-6:
The ZigZag file is being dragged to the Junk folder on the left side of the window in order to move it there.

3. **Release the mouse button.**

   When the mouse arrow hovers over the place to which you'd like to move the file, take your finger off the mouse button.

Moving a file by dragging its name is pretty easy, actually. The hard part often comes when you try to put the file and its destination on-screen at the same time. You often need to use both Explorer and My Computer to put two windows on-screen. When you can see the file and its destination, start dragging.

Both Explorer and My Computer do something awfully dumb to confuse people, however: When you drag a file from one folder to another on the same drive, you *move* the file. When you drag a file from one folder to another on a different drive, you *copy* that file.

I swear I didn't make up these rules. And it gets more complicated: You can click on the file and hold down Shift to reverse the rules. Table 12-1 can help you keep these oafish oddities from getting too far out of control.

Table 12-1	Moving Files Around
To Do This	*Do This*
Copy a file to another location on the same disk drive	Hold down Ctrl and drag it there.
Copy a file to a different disk drive	Drag it there.
Move a file to another location on the same disk drive	Drag it there.
Move a file to a different disk drive	Hold down Shift and drag it there.
Make a shortcut while dragging a file	Hold down Ctrl+Shift and drag it there.
Remember these *obtuse* commands	Refer to the handy Cheat Sheet at the front of this book.

Here's an easy way to remember this stuff when the book's not handy: Always drag icons while holding down the *right* mouse button. Windows 95 is then gracious enough to give you a menu of options when you position the icon, and you can choose among moving, copying, or creating a shortcut.

✔ To copy or move files to a floppy disk, drag those files to the icon for that floppy disk, which you should find along the top of the Explorer window.

✔ When you drag a file someplace in Windows 95, look at the icon attached to the mouse pointer. If the document icon has a *plus sign* in it, you're *copying* the file. If the document icon is *blank,* you're *moving* the file. Depending on where you are dragging the file, pressing Ctrl or Shift toggles the plus sign on or off, making it easier to see whether you're currently copying or moving the file.

✔ After you run a program's installation program to put the program on your hard drive, don't move the program around. An installation program often wedges a program into Windows pretty handily; if you move the program, it may not work anymore.

Selecting More Than One File or Folder

Windows 95 lets you grab an armful of files and folders at one swipe; you don't always have to piddle around, dragging one item at a time.

To pluck several files and folders from a list, hold down Ctrl when you click on the names. Each name stays highlighted when you click on the next.

To gather several files or folders sitting next to each other, click on the first one. Then hold down the Shift key as you click on the last one. Those two items are highlighted, along with every file and folder between them.

Windows 95 lets you *lasso* files and folders as well. Point slightly above the first file or folder you want; then, while holding down the mouse button, point at the last file or folder. The mouse creates a lasso to surround your files. Let go of the mouse button, and the lasso disappears, leaving all the surrounded files highlighted.

- ✔ You can drag these armfuls of files in the same way as you drag one.

- ✔ You can delete these armfuls, too.

- ✔ You can't rename an armful of files all at once. To rename them, you have to go back to piddling around with one file at a time.

Renaming a File or Folder

If you're a he-man stuck with a name like Pink Gardenia, you can petition the courts to change it to Blue Gardenia. Changing a filename requires even less effort: Click on the file or folder's name to select it, wait a second, and click on the file's name (its title running beneath or next to it).

The old filename gets highlighted and then disappears when you start typing in the box the file or folder's new name. Press Enter or click on the desktop when you're through, and you're off.

- ✔ When you rename a file, only its name changes. The contents are still the same, it's still the same size, and it's still in the same place.

- ✔ You can't rename groups of files this way. The programs spit in your face if you even try.

- ✔ You can rename folders this way, too. (Renaming a folder can confuse Windows, however, which grows accustomed to folders the way they're first set up.)

Sometimes it's tricky clicking on filenames to rename them. If you're having trouble, just click on the file or folder with your right mouse button and choose Rename from the menu that pops up. Handy button, that right mouse button.

Using Legal Folder Names and Filenames

DOS is pretty picky about what you can and can't name a file or folder, so Windows 95 plays along. If you stick to plain old letters and numbers, you're fine. But don't try to stick any of the following characters in there:

```
: / \ * | < > ? "
```

If you use any of those characters, Windows 95 bounces an error message to the screen, and you have to try again.

These names are illegal:

```
1/2 of my Homework
JOB:2
ONE<TWO
He's no "Gentleman"
```

These names are legal:

```
Half a Term Paper
JOB2
Two is Bigger than One
A #@$%) Scoundrel
```

✔ As long as you remember the characters you can and can't use for naming files, you'll probably be okay.

✔ Like Windows 3.1, Windows 95 programs *brand* files with their own three-letter extension so that Windows 95 knows what program created what file. Normally, Windows 95 hides the extensions so that they're not confusing. But if you happen to spot filenames like SAVVY.DOC, README.TXT, and NUDE.BMP across the hard disk, you'll know that the extensions have been added by the Windows 95 programs WordPad, Notepad, and Paint, respectively. In Windows 3.1, you know what program created what file by looking at the file's extension; with Windows 95, you just look at the file's icon for heritage clues.

If you really want to see a filename's extension, click on Options from the folder's View menu and then click on the tab marked View. Finally, click on the little box that says Display the full MS-DOS path in the title bar. The extensions then show up in that particular folder. (Click on the box again to remove the extensions.)

You may see a filename with a weird tilde thing in it, such as WIGWAM~1.TXT. That's Windows 95's special way of dealing with long filenames. Most older programs expect files to have only eight characters; Windows 95 whittles long filenames down so those older programs can use them. (Windows 95 remembers the long filename for itself.)

Copying a Complete Floppy Disk

To copy files from one disk to another, drag 'em over there, as described a few pages back. To copy an entire disk, however, you have to use the Diskcopy command.

What's the difference? When you're copying files, you're dragging specific filenames. But when you're copying a disk, the Diskcopy command duplicates the disk exactly: It even copies the empty parts! (That's why it takes longer than just dragging the files over.)

The Diskcopy command has three main limitations:

- ✔ It can copy only floppy disks that are the same *size* or *capacity.* Just as you can't pour a full can of beer into a shot glass, you can't copy one disk's information onto another disk unless they hold the same amount of data.
- ✔ It can't copy the hard drive or a RAM drive. Luckily, you really have no reason to copy them, even if you know what a RAM drive is.
- ✔ It's a *DOS command,* meaning you have to type it in by hand.

Here's how to make a copy of a floppy disk:

1. **Put your floppy disk in your disk drive.**
2. **Click on the Start button and click on R̲un from the menu that pops up.**
3. **Type the following information:**

   If you're copying the disk in drive A, type this command and then press the Enter key:

   ```
   DISKCOPY A: A:
   ```

   That's the word DISKCOPY, a space, the letter A followed by a colon, another space, and the letter A followed by a colon.

   If you're copying the disk in drive B, type this command and then press the Enter key:

   ```
   DISKCOPY B: B:
   ```

Everything's the same as before, but you substitute the letter B for the letter A.

4. Follow the instructions on-screen.

  ✔ With all these limitations, why bother with the Diskcopy command? Well, because it makes a *complete* copy of a disk, it also copies any hidden files that other copy programs may not catch.

  ✔ Microsoft says it's coming up with a better way to make complete copies of disks in the *real* version of Windows 95, slated to arrive late this year.

  ✔ All this *capacity* and *size* stuff about disks and drives is slowly digested in Chapter 2.

  ✔ The Diskcopy command can be handy for making backup copies of your favorite programs.

Creating a Folder

To store new information in a file cabinet, you grab a manila folder, scrawl a name across the top, and start stuffing it with information.

To store new information in Windows 95 — a new program, for example — you create a new folder, think up a name for the new folder, and start moving or copying files into it.

New, more organized folders make finding information easier, too. For example, you can clean up a crowded Letters folder by dividing it into two folders: Business and Personal.

Here's how to use Explorer to create a new folder — a folder called Business — that lives in your Letters folder:

1. On the left side of the Explorer window, click in the area in which you want the new folder to appear.

If you want a new Games folder in your Windows folder, for example, you click on the Windows folder on the Explorer's left side. In the Letters example, you click on the Letters folder, as shown in Figure 12-7, because you want the Business folder to appear in the Letters folder.

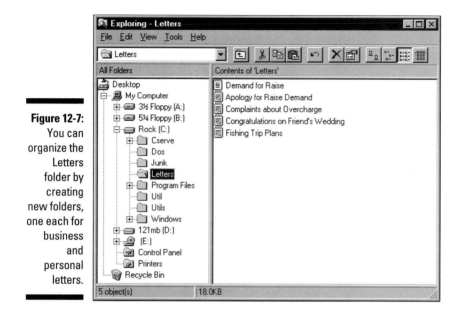

Figure 12-7:
You can
organize the
Letters
folder by
creating
new folders,
one each for
business
and
personal
letters.

Click on the Letters folder, and its current contents spill out into Explorer's right side.

2. Click on Explorer's right side with your right mouse button and choose New; when the menu appears, choose Folder.

The My Computer window lets you create a folder when you right-click in any window; Explorer lets you create a folder only when you right-click within its right-hand side. A box pops up and asks you to think of a name for your new folder.

3. Type the new folder's name and press Enter.

Windows 95 can sometimes be picky about names you give to folders and files. For the rules, check out the "Using Legal Folder Names and Filenames" section earlier in this chapter.

After you type the folder's name and press Enter, the new Business folder is complete, ready for you to start moving your business letter files there. For impeccable organization, follow the same steps to create a Personal folder and move your personal files there, using the "dragging" process shown in Figure 12-8 (and explained in the "Copying or Moving a File" section in this chapter).

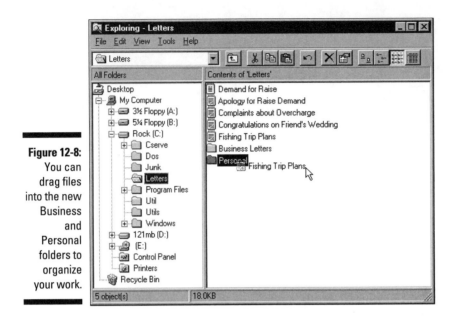

Figure 12-8:
You can
drag files
into the new
Business
and
Personal
folders to
organize
your work.

✔ Want to install a new Windows program that doesn't come with an installation program? Create a new folder for it and copy its files there. Then head to Chapter 11 to see how to put the new program's name in the Start menu for easy clicking.

✔ To move files into a new folder, drag them there. Just follow the directions in the "Copying or Moving a File" section.

✔ When copying or moving lots of files, select them all at the same time before dragging them. You can chew on this stuff in the "Selecting More Than One File or Folder" section.

✔ Just as with naming files, you can use only certain characters when naming folders. (Stick with plain old letters and numbers, and you'll be fine.)

Seeing More Information about Files and Folders

Whenever you create a file or folder, Windows 95 scrawls a bunch of secret hidden information on it: its size, the date you created it, and even more trivial stuff. To see what Windows 95 is calling the files and folders behind your back, select <u>V</u>iew from the menu bar and then select <u>D</u>etails from the menu.

In fact, you can simply click on the right-most button on the toolbar, which lives atop the My Computer and Explorer windows. Each of the four buttons on the right arranges the icons in a different way, as shown in Figure 12-9, showing different amounts of information. (And clicking on those buttons simply changes the way Windows 95 displays the icons — it doesn't hurt anything.)

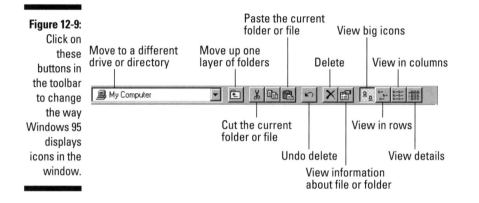

Figure 12-9: Click on these buttons in the toolbar to change the way Windows 95 displays icons in the window.

✔ Toolbar not living on top of your window? Then put it there by choosing Toolbar from the View menu. That little bar of buttons now appears atop your window like a mantel over a fireplace.

✔ If you can't remember what those little toolbar buttons do, rest your mouse pointer over them and make it look lost. Windows 95 displays a helpful box summing up the button's mission, and a further explanation often appears along the window's bottom.

✔ Although some of the additional file information is handy, it can consume a lot of space, limiting the number of files you can see in the window. Displaying only the filename is often a better idea. Then, if you want to see more information about a file or folder, try the following tip.

✔ Hold down Alt and double-click on a file or folder to see its size, date, and other information.

✔ With the Alt+double-click trick (described in the preceding paragraph), you can change a file's attributes as well. Attributes are too boring to be discussed further, so duck beneath the technical stuff coming up.

At first, Windows 95 displays filenames sorted alphabetically by name in its Explorer and My Computer windows. But, by right-clicking in a folder and choosing the different sorting methods in the Arrange Icons menu, you display them in a different order. Windows puts the biggest ones at the top of the list, for example, when you choose sort by Size. Or you can choose sort by Type to keep files created by the same application next to each other. Or you can choose sort by Date to keep the most recent files at the top of the list.

Who cares about this stuff, anyway?

Windows 95 gives each file four special switches called *attributes*. The computer looks at the way those switches are set before it fiddles with a file.

Read Only: Choosing this attribute allows the file to be read but not deleted or changed in any way.

Archive: The computer sets this attribute when a file has changed since the last time it was backed up with the special DOS or Windows 95 BACKUP command.

Hidden: Setting this attribute makes the file invisible during normal operations.

System: Files required by a computer's operating system have this attribute set.

The Properties box makes it easy — perhaps too easy — to change these attributes. In most cases, you should leave them alone. They're just mentioned here so you'll know what computer nerds mean when they tell cranky people, "Boy, somebody must have set *your* attribute wrong when you got out of bed this morning."

Dragging, Dropping, and Running

You can drag files around in Windows 95 to move them or copy them. But there's more: You can drag them outside of the Explorer or My Computer window and drop them into other windows to load them into other files and programs, as shown in Figure 12-10.

For example, drag the Egyptian Stone file into the Paint window and let go of the mouse button. Paint loads the Egyptian Stone file, just as if you'd double-clicked on it in the first place.

This feature brings up all sorts of fun ideas. If you have a sound card, you can listen to sounds by dropping sound files into the Media Player or Sound Recorder windows. You can drop text files into Notepad to load them quickly. Or you can drop WordPad files into WordPad.

 ✔ Okay, the first thing everybody wants to know is what happens if you drag a sound file into WordPad? Or a WordPad file into Notepad? Or any other combination of files that don't match? Well, Windows 95 either embeds one file into the other — a process described in Chapter 9 — or sends you a box saying that it got indigestion. Just click on the OK button, and things will return to normal. No harm done, either way.

 ✔ The second question everybody asks is why bother? You can just double-click on a file's name to load it. That's true. But this way is more fun and occasionally faster.

 ✔ Never dragged and dropped before? Chapter 4 contains complete instructions.

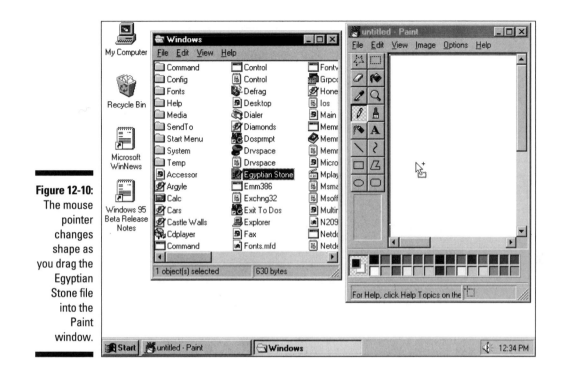

Figure 12-10:
The mouse
pointer
changes
shape as
you drag the
Egyptian
Stone file
into the
Paint
window.

✔ Old-time Windows users will want to know if they can load files by dropping them onto taskbar icons along the screen's bottom. Not any more;
Windows 95 lets you drop things only into *open* windows. But if you drag
the object over to the taskbar icon that you're interested in and let the
mouse pointer hover over it for a while, the icon blossoms into an open
window, ready to receive the object. (Yep, there's a lot of mouse-pointer
hovering in Windows 95.)

Making My Computer and Explorer List Missing Files

Sometimes Windows 95 snoozes and doesn't keep track of what's *really* on the
disk. Oh, it does pretty well with the hard drive, and it works pretty well if
you're just running Windows programs. But it can't tell when you stick in a new
floppy disk. Also, if you create a file from within a DOS program, Windows 95
may not know that new file is there.

If you think the Explorer or My Program window is holding out on you, tell it to
refresh, or take a second look at what's on the floppy disk or hard drive.

You can click on <u>V</u>iew from the menu bar and choose <u>R</u>efresh from the pull-down menu, but a quicker way is to press the F5 key. (It's a function key along the top or left side of the keyboard.) Either way, the programs take a second look at what they're supposed to be showing and update their lists if necessary.

Press the F5 key whenever you stick in a different floppy disk and want to see what files are stored on it. Windows 95 then updates the screen to show that *new* floppy's files, not the files from the first disk.

Formatting a New Floppy Disk

New floppy disks don't work straight out of the box; your computer will burp out an error message if you even try to use them fresh. Floppy disks must be formatted, and unless you paid extra for a box of *preformatted* floppy disks, you must format them yourself. The My Computer program handles this particularly boring chore quite easily. It's still boring, though, as you'll discover when repeating the process twelve times — once for each disk in the box.

Here's the procedure:

1. **Place the new disk into drive A or drive B and close the latch.**

2. **In either Explorer or the My Computer window, click on the drive's icon with your right mouse button and choose For<u>m</u>at from the menu.**

3. **If you're formatting a *high-capacity* disk in drive A, then select the <u>F</u>ull setting under Format type and select <u>S</u>tart in the top-right corner.**

    Your disk drives whir for several minutes, and then Windows 95 asks whether you'd like to format another.

4. **Click on the Close button when Windows 95 is through.**

    Then remove the floppy disk and return to Step 1 until you've formatted the entire box.

✔ You can format disks in your drive B by clicking on the drive B icon with your right mouse button. Likewise, you can change a disk's capacity by clicking on the little arrow in the <u>C</u>apacity: box. Don't know the capacity of your disks? Then head for the handy chart in Chapter 2.

✔ Don't get your hopes up: The <u>Q</u>uick (Erase) option won't speed things up unless your disk has already been formatted once before.

✔ If you want to be able to boot your computer from a disk, check the Copy s<u>y</u>stem files option. These System Disks can come in handy if your hard drive ever goes on vacation.

✔ In fact, if Windows 95 ever goes on vacation, you should have an emergency disk. The Add/Remove Programs icon in the Windows 95 Control Panel makes one for you. (And it's covered in Chapter 10.)

Chapter 13
The *Free* Programs!

*W*indows 95 comes with a lot of free programs, but it doesn't install them all onto your hard drive automatically; some of them stay on the installation disks. If you installed Windows 95 over Windows 3.1, some of your older programs will still be kicking around, too. The point? You probably won't see all of this chapter's programs on your particular computer.

These little programs won't work wonders, though. Microsoft programmers squirm a little in their chairs if you even call them *programs*. No, Microsoft calls these things *applets* — mini programs designed to demonstrate what a *real* Windows program could do if you head back to the software store and buy one. If your needs are simple, these simple programs might fill them. But when your needs start growing, your software budget will probably have to grow, as well.

Word Processing with WordPad

You'll find most of the little programs that come with Windows 95 listed under the Accessories section of the Programs menu (which lurks in the menu that leaps up from the Start button). The icon for WordPad looks pretty fancy — a distinguished-looking fountain pen, like the ones that get ink on your hands:

Wordpad

Although the icon is fancy, WordPad isn't quite as fancy as some of the more expensive word processors on the market. You can't create multiple columns, for example, like the ones in newspapers or newsletters, nor can you double-space your reports. But WordPad works fine for letters, simple reports, and other basic documents. You can change the fonts around to get reasonably fancy, too, as shown in Figure 13-1.

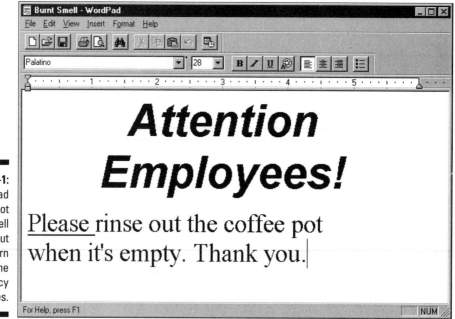

Figure 13-1: WordPad may not have a spell checker, but it can churn out some fairly fancy pages.

WordPad also can handle the Windows *TrueType fonts* — that font technology that shapes how characters appear on-screen. You can create an elegant document by using some fancy TrueType fonts and mail it on a disk to somebody else. That person can view it in WordPad, just as you did. (Before TrueType, people could see only the fonts they had laboriously installed on their own computers.)

Plus, WordPad can handle all that embedding and linking stuff talked about in Chapter 9.

- ✔ WordPad works well for most word-processing needs: writing letters, reports, or term papers on somber philosophers with weird last names. Unless you're a lousy speller, you'll find WordPad easy to use, and you'll like its excellent price.

- ✔ If you're ditching your typewriter for Windows, remember this: On an electric typewriter, you have to press the Return key at the end of each line or else you start typing off the edge of the paper. Computers, in contrast, are smart enough to sense when words are about to run off the end of the screen. They automatically drop down a line and continue the sentence. (Hip computer nerds call this phenomenon *word wrap*.)

  Press Enter only when you're done typing a paragraph and want to start a new one. Press Enter twice to leave a blank line between paragraphs.

- ✔ WordPad replaces the old Write word processor from Windows 3.1, and it does almost everything Write could do. You won't find any way to add headers or footers, however, nor will WordPad let you double-space your documents. Finally, none of the new applications that come with Windows 95 let you search for funny characters such as Tabs or Paragraph marks.

Opening and saving a file

In a refreshing change of pace, all Windows 95 programs enable you to open and save a file in exactly the same way: Select File at the top of the program's window, and a menu tumbles down. Choose Open or Save, depending on your whim. A box pops up, listing the files in the current folder. Select the name of the file you want to open (click on it) or type the name of a new file. Then choose OK. That's it.

- ✔ If you'd like to open a file you spot listed in Explorer or the My Computer window, double-click on the file's name. Windows 95 yanks the file into the right program and brings both the program and the file to the screen.

- ✔ You can find more explicit instructions on opening a file in Chapter 6.

- ✔ Folders and equally mind-numbing concepts are browbeaten in Chapter 12.

- ✔ When you save a file for the first time, you have to choose a name for it, as well as a folder to put it in. WordPad subsequently remembers the file's name and folder, so you don't have to keep typing them in each time you save your current progress.

- ✔ WordPad can create files in three formats: A plain text file known as *ASCII*, a Word 6 file, or a *Rich Text Format*. All three formats are covered in the next section.

✔ Sometimes you open a file, change it, and want to save it with a different name or in a different folder. Choose Save As, not Save; WordPad then treats your work as if you were saving it for the first time — it asks you to type in a new name and a location.

✔ Although you can make up filenames on the fly in WordPad, you can't use WordPad to create new folders. That duty falls to Explorer or My Computer, discussed in Chapter 12.

Saving a WordPad file in different formats

Just as you can't drop a Ford engine into a Volvo, you can't drop a WordPad file into another company's word processor. All brands of word processors save their information in different ways in order to confuse the competition.

WordPad can read and write in three file formats. As soon as you try to create a new file, WordPad forces you choose between three formats: a Word 6 document, a Rich Text Document, and a Text Only Document. Each format meets different needs.

✔ **Word 6 Document:** This creates files that can be read by Microsoft's *real* (and expensive) word processor, Microsoft Word. Many of the most popular competing word processors can read Word 6 files, too. You'll probably be safe with this format.

✔ **Rich Text Document:** These files can also be read by a wide-variety of word processors. Like the Word 6 documents, Rich Text documents can store **boldfaced** and *italicized* words, as well as other special formatting. These files can be *huge*, however. Don't choose this format unless it's the only format your friend's word processor will accept.

✔ **Text Only Document:** Almost all brands of word processors can read plain old text, making Text Only Document the safest format if you plan on exchanging files with friends. The Text Only document can't have any boldface type, italic type, columns, or any other fancy stuff, however. *Nerdly note:* Text Only files are also called *ASCII* files (pronounced *ASK-ee*).

If somebody asks you to save a WordPad file in a different format, choose Save As from the File menu. Click on the arrow next to the Save file as type box and choose the new format from the drop-down list. Type a new name for the file into the File name box and press Enter. *Voilà!* You've saved your file in the new format.

✔ The other word processor that comes with Windows 95, Notepad, can't handle anything *but* Text Only files. Notepad can't load WordPad's Word 6 files, and if it opens the Rich Text Documents, the files look *really* weird. (WordPad can easily read Notepad's files, though.) Notepad gets its due later in this chapter.

✔ Although most word processors can read and write ASCII files, problems still occur. You lose any formatting, such as italicized words, special indents, or embedded pictures of apples.

✔ ASCII stands for American Standard Code for Information Interchange. A bunch of technoids created it when they got tired of other technoids saving their information in different ways. Today, most programs grudgingly read or write information using the ASCII format. In fact, ASCII files can even be exchanged with computers from different home planets, such as the Apple Macintosh and Unix workstations, with only minor technical glitches.

Other WordPad stuff

✔ WordPad is always in Insert mode: When you add something in the middle of a sentence, all the words move to the right to make room for the incoming stuff. WordPad doesn't support the Overwrite mode, where the incoming letters are written right over the old stuff. The Insert key on the keyboard won't do anything, even if you push it really hard.

✔ A faster way to open a file is to press and release the Alt key and then press F and then O. If you memorize the keyboard commands, you won't have to trudge through all the menus with the mouse. If you don't remember the key commands, check out the handy chart in Table 13-1. You'll find other time-savers listed, as well.

✔ To open a file, feel free to "drag" its name from the Explorer or My Computer window and drop the name directly into WordPad's open window. Whoosh! WordPad will immediately suck the file's contents into the open window.

✔ Want to change your page margins? Click on File and choose Page setup when the menu drops down. The Page Layout dialog box lets you specify top, bottom, and side margins.

✔ Saved a file in WordPad, but now you want to delete it? Head for Explorer or My Computer and delete it there. WordPad's an overly sensitive program; it can only *create* files, not destroy them.

Table 13-1	WordPad Shortcut Keys
To Do This	*Do This*
Open a file	Press Alt, F, and O.
Save a file	Press Alt, F, and S.
Save a file under a new name	Press Alt, F, and A.
Print a file	Press Alt, F, and P.
Select the entire document	Click rapidly three times in the left margin.
Select one word	Double-click on it.
Add *italics* to selected text	Hold down Ctrl and press the letter I (press Ctrl+I).
Add **boldface** to selected text	Hold down Ctrl and press the letter B (press Ctrl+B).
Add <u>underline</u> to selected text	Hold down Ctrl and press the letter U (press Ctrl+U).

Drawing pictures with Paint

Love the smell of paint and a fresh canvas? Then you'll hate Paint. After working with real fibers and pigments, you'll find the computerized painting program that comes with Windows 95, Paint, to be a little sterile. But at least there's no mess. Paint creates pictures and graphics to stick into other programs. The icon for Paint is a picture of a palette, found in the Accessories menu (which leaps out from the Start menu's Programs' menu):

Paint

Paint offers more than just a paintbrush. It has a can of spray paint for that *airbrushed* look, several pencils of different widths, a paint roller for gobbing on a bunch of paint, and an eraser for when things get out of hand. Figure 13-2 was drawn with Paint.

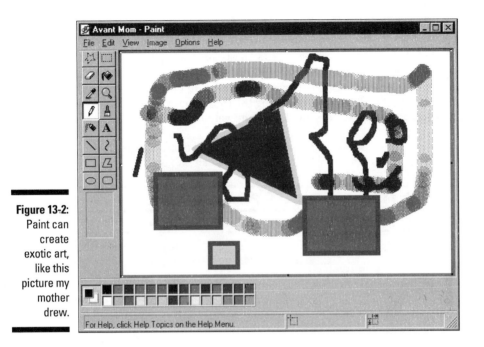

Figure 13-2:
Paint can create exotic art, like this picture my mother drew.

In addition to capturing your artistic flair, Paint can team up with a digital camera or scanner to touch up pictures in your PC. You can create a flashy letterhead to stick into letters in WordPad. You can even create maps to paste into your party fliers.

✔ Drawings and pictures can be copied from Paint and pasted into just about any other Windows 95 program.

✔ Remember that *cut and paste* stuff from Chapter 9? Well, you can cut out or copy chunks of art from the Paint screen using the *select* or *free-form select* tools described later in this section. The art goes onto the Windows 95 Clipboard, where you can grab it and paste it into any other Windows program. (Paint doesn't support "Scraps," also covered in Chapter 9.)

✔ Paint enables you to add text and numbers to graphics, so you can add street names to maps, put labels inside drawings, or add the vintage year to your wine labels.

Paint replaces Paintbrush from Windows 3.1. In fact, if you installed Windows 95 over Windows 3.1, the Paint icon will be labeled *Pbrush* instead of Paint. Unlike Paintbrush, the Paint program no longer saves files in PCX format. If you used PCX files, you might want to copy your old version of Paintbrush back onto your hard drive. (The old version can also do a few other things that Paint can't, like erasing in straight lines when you hold down the Shift key.)

Figuring out how to draw something

Paint comes with a row of drawing tools along the left side of the window. Not even Jeanne Dixon can figure out what they do, so Table 13-2 explains them. Remember this, though: If you hold the mouse pointer over a mysterious-looking tool, a box pops up listing the tool's name, and a description of the tool appears along the bottom of the Paint window.

Below the drawing tools panel lies the *palette bar,* which is shown in Figure 13-3. *Palette* is a fancy name for the colors you can dab onto your drawing.

Table 13-2	Paint Tools
What It Looks Like	*What It's Called and What It Does*
	Free-Form Select: Grabs irregular chunks of the screen for cutting or copying to the Clipboard and pasting elsewhere.
	Select: Grabs a rectangular chunk of the screen for cutting or copying to the Clipboard and pasting elsewhere.
	Eraser: Rubs out *everything,* leaving nothing showing but the current background color.
	Fill With Color: Pours color into an area, filling it up to its boundaries.
	Pick Color: Picks up a color from the current picture.
	Magnifier: Enlarges portion of the picture for easier viewing of details.
	Pencil: Just like it sounds, this pencil draws freehand. *Very* hard to use.
	Brush: Works more like a felt pen with an adjustable tip.
	Airbrush: Adds *spray paint* on the drawing. Good for touching up pictures of bus stop benches.
	Text: Enables you to add text, along with standard effects like **bold** and *italics.*
	Line: Draws a straight line between two points. (Hold down the Shift key to make vertical or horizontal lines.)
	Curve: Draws a line and then lets you bend it, twice. Truly weird.
	Rectangle, Polygon, Ellipsis, and **Rounded Rectangle:** Click on these tools to create shapes that look just like the icons.

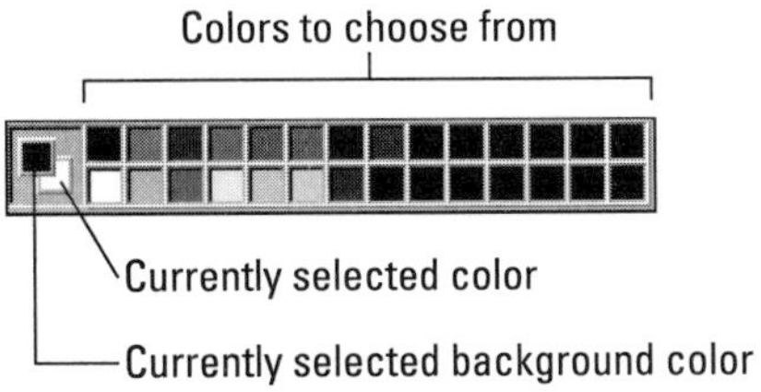

Figure 13-3:
You use the
palette bar
to choose
different
colors.

Colors to choose from

Currently selected color

Currently selected background color

The key to using Paint is to realize that you're always working with *two* colors: the color of the background and the color you're dabbing on top of it. Paint starts out with the drab combination of black lines on a white background.

 To change the color of the *foreground* — the color you use to draw things — click on one of the colors in the palette with the *left* mouse button. To change the color of the *background* — the color you're drawing *on* — click on that color in the palette with the *right* mouse button. You'll see your new background color when you start a new drawing.

Some of the tools have adjustable tips. When you click on the tool, look in the box beneath the tool bar. If a variety of tips appear, you can click on those tips to change the size and shape of your tool. (The best way to figure them out is to just click and play.)

After you select colors, click on the tool you're after in the toolbar and then start slapping paint around. Here are a few tips to help you with some of the tools' less-than self-explanatory features:

- **Eraser:** This eraser doesn't really erase colors so much as it changes them to a different color. Because the background color is usually white, moving the eraser over your drawing usually leaves white splotches. To leave *different colored* splotches, click on a different color in the palette using the right mouse button.

  The Eraser can also erase specific colors, ignoring the other colors. For example, if you don't like the yellow in a drawing, click on the Eraser tool and then click on yellow in the palette along the bottom. Then click on the preferred color in the palette — say, purple — with the right mouse button. When you hold down the right mouse button and move the pointer over the drawing, all the yellow parts magically change to purple.

- **Pencil:** Although Paint puts this tool in your hand when it is first loaded, the pencil is probably the most difficult tool to use. Use the other tools to create shapes and then click on the pencil for minor touch-ups.

- **Cutting/Moving pieces:** When you cut pieces out of a drawing, sometimes you leave white holes; other times the holes are a different color. The trick? Holes take on the shade of the currently selected *background* color.

> ✔ **Pasting:** You can paste anything you want into Paint, and Paint is most accommodating. In fact, if you're trying to paste something that's bigger than the size of the current Paint window, Paint respectfully asks whether it should make the window bigger so that everything will fit. (The version in Windows 3.1 wasn't that nice.)

Making new wallpaper in Paint

Anything you make in Paint can be turned into wallpaper and used as a backdrop. Just save your fun new file in the Windows folder. When you head for the Control Panel's Display area, the new file is listed with the other potential wallpaper files. Or you can bypass that step by saving the file and clicking on the Set as Wallpaper (Tiled) or Set as Wallpaper (Centered) options from the Paint program's File menu.

Save your file before you try to click on either of the "Set as Wallpaper" options, however, or Point will yell at you. Finally, if you don't have a color monitor and a mouse, you'll find Paint unwieldy. More detailed wallpaper installation information awaits in Chapter 10.

Calling other Computers with HyperTerminal

The old modem program that came with Windows, Terminal, could handle the basics of logging onto a BBS and grabbing files, but it wasn't fancy enough for today's more-sophisticated Internet surfers. Terminal does not come with Windows 95, but its replacement, HyperTerminal, makes modeming a lot easier.

HyperTerminal can automatically figure out what settings to use for most places you call. And because Windows 95 figures out what brand of modem you're using as part of the installation process, HyperTerminal automatically knows your modem's language.

> ✔ HyperTerminal does more stuff automatically than Terminal, making it a little easier to use. HyperTerminal can do more things than Terminal, however, which brings its friendliness level back down by quite a few notches.

> ✔ In fact, installing and setting up a modem and flipping all the switches in the right direction are notoriously difficult tasks. You need to worry about gross things like modem speed, parity, stop bits, and other buzz word stuff — stuff that's much too advanced for this book. If you just purchased a modem, lure a computer guru friend over to help install the thing and get it modulating in the right directions. After it has been tweaked in just the right way, a modem is pretty easy to use.

✔ Modems are computer gizmos that can translate the computer's digital information into sound and squirt it over the phone lines to other modems. They come in two types: internal and external. _Internal modems_ plug into the nether reaches of the computer, and _external modems_ have a cable that plugs into a serial port on the computer's rump. Both types do the same thing, but the external ones have little lights on them that blink as the sound flows back and forth.

✔ The older Terminal program that came with Windows could only download files using two settings: XMODEM and Kermit. The program that comes with Windows 95's HyperTerminal, supports the much speedier ZMODEM and YMODEM formats, as well. Modem hounds can choose among ANSI, Minitel, TTY, Viewdata, VT100, and VT52 terminal emulation.

✔ World travelers with Windows 95 on their laptops will appreciate HyperTerminal's support for dialing codes used by a wide variety of countries, from Afghanistan to Zimbabwe.

✔ HyperTerminal works only with _text-based_ on-line services, such as CompuServe, GEnie, MCI Mail, or computer bulletin boards. It doesn't work with graphics-based bulletin boards, such as Prodigy and America Online.

Don't pick up the phone while the modem is using it to transmit information. Just picking up the handset can garble the signal and possibly break the connection.

After HyperTerminal is finally up, running, and downloading a file, you'll spot a little modem icon next to the clock along the bottom of the taskbar. Double-click on the little modem, and HyperTerminal displays statistics on how fast your modem is slinging data.

Dialing Phones Automatically with Phone Dialer

The Windows 95 phone dialer spiffs up your desktop telephone, even if it's a really cheap one. First, it lets you assign your most frequently dialed phone numbers to push buttons: Just click on the button, and Phone Dialer dials the number. In addition, Phone Dialer keeps track of calls you make using the program. Can't remember whether you made that important call yesterday morning? Choose Show Log from the Tools menu, and you see a list of the phone numbers you've dialed, when you dialed them, and how long the conversation lasted.

If Windows 95 has already been introduced to your modem, you won't see the window shown in Figure 13-4 the first time you load Phone Dialer from the Start menu. If you're setting the program up for the first time, you need to tell

Windows 95 four things: Your country, your area code, whether you need to dial a number like "9" to get an outside line, and whether your phone is touch-tone. (You only need to fill this stuff out once.)

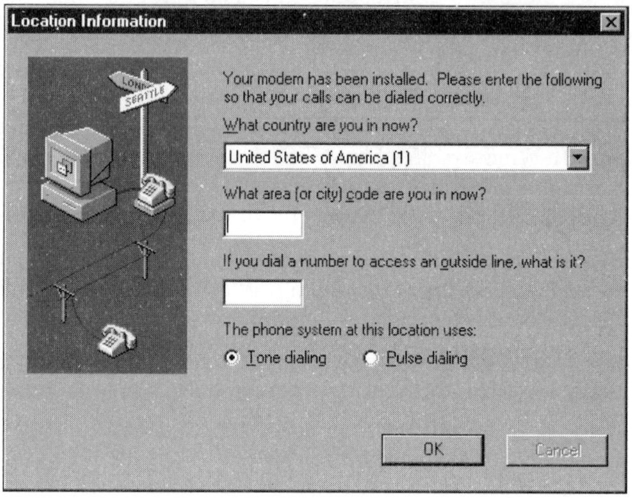

Figure 13-4:
The Phone Dialer needs to know some basic information about your modem and phone before it will work.

Here's how to store your favorite radio station or pizza delivery service (or whatever) into the Phone dialer.

1. **Click on one of the buttons along the program's right side, as shown in Figure 13-5.**

   The box on the top is probably handiest. A box will appear, ready for you to type in the name and phone number of the place you're calling.

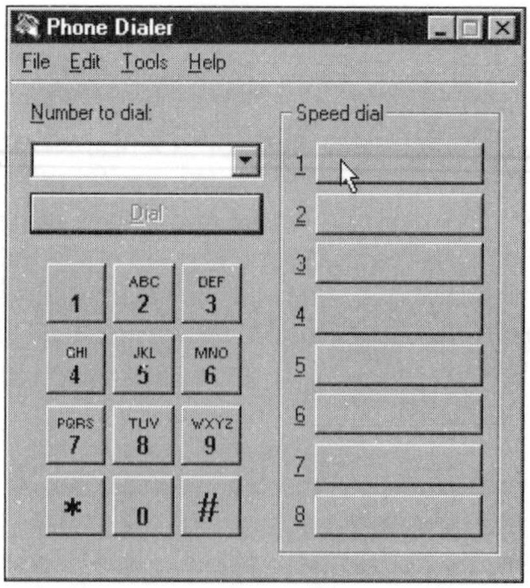

Figure 13-5:
Click on one of the buttons along the program's right side.

2. Type the name of the place you're calling into the Name box; then press Tab and type the place's phone number into the Number to dial box.

Start typing the place's name, and the letters appear in the top box. Press Tab to move the cursor to the second box, where you can type the phone number, as shown in Figure 13-6. You can use the numbers on your keyboard's numeric keypad or the ones along the top of your keyboard, whichever you prefer. (The Function keys won't work, however.)

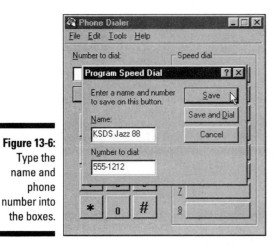

Figure 13-6:
Type the name and phone number into the boxes.

3. Click on the Save button.

The Phone Dialer reappears, showing its newly configured dial button, as shown in Figure 13-7. To dial the number, click on the button.

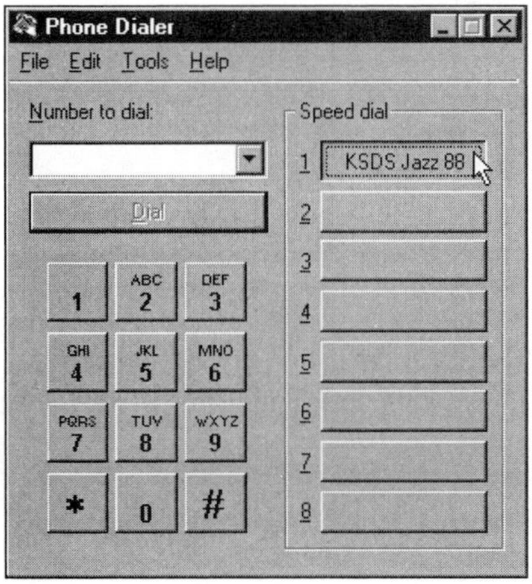

Figure 13-7:
Click on the button to dial that particular number.

- The Phone Dialer can be handy for making those complicated long distance calls with too many digits to remember.

- The Phone Dialer offers a few more options for dialing than are found in the old Windows 3.1 Cardfile. The Phone Dialer can dial using a Calling Card number, turn call waiting on and off, and dial extra numbers to reach outside lines.

- Using Phone Dialer on your laptop in the hotel room? Phone Dialer will automatically set up your call for dozens of countries, from Albania to Zambia (and Afghanistan and Zimbabwe, too). Lots of international stuff in Windows 95.

CD-Player

Adding a CD-ROM drive to a computer doesn't always add multimedia as much as it adds Bachman Turner Overdrive to the lunch hour. It's a well-known fact that most multimedia computer owners pop a musical CD into their computer's disk drive now and then.

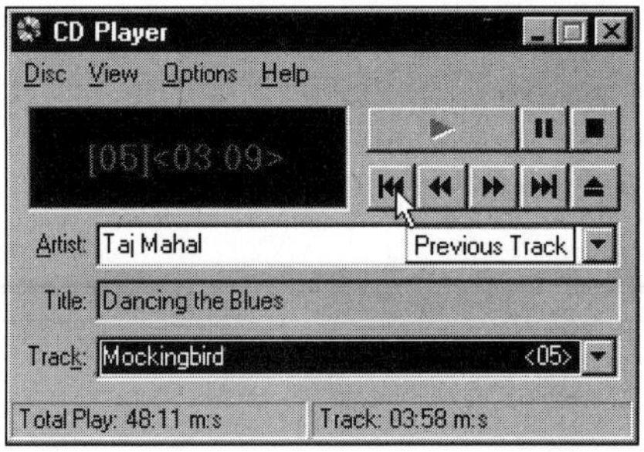

Figure 13-8:
The Windows 95 CD Player lets you keep track of your songs.

CD Player
Disc   View   Options   Help
[05]<03 09>   ▶ ❚❚ ■
⏮ ◀◀ ▶▶ ⏭ ⏏
Artist: Taj Mahal   Previous Track ▼
Title: Dancing the Blues
Track: Mockingbird   <05> ▼
Total Play: 48:11 m:s   Track: 03:58 m:s

Windows 3.1's Media Player could play music CDs, but Windows 95 comes with a full-fledged CD Player, shown in Figure 13-8.

The CD Player lets you add song titles to the menu, as well as create your own play lists. If you're feeling random, choose the Random Order setting under Options to make Windows 95 to act like a juke box. Now, if it could just come with a pool table.

- Music too loud? Just click on the little speaker in the corner of the taskbar. An easy-to-use sliding bar lets you lower the volume — no more frantic searching to save your ears.

 ✔ Don't remember what some of those buttons do? Just rest your mouse
   pointer over them, and Windows 95 sends a message to the screen to help
   you out. In Figure 13-8, for example, the CD Player says those two triangles
   let you jump to the previous track on the CD.

 ✔ Looking for a certain song, but can't remember which one it is? Then
   choose the Intro Play option under Options. It automatically plays the first
   few seconds of every song on the CD until you recognize the one you're after.

 ✔ As soon as you insert an audio CD, Windows 95 begins playing it — as long
   as your CD-ROM drive supports that feature. To stop Windows 95 from
   immediately playing the CD, hold down the Shift key while inserting the CD
   into the CD-ROM drive.

The Techie Programs

Windows 95 comes with several technical programs designed to make the nerd
feel at home. The Windows 95 installation program doesn't automatically install
all of these programs, however. If you want to go back and add them, grab your
Windows 95 installation disks (or compact disc) and head for Chapter 17. That
chapter explains how to use the Control Panel's Add/Remove Programs feature
to make Windows 95 toss a few more goodies onto your hard drive.

Meanwhile, the next few sections describe some of the more technical programs in Windows 95.

The Disk Defragmenter

What it does: When a computer reads and writes files to and from a hard disk,
it's working like a liquor store stock clerk after a labor day weekend: It has to
reorganize the store, moving all the misplaced beer cans out of the wine aisles.
The same disorganization happens with computer files. When the computer
moves files around, it tends to break the files into chunks and spread them
across your hard drive. The computer can still find all the pieces, but it takes
more time. A Disk Defragmenter reorganizes the hard drive, making sure that all
the files' pieces are next to each other.

What it looks like: The Disk Defragmenter, shown in Figure 13-9, can sometimes
speed up your hard drive.

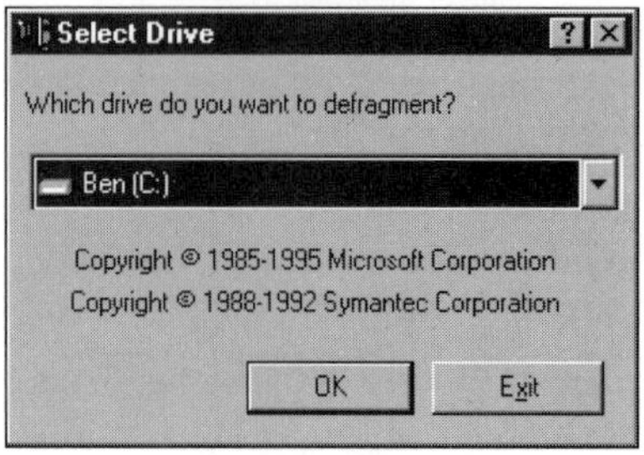

Figure 13-9:
Defragment
your hard
drive if your
computer's
been acting
more
sluggish
than usual.

Select Drive   ? ✕

Which drive do you want to defragment?

Ben (C:)   ▼

Copyright © 1985-1995 Microsoft Corporation
Copyright © 1988-1992 Symantec Corporation

OK   Exit

Why bother with it: Your hard drive can grab files more quickly if all the files' pieces are stored next to each other. The Disk Defragmenter organizes the files, speeding up access times.

Where it lives: Click on the Start button and then choose Programs, Accessories, System Tools, and, finally, Disk Defragmenter.

How to use it: When the program pops up, click on the drive you'd like defragmented. The program will look at the drive and say whether the drive needs any work. Take the program's advice. (You probably won't have to use the program more than every couple of months, depending on how often you're using your computer.)

ScanDisk

What it does: Sometimes a computer goofs and loses track of where it has stored information on a hard disk. ScanDisk examines a hard disk for any errors and, if it finds anything suspicious, offers to fix the problem.

What it looks like: ScanDisk, shown in Figure 13-10, can sometimes repair errors on your hard disk.

Why bother with it: ScanDisk not only finds hard disk errors, but, if you click in the Automatically fix errors box, it fixes them.

Where it lives: Click on the Start button and then choose Programs, Accessories, System Tools, and, finally, ScanDisk.

How to use it: After loading the program, click on the drive you'd like to check. Then click on the Automatically fix errors box until a check mark appears and click on the Start button. If you still have problems, rerun the program, but choose the Thorough option to make ScanDisk work a little harder. (The Thorough option takes an extra five or ten minutes.)

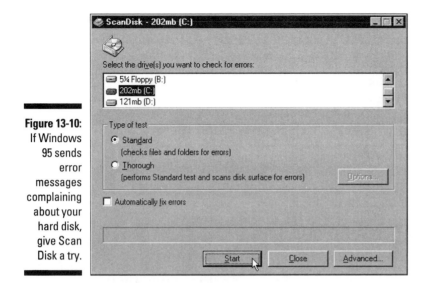

Figure 13-10:
If Windows
95 sends
error
messages
complaining
about your
hard disk,
give Scan
Disk a try.

The Optional Programs

Windows 95 doesn't automatically install *all* its possible freebie programs. If you followed the normal installation, you won't find the following programs listed on any menus. The next few sections tell you which programs you're missing — as well as how to install them.

My version of Windows 95 doesn't have the right programs!

Depending on the buttons you punched when you installed Windows 95, you'll find different varieties of programs installed on your hard drive. Very few people get all the programs installed. If you feel left out and want some of the optional programs mentioned in this chapter, follow these steps:

1. **Double-click on the Control Panel's Add/Remove Programs icon.**

   You can load the Control Panel by clicking on Settings in the Start menu.

2. **Click on the Windows Setup tab.**

   It's the tab in the middle of the three along the top; a box will appear showing the various components of Windows 95, as well as the amount of space they'll need to nestle onto your computer's hard drive.

3. Click in the little box by the programs or accessories you'd like to add.

A check mark appears in the box of the items you select. To select part of a category — a portion of the accessories, for example — click on the category's name and click on the Details button. Windows 95 lists the items available in that category so that you can click on the ones you want. If you clicked on the Details button, click on the OK button to continue back at the main categories list.

4. Click on the OK button and insert your installation disks when asked.

Windows 95 will copy the necessary files from your installation disks onto your hard drive. You can remove Windows 95 accessories the same way, but by *removing* the check mark from the box next to their name.

The Microsoft Network On-Line Service

Most people have heard about *on-line services,* where you can hook your computer up to the phone lines and, under the pretense of making direct deposit payments through your checking account, swap pictures of your cat wearing a beret with new-found friends on the Cat User Group.

Smelling money, Microsoft started its own on-line service to compete with CompuServe, America Online, Prodigy, GEnie, the Internet, and the plethora of other on-line services that hatch each day.

Windows 95 comes with software that's itching to access *The Microsoft Network.* Shown in Figure 13-11, The Microsoft Network looks more like a Windows program than an on-line service. It uses the same folders and format used by Windows 95.

✔ Don't bother searching through the Windows 95 box for mail-in forms in order to subscribe to The Microsoft Network. Instead, you'll find the sign-up form right on the Start button's menu, listed under Programs. Point and click, and Windows 95 starts dialing. (That's why all the other online services are a little bit worried about the competition.)

✔ Just as you can place pictures, sounds, and charts in a Windows word processor file, you can place pictures, sounds, and charts in messages swapped over The Microsoft Network. For example, you can easily paste a picture of yourself (or your cat) into a message to a friend.

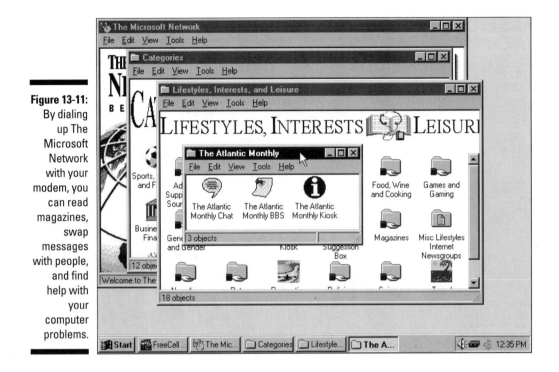

Figure 13-11:
By dialing up The Microsoft Network with your modem, you can read magazines, swap messages with people, and find help with your computer problems.

✔ The Microsoft Network offers the standard on-line fare: electronic mail, bulletin boards, "chat rooms," file libraries, and Internet newsgroups. Because Microsoft's running the show, you'll be able to find lots of technical support for Microsoft products on-line, as well.

✔ The Microsoft Network will be accessible in more than 35 countries. Vacation planners can send messages to London, asking for the names of the best pubs before traveling there.

FreeCell

The Windows 3.1 favorite time waster, Solitaire, has been passed up by a new contestant: FreeCell. FreeCell has been a "real" card game for years; it entered the Microsoft world with Windows NT (an earlier, "big" version of Windows that didn't excite very many people).

Microsoft has tossed FreeCell to the masses in Windows 95. Although FreeCell looks a lot like Solitaire, it plays a lot differently. Shown in Figure 13-12, FreeCell works with double-clicks: Instead of making you drag the cards around, FreeCell simply jumps them into place.

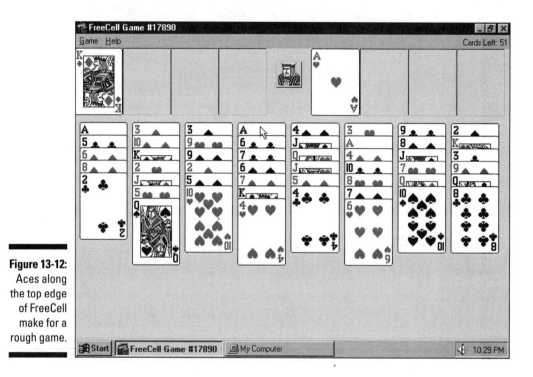

Figure 13-12:
Aces along the top edge of FreeCell make for a rough game.

The object is pretty simple: Sort the cards in order by suit and number from Ace to King on the four right-hand squares. While moving the cards up there, you can move other cards temporarily to the four "free cells" — temporary card-storage areas — on the left-hand side.

- FreeCell comes with 32,000 different games. So far, none of them have been proven unbeatable.

- If you're looking for a challenge, try games number 285; 27,006; or 31,465. In fact, you might find one or two other difficult ones, as well.

- Moved the wrong card? Quick, press F10. That's the Undo button, but only if you press it before clicking on another card.

- After you've won 65,535 games, FreeCell resets your winning streak statistics to zero. Be forewarned.

Hearts

Windows 95 has no shortage of card games, that's for sure. If you're tired of Solitaire and FreeCell, you might give Hearts a try. Shown in Figure 13-13, it's the same version of Hearts that came with Windows for Workgroups.

The game works just like *real* Hearts. One person tosses a card onto the table, everybody else tosses down a card of the same suit, and the person with the highest card grabs the pile. The tricky part? You want the *lowest* score — any card with a heart is one point, and the queen of spades is worth 13 points.

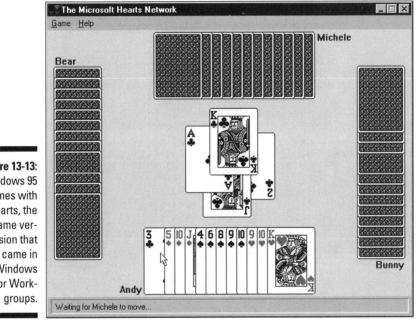

Figure 13-13: Windows 95 comes with Hearts, the same version that came in Windows for Workgroups.

✔ There's a catch. If one player grabs all the hearts and the queen of spades, that player doesn't get any points, and all the other players are penalized 26 points.

✔ Nobody around at the office network? The computer fills in for the other three players, and you can still play. You don't need a network to play Hearts.

✔ ***Cheat alert:*** The computer automatically sorts your cards by suit at the screen's bottom. However, it doesn't sort the cards that represent the other player's hands — the cards around the edges. Therefore, you can't get an idea of what cards the other players have by watching the position of their cards.

✔ If you migrated from Windows for Workgroups, you're probably already used to playing Hearts over the network. Windows 95 keeps Hearts in the mix of games, along with Solitaire.

Backup

Everybody knows you're supposed to make backup copies of your computer's information. The problem is finding the time to do it.

The Microsoft Backup program, shown in Figure 13-14, isn't anything special except in one key area: It can handle long file names. Because the old-school, DOS-based backup programs can only handle eight-character file names, they can't make reliable backups in Windows 95.

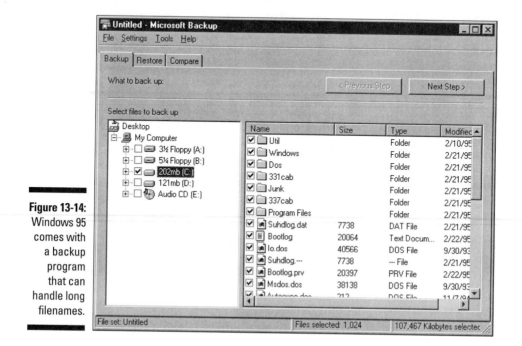

Figure 13-14: Windows 95 comes with a backup program that can handle long filenames.

To keep Windows 95 users from treading dangerously, Microsoft tossed a backup program in with Windows 95 until all the other companies update their backup programs. After you tell the backup program which programs to save, it copies them to floppy disks or a tape backup unit.

If you haven't bought a tape backup unit yet, now might be a good time to put one on your shopping list. They've come way down in price, and copying huge hard drives onto hundreds of floppies is a bore, even if Windows 95 *does* let you play FreeCell while you're doing it.

Briefcase

Want to move files between your laptop and desktop — and still come up with the right file when you need it? Briefcase lets you connect two computers with a serial or parallel cable and shoot files between them. Best yet, Briefcase can tell which one is most up-to-date, so you'll always be keeping the current copy.

Of course, if you want a more full-featured version, you'll stick with Traveling Software's LapLink. That program's been doing the same thing for years (and it comes with the cables you need, too).

Microsoft Exchange

Having an electronic mail box is like having a Post Office box. Instead of having your stuff dumped at your doorstep, you have to head for the P.O. Box to see what's been stuffed inside it.

Dozens of services offer electronic mail, and sometimes it can be confusing keeping track of everybody's address. In fact, many people have several addresses of their own — one on CompuServe, one on Prodigy, one on the Internet, and one on that new service that just opened up.

The Microsoft Exchange lets you enter everybody's address into one place. Then, when you send mail, you can concentrate on the mail — not the envelope. When you're done writing, push the Send button, and Microsoft Exchange automatically sends the letter to the right place. And while it's there, it grabs any incoming mail you might have.

How Did Windows 3.1 Hold Up?

Like an evolving creature, Windows 95 has changed Windows 3.1 fairly drastically. To see whether your favorite programs have been improved, removed, or destroyed, check out Table 3-3; it lists Windows 3.1 programs and their Windows 95 replacements. (Chapter 15 contains even more information to help Windows 3.1 users make their move.)

Table 13-3	Windows 3.1 Programs and their Windows 95 Replacements
The Windows 3.1 Program	*Its Windows 95 Equivalent*
Program Manager	Start Button. (Program Manager is still included, in case you prefer to stick with it.)
File Manager	Explorer and My Computer programs. (File Manager is still included, in case you like it better.)
Write	WordPad; both adds and removes features.
Paintbrush	Paint; both adds and removes features.
Cardfile, Calendar	Gone with no replacements, although Windows 95 leaves the Windows 3.1 versions on the hard disk in case you've upgraded.
Character Map, Calculator, Notepad, Media Player, Sound Recorder, MS-DOS Prompt, Solitaire, Clipbook Viewer, Hearts	Still the same in Windows 95.
Terminal	Replaced with HyperTerminal, a telecommunications program with many more features.
Control Panel	Replaced by Control Panel window, a similar collection of icons.
PIF Editor	Replaced by Properties sheet: Click on a DOS program's icon with the right mousebutton and choose Properties from the menu to tweak the program's settings.
Clock	Replaced by a permanent clock on the taskbar.

Those Windows 3.1 Leftovers

If you installed Windows 95 over Windows 3.1 (or Windows for Workgroups — they're almost the same thing), you'll find a few of your older Windows programs still hanging around. Here's what's left.

Notepad

Windows comes with two word processors, WordPad and Notepad. WordPad is for the letters you're sprucing up for other people to see. Notepad is for stuff you're going to keep for yourself.

Notepad is quicker than WordPad. Double-click on its icon, and it leaps to the screen more quickly than you could have reached for a notepad in your back pocket. You can type in some quick words and save them on the fly.

Understanding Notepad's limitations

Notepad's speed comes at a price, however. Notepad stores only words and numbers. It doesn't store any special formatting, such as italicized letters, and you can't paste any pictures into it, as you can with WordPad. It's a quick, throw-together program for your quick, throw-together thoughts.

- ✔ Notepad tosses you into instant confusion: All the sentences head right off the edge of the screen. To turn one-line, runaway sentences into normal paragraphs, turn on the *word wrap* feature by selecting Word Wrap from the Edit menu. (You have to turn it on each time you start Notepad, strangely enough.)

- ✔ Notepad prints kind of funny, too: It prints the file's name at the top of every page. To combat this nonsense, select File and then choose Page Setup. A box appears, with a funny code word in the Header box. Delete the word and click on the OK button. If you want to get rid of the automatic page numbering, clear out the Footer box as well.

- ✔ Here's another printing problem: Notepad doesn't print exactly what you see on-screen. Instead, it prints according to the margins you set in Page Setup under the File menu. This quirk can lead to unpredictable results.

Turning Notepad into a log book

Although Notepad leans toward simplicity, it has one fancy feature that not
even WordPad can match. Notepad can automatically stamp the current time
and date at the bottom of a file whenever you open it. Just type **.LOG** in the
very top left-hand corner of a file and save the file. Then, whenever you open it
again, you can jot down some current notes and have Notepad stamp it with the
time and date. It looks similar to what is shown in Figure 13-15.

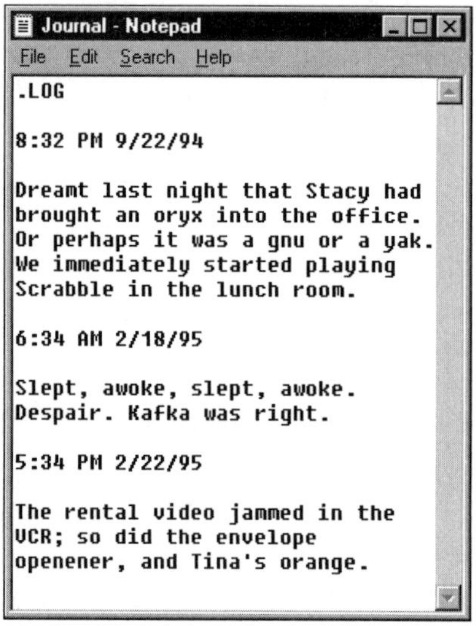

Figure 13-15:
Add the
word .LOG
to the top of
the file, and
Notepad
stamps it
with the
time and
date
whenever
you open it.

```
.LOG

8:32 PM 9/22/94

Dreamt last night that Stacy had
brought an oryx into the office.
Or perhaps it was a gnu or a yak.
We immediately started playing
Scrabble in the lunch room.

6:34 AM 2/18/95

Slept, awoke, slept, awoke.
Despair. Kafka was right.

5:34 PM 2/22/95

The rental video jammed in the
VCR; so did the envelope
openener, and Tina's orange.
```

 ✔ Don't try the .LOG trick by using lowercase letters and don't omit the
   period. It doesn't work.

 ✔ To stick in the date and time manually, press F5. The time and date
   appear, just as they do in the .LOG trick.

Calculator

Calculator is, well, a calculator. It looks simple enough, and it really is — unless
you've mistakenly set it for Scientific mode and see some nightmarish logarith-
mic stuff. To bring it back to normal, select View and choose Standard.

To punch in numbers and equations, click on the little buttons, just as if it were a normal calculator. When you press the equal sign (=), the answer appears at the top. For an extra measure of handiness, you can copy the answers to the Clipboard by pressing Ctrl+C (holding down the Ctrl key while pressing C). Then click in the window where you want the answer to appear and press Ctrl+V. That method is easier than retyping a number like 2.449489742783.

✔ Unlike in other Windows programs, you can't copy Calculator's answer by running the mouse pointer over the numbers. You have to press Ctrl+C or choose Copy from the Edit menu.

✔ If the mouse action is too slow, press the Num Lock key and punch in numbers with the numeric keypad.

✔ In Windows 95, Calculator fixes the subtraction and decimal point problems found in the Windows 3.1 version. It's been verified to be at least as accurate as the Star Trek key chain calculators.

Adding the à in Voilà (Character Map)

To add weird foreign characters, such as *à*, *£*, or even *Ð*, choose Character Map from the Start menu's Program Accessories menu. A box like the one shown in Figure 13-16 appears, listing every available character and symbol.

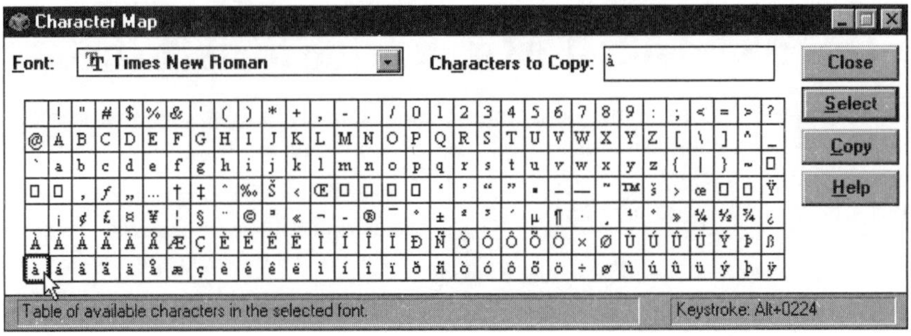

Figure 13-16:
You can use the Character Map to find foreign characters and stick them in your work.

Follow these steps to put a foreign character in your work:

1. **Make sure that the current font — the name for the style of the characters on the page — shows in the Font box.**

   Not showing? Then click on the down arrow and click on the font when it appears in the drop-down list.

2. **Scan the Character Map box until you see the symbol you're after; then pounce on that character with a double-click.**

    It appears in the Characters to Copy box.

3. **Click on Copy to send the character to the Clipboard.**

4. **Click on the Close button to close the Character Map.**

5. **Click in the document where you want the new symbol or character to appear.**

6. **Press Ctrl+V, and the new character pops right in there.**

    (Give it a second. Sometimes it's slow.)

The symbols in the Character Map box are easier to see if you hold down the mouse button and move the pointer over them.

✔ When working with foreign words, keep the Character Map handy as an icon, ready for consultation.

✔ For some fun symbols like ✎, ⌨, ✂, ⌦, ☀, ♞, or ☑, switch to the Wingdings font. It's full of little doodads to spice up your work.

✔ You can grab several characters at a time by double-clicking on each of them and then copying them into your work as a chunk. You don't have to keep returning to the Character Map for each one.

That weird Alt+0208 stuff is too trivial to bother with

In the bottom right-hand corner, Character Map flashes numbers after the words `Keystroke: Alt+`. Those numbers hail back to the stone-tablet days of adding foreign characters when word processing. Back then, people had to look up a character's code number in the back of a boring manual.

If you remember the code numbers for your favorite symbols, however, you can bypass Character Map and add them directly to documents. For example, the code number listed in the bottom corner for é is 0233.

Here's the trick: Press and release Num Lock, hold down Alt and type 0233 with the numeric keypad. Let go of the Alt key, and the é symbol appears.

If you constantly use one special character, this method may be faster than using Character Map. (Press and release Num Lock when you're finished.)

Calendar

Some cynics say that the free Windows programs aren't really programs. They're merely *demonstrations* of what Windows can do. The old Windows 3.1 Calendar fits in with that school of thought because it's too lame to be a *real* program. First, when Calendar is an icon, it always thinks the date is the 12th of the month. The icon never displays the current date (except on the 12th). The Calendar icon looks like this:

Calendar

Second, you can't list appointments that are longer than 80 characters. And the words start running off the page before you type even half that much, as shown in Figure 13-17. This problem has no solution; even when Calendar fills the whole screen, its tiny calendar page stays the same size.

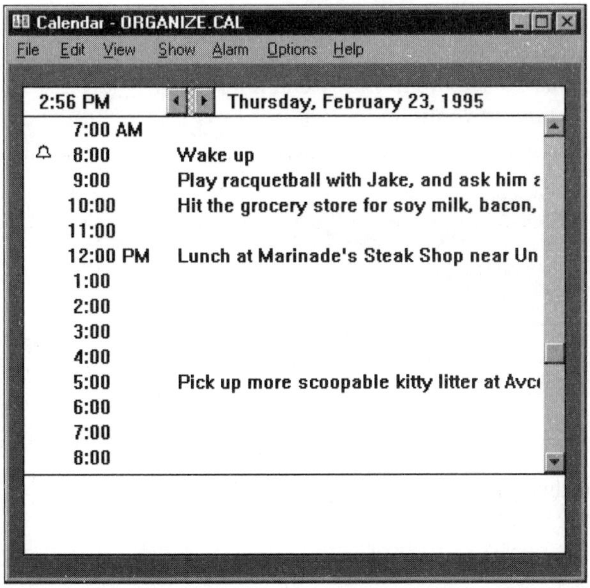

Figure 13-17: The appointments in the Windows 95 calendar fall off the edge of the page. This weirdness isn't your fault.

When you click on one of those appointments, the view gets even worse, as shown in Figure 13-18.

Clicking on the *Lunch at Marinade's Steak Shop* appointment doesn't bring you to the word *Lunch*. Instead, Calendar jumps to the middle of the sentence, as shown in Figure 13-18, making it hard to tell what's going on. This strange behavior isn't your fault.

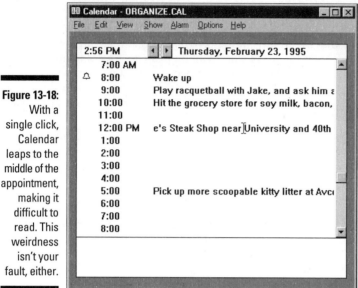

Figure 13-18:
With a
single click,
Calendar
leaps to the
middle of the
appointment,
making it
difficult to
read. This
weirdness
isn't your
fault, either.

Calendar works best when it's doing something simple, such as displaying a monthly calendar. To see the monthly calendar, select <u>V</u>iew and then select <u>M</u>onth from the pull-down menu (see Figure 13-19). Or just press F9 — whichever comes to mind sooner.

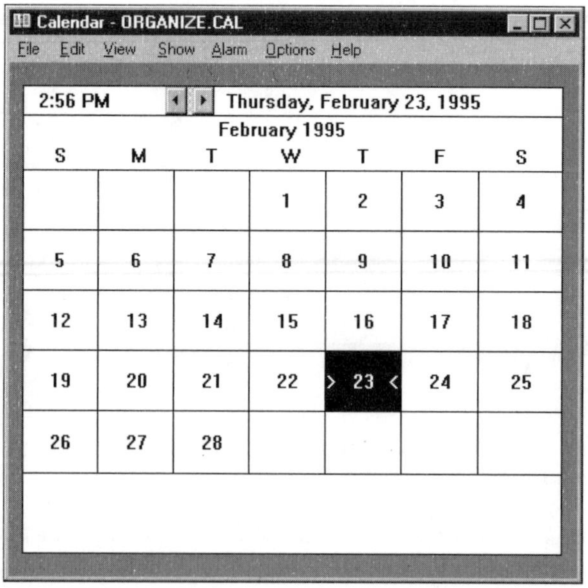

Figure 13-19:
A press of
the F9 key
makes
Calendar
display a
monthly
view.

The monthly view doesn't show any upcoming appointments, though. You have to mark important days yourself by clicking on them and pressing F6 (or by choosing Mark from the Options pull-down menu).

Calendar doesn't search for upcoming appointments, either. You can't search for *Tina* to find out when you're next scheduled for lunch. You can only stumble across the information yourself by viewing appointments in the *Day* mode (press F8) and clicking on the little right- and left-pointing arrows at the top of the screen until you see the name. (And, if the name is off the edge of the page, you'll *never* see it.)

Calendar has one redeeming factor: You can set an alarm by clicking next to an appointment and pressing F5 (or choosing Set from the Alarm pull-down menu). You can set the alarm to go off ten minutes before the appointment, thank goodness.

Table 13-4	Calendar Shortcut Keys
To Do This	*Do This*
View an entire month	Press F9.
View a single day	Press F8.
Jump to a specific date	Press F4.
Set an alarm for a selected time	Press F5.
Add a special mark to a day	Press F6.
Enter an appointment on a specific time	Press F7.
Find help	Press F1.
Track your appointments	Buy a better program.

✔ If you find Calendar difficult to use, don't blame yourself. Everybody else does, too. It's fine for figuring out the date of the third Tuesday in a month, but it's terrible for planning appointments.

✔ Calendar is a remnant from Windows 3.1, so you won't find it on your hard disk unless you've installed Windows 95 over Windows 3.1. Because Calendar is a Windows 3.1 leftover, it won't be able to read or write file names with more than eight characters.

✔ Calendar always loads the day view first. If you want to see the current month, press F9.

✔ Try the shortcut keys in Table 13-4 before giving up on Calendar completely.

✔ Oh yeah — Calendar won't let you change your computer's time or date. If your computer's internal clock is off, double-click on the little clock on the taskbar, usually found in the bottom-right corner of your screen.

Cardfile

The old Cardfile from Windows 3.1 works pretty much like the standard flip-through-the-business-cards gizmo organized people keep on their desks. Even the icon looks the same:

Cardfile

The actual program looks like a business card holder, too, as shown in Figure 13-20.

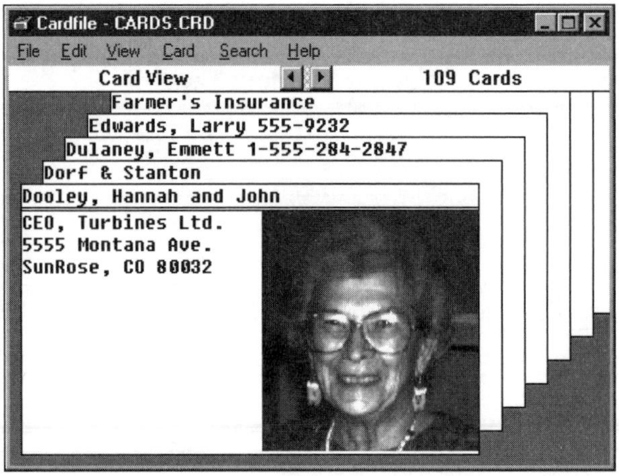

Figure 13-20:
You can paste pictures, as well as text, onto the cards in Cardfile.

To fit more names on-screen, Cardfile can display just the top line of each card. Select View and choose List from the menu. Figure 13-21 shows a list made up of the top lines of several cards.

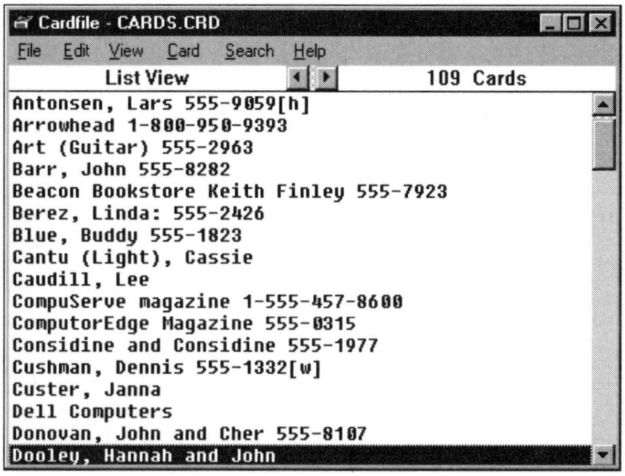

Figure 13-21:
In the List
mode, when
you type a
single letter,
Cardfile
jumps to the
first card
starting with
that letter.

Cardfile provides you with a quick and easy way to keep track of people. It's simple, and yet it lets you add pictures, sounds, or even huge text files with that Object Linking and Embedding stuff from Chapter 9. Remember that it's an old Windows 3.1 program, though, so you're limited to file names of only eight letters.

Adding a new card

When you're ready to start typing all your business cards, choose Add from the Card pull-down menu (or press F7). Cardfile gives you a blank line where you can type the person's name and phone number. Press Enter and then fill out the rest of the card.

✔ After you type the name, enter the person's phone number and area code so that Cardfile can automatically dial the phone number. (The upcoming "Autodial" section explains how to make it dial the number.) Put a **1** in front of the number if it's long distance.

✔ To paste a picture into a card, click on Picture from the Edit menu. Then paste it from the Clipboard by pressing Ctrl+V (holding down Ctrl while pressing V). Drag the picture until it's positioned just so and let go of the mouse button. (Use Paint to copy the picture to the Clipboard.)

✔ You can't edit both the picture and the text at the same time. To switch Cardfile to the proper editing mode, choose either Picture or Text from the Edit menu. A check mark appears next to the one you can currently edit.

✔ To edit the picture, switch to the Edit Picture mode described earlier and double-click on the picture. Paint appears with the image, ready for you to add a mustache. When you're finished, close Paint and the updated image appears in Cardfile.

Making Cardfile dial phone numbers automatically

If you have a computer gizmo called a *modem* connected to the computer, Cardfile automatically dials the number at the top of the card when you press F5. When Cardfile tells you to pick up the phone, pick it up and start talking.

✔ For this trick to work, you need a modem connected between the computer and the phone lines. You also need a plain old telephone plugged into the modem's phone jack. (Some expensive multiline phones can't handle this autodial stuff.)

✔ Cardfile dials any numbers it finds along the top of the card, so put a 1 in front of any long-distance numbers. (Don't put other numbers up there, like the person's shoe size, or the modem will dial those numbers, too.) Finally, if you need to dial a 9 for an outside line, press F5 and click on the Setup button. Click in the Use Prefix box and type the number **9** in the Prefix box.

Rooting through the cards for somebody's phone number

Cardfile complicated matters by offering two kinds of searches. It can search the names along the top of the cards, or it can search the information stored on the card itself. However, Cardfile can't be bothered to search *both* parts of the card at the same time.

✔ To search through the *names* at the top of the cards, select Search and then choose Go to (or just press F4). Type the name of the person you're after and press Enter. Cardfile dashes to the first card that matches that name. Not the right person? Then press F4 again and type the name again. (You have to retype the name every time you repeat the process. It can take a *long* time to find the right Mr. Smith card. However, if you know Mr. Smith's first name — say, Pat — you can speed up the process by typing **Smith, Pat** in the box.)

✔ To search through the *information* stored on the cards, select Search and then choose Find from the menu. Type in the word you're after and press Enter. Not the right card? Then press F3 to keep searching through the other cards.

Sound Recorder and Media Player

If you've bought and installed a sound card for your computer, you can play and record sounds with Sound Recorder. It looks and works pretty much like a tape recorder. Here's one warning, however: Don't get carried away when recording particularly long sounds. They take a *lot* of space on the hard drive.

Media Player can't record, but it can play from a wide variety of devices. It can play sounds from a sound card, as well as connect to MIDI keyboards. It can access CD-ROM drives for both sound and data. It even plays videodiscs.

- ✔ Windows 95 comes ready to run with some of the most popular sound cards. Other sound cards or CD-ROM drives come with special drivers on a floppy disk that is boxed with the package.

- ✔ Sound cards and CD-ROM drives are covered in Chapter 2.

- ✔ *MORE Windows For Dummies,* a "next-step-up" Dummies book, shows you how to use Sound Recorder and Media Player to play and record sounds, listen to compact discs, and even watch movies.

- ✔ Or if you're *really* entranced by flashing lights and screaming sounds, check out *Multimedia & CD-ROMs For Dummies.* It shows you how to buy, set up, and use all those cool multimedia gizmos everybody's talking about.

Solitaire

Windows 95 Solitaire works just like the card game, so here are just a few pointers for the computerized version:

- ✔ When the boss comes by, click on the minimize button, that underscore-looking thing in a box in the upper-right corner. If you can't move the mouse quickly enough, hold down Alt and press the spacebar, followed by the letter N. In either case, Solitaire turns into an icon at the bottom of the screen. Double-click on the icon to resume play when the boss passes.

- ✔ Using Windows isn't easy on a laptop, and Solitaire can be a nightmare. You can play Solitaire with a keyboard by using an awkward combination of Tab, Enter, and the arrow keys. But a laptop's black-and-white screen makes it difficult to tell when a card is being placed on the right color.

- ✔ Sharp-eyed players will notice some background fun: The bats flap their wings, the sun sticks out its tongue, and a card slides in and out of a dealer's sleeve. These shenanigans only occur when you play in *timed* mode. To start the fun, choose Options from the Game menu and make sure that there's an X in the Timed Game box.

Minesweeper

Despite the name, Minesweeper does not cause any explosions, even if you accidentally uncover a mine. And it works better on laptops than Solitaire does. Minesweeper is more of a math game than anything else. No jumping little men here.

Start by clicking on a random square. If you click on a hidden mine, you lose on the first click; otherwise, some numbers appear in one or more of the little squares. The number says how many mines are hidden in the squares surrounding that square.

Each square is surrounded by eight other squares. (Unless it's on the edge; then there are only five. And only three squares surround corner squares.) If, through the process of elimination, you're sure a mine exists beneath a certain square, click on it with the right mouse button to put a little flag there.

Eventually, through logical deduction (or just mindless pointing and clicking), you either accidentally click on a mine and are blown up, or mark all the mine squares with flags and win the game.

The object of the game is to win as fast as you can.

The 5th Wave

By Rich Tennant

"We expect Windows 95 in any day! So if you want to go ahead and prepay to reserve a copy..."

Chapter 14

Uh, How Do I Run My Old DOS Programs?

. . . .

In This Chapter

▶ Running DOS programs under Windows 95

▶ Making your own PIFs for DOS programs

▶ Changing fonts in a DOS window

▶ Halting runaway DOS programs

. . . .

*W*indows 95 programs are used to a communal lifestyle where they all eat from the same granola trough. They can share the computer's memory without bickering. DOS programs, however, hail from a different computing era. Windows 95 must nurse DOS programs along, or the DOS programs won't run.

In fact, Windows keeps a special chart called a *PIF* (an acronym for *program information file*) for each problem-causing DOS program. A PIF (rhymes with *sniff*) contains the care and feeding instructions that Windows needs to make a particular DOS program happy.

The information in these PIFs can include some pretty meaty stuff. This chapter chops it into easily digestible chunks, but you may want to keep a napkin around, just in case.

Running DOS Programs under Windows

Some DOS programs are easy to run under Windows 95. Just head for the Start menu (or Explorer or the My Computer window), double-click on that program's icon, and stand back while it heads for the screen. Sometimes the DOS program fills the entire screen while Windows waits in the background. Other times, the program runs happily in its own window, oblivious to everything around it.

But some DOS programs refuse to run under Windows 95 at all. They were designed to use *all* of a computer's resources, so they balk if they think that Windows 95 is just tossing them a few scraps.

To trick these DOS programs into feeling at home, Windows 95 gives each problem-causing DOS program its own PIF containing the special instructions needed to trick that program into running in Windows.

For example, a PIF may tell Windows 95 to put the DOS program in a window or to make the program fill the entire screen. PIFs tell Windows 95 the type of memory that the DOS program craves and how much of that memory it wants. Other settings are cosmetic, such as specifying what type of font to use.

Windows 95 can automatically create PIFs for the most popular DOS programs. In fact, when you're double-clicking on a DOS program's icon, you're probably double-clicking on that program's PIF. Windows 95 consults the PIF and then runs the program accordingly.

✔ When Windows 95 installs itself, it searches to see what programs you've already installed on the computer. When it finds a troublesome DOS program that it recognizes, it tosses a PIF for that program into the computer and puts an icon for that PIF on the Start menu and in the My Computer and Explorer programs. The PIF also serves as a shortcut, telling Windows 95 where the DOS program lives on the computer.

✔ If you've installed a new DOS program and want to run it under Windows 95, check out the section in Chapter 11 about putting a favorite program into the Start menu. If Windows 95 recognizes that new DOS program, it creates a PIF and everything is hunky-dory.

✔ Some DOS programs come with their own Windows PIFs. When you install such a program, it tosses its PIF onto the hard drive. PIF names usually start with the program's filename and end in the letters PIF. When Windows 95 installs itself, it searches the hard drive looking for PIFs. If it finds any, it updates them and uses them as shortcuts for the DOS program.

✔ If you double-click on a DOS program that doesn't have a PIF, Windows 95 uses general-purpose settings that allow almost any DOS program to run without problem. If there is a problem, you'll have to make your own PIF, a process described in the very next section.

Getting Your Own PIFs for DOS Programs

If a DOS program isn't working under Windows 95, call the company that made it and tell the company that you need its PIF for Windows 95. If the company doesn't have one, call your computer dealer or bribe a computer guru to make one for you.

Until then, choose the Sh<u>u</u>t down command from the Start menu and choose the Restart the computer in <u>M</u>S-DOS mode from the box that pops up. Windows leaves the screen, and a DOS prompt appears, ready for you to run your DOS program.

When you're ready to go back to Windows 95, exit your DOS program and type **EXIT** at the C:\> thing to get your windows back on-screen.

Don't bother trying to make your own PIF. This is heavy stuff, meant for advanced users who *enjoy* piddling with PIFs. Besides, some DOS programs won't run under Windows 95 no matter how much PIF coddling they get. Until you become a PIF manufacturer, you're better off sticking with Windows 95 programs when running Windows 95. Most companies are writing Windows 95 versions of their DOS programs, so there's less need to run a DOS program in Windows 95 anyway.

Figuring Out the DOS Window's Buttons

When a DOS program fills the whole screen, it looks like a general, run-of-the-mill DOS program. But when it runs in a window, you'll notice little buttons along the program's top edge. Those buttons are the toolbar. (And if you don't see them, click on the icon in the window's uppermost-left corner and choose <u>T</u>oolbar from the menu that dangles down.) See Figure 14-1 for a look at the toolbar.

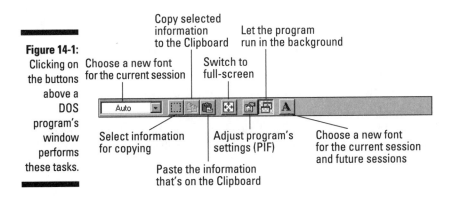

Figure 14-1:
Clicking on the buttons above a DOS program's window performs these tasks.

Copy selected information to the Clipboard

Let the program run in the background

Choose a new font for the current session

Switch to full-screen

Select information for copying

Adjust program's settings (PIF)

Choose a new font for the current session and future sessions

Paste the information that's on the Clipboard

Figure 14-1 shows what each button is supposed to do. If you don't want to remember all that, just remember this:

Rest your mouse pointer over any confusing button in Windows 95 or one of its programs, and a window pops up to explain that button's reason for living.

✔ First question: What's the difference between the two Font buttons? Well, they both change the size and style of the font in the current window, but the button on the left changes the font for the *current* session; the one on the right does that, too, but it also remembers your choice for that program's *future* sessions.

✔ Clicking on the little button with the outward-pointing arrows makes the DOS program run in full-screen mode. To cram the program back into a window, press Alt+Enter.

The Background button lets your DOS program work in the background — sorting a database, calculating a spreadsheet, or downloading a file — even when the program's not running on the top of the pile. If the program needs to be able to run in the background, then click on that button. Otherwise, clicking on the Background button only slows things down.

Changing Fonts in a DOS Window

DOS programs are used to roaming free and wild, but Windows 95 can force them to run inside a window, just like any Windows 95 program. A DOS window functions pretty much like any other window: You can move it around, tug on its borders to change its size, or shrink it into an icon if it's getting in the way.

If the DOS program normally fills the whole screen under Windows 95, try this to run it inside a window: Hold the Alt key and press Enter. The DOS program hops into a window on-screen.

Unfortunately, a DOS window sometimes won't fit comfortably on the screen. To fix that oversight, change the size of the font used by the window. That action makes the letters larger or smaller so that the information fits better on the screen. Follow these steps to change the font size for a DOS window:

1. Click on the button with the capital A on it, as shown in Figure 14-1.

It's that button along the top, toward the right. The dialog box shown in Figure 14-2 then appears. The little numbers on the right side of the dialog box, which start with 2 × 4, are the sizes of the available fonts.

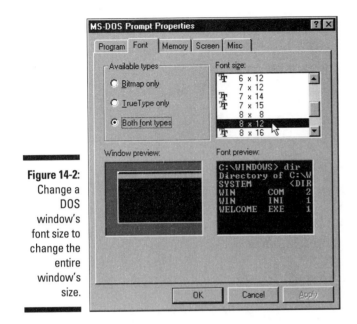

Figure 14-2:
Change a
DOS
window's
font size to
change the
entire
window's
size.

2. **Click on the different numbers and look in the preview boxes to see how the words on the DOS program window will look in that font size.**

The window's total size in relation to the desktop appears in the Window preview box; the size of the letters appears in the Font preview box. Figure 14-2, for example, shows the font size 8 × 12 selected; the Window preview box shows that a window of that size would cover almost the entire desktop.

Smaller font-size numbers make for smaller words and a smaller DOS window. For example, the 6 × 8 font shrinks the DOS window to the more manageable size shown in Figure 14-3.

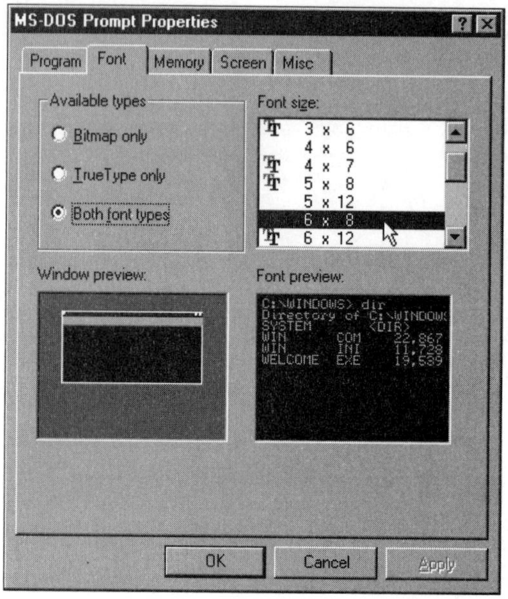

Figure 14-3:
Smaller
fonts make
for smaller
windows.

You can make the fonts larger, too, so that they're easier to read. If you're using a laptop on a plane, try some of the larger fonts so that the passenger sitting next to you won't have to strain so hard to see what you're doing.

✔ The changing-fonts trick works only with DOS programs that display mostly text — like spreadsheets and word processors. DOS programs that use graphics don't work too well in windows. Their displays don't completely fit in a window, and the colors almost always look weird.

✔ You can change a DOS window's size by dragging the borders, but that's pointless. A DOS program's display doesn't shrink or grow in size like a Windows 95 program does. If you drag the border in, you just cover up your view of the program.

✔ If you want to cut or paste anything from a DOS program in a window, head back to Chapter 9 for information about the DOS window versions of cut, copy, and paste.

Although TrueType fonts usually look better than Bitmap fonts in Windows programs, that doesn't hold true as often with DOS programs. Test both Bitmap and TrueType fonts before making a final selection.

Halting Runaway DOS Programs

Like startled Arkansas farmers who wake up in the belly of a spaceship, some DOS programs simply freak out when they find themselves running under Windows 95. For example, some freeze up solid, stubbornly beeping each time you press a key.

To halt a runaway DOS program, first look at the top of the DOS window. If the first word along the top says Mark or Select, then Windows 95 thinks that you're trying to copy information from the DOS window. Press Esc to restore order. If you really were trying to copy something, head for Chapter 9.

If pressing Esc doesn't work, try holding the Alt key and pressing Enter. That action tells Windows 95 to let the temperamental program have the entire screen. For example, if a program suddenly switches from text to graphics in a window, Windows 95 sometimes freezes the program until you use the Alt+Enter trick.

That didn't work, either? Then things are getting serious. If the confused DOS program is in a window, follow these steps:

1. **Press Ctrl+Alt+Delete.**

2. **When the list of currently running programs appears, click on your runaway program's name.**

3. **Click on the ominous-looking End Task button.**

4. **When Windows 95 asks whether you're sure, click on the Yes button.**

Hopefully, these steps will rip the DOS program from the computer's memory; use these steps pretty much as a last resort.

If the frozen DOS program is running full-screen, hold the Ctrl key, press and hold Alt, and then press Delete (Ctrl+Alt+Delete). When Windows 95 asks whether you're sure that you want to close the program, press End Task.

If you click on the End Task button or press the Ctrl+Alt+Delete combination, you lose any unsaved work in the DOS program.

- ✔ Only use the End Task or Ctrl+Alt+Delete method as a last resort. If at all possible, quit the DOS program in an orderly fashion. For some programs, you hold down the Alt key and press X; in others, you press F10 or Esc. Almost all programs are different. (That's one reason why people are switching to Windows 95; its commands are more predictable.)

- ✔ After you use End Task or Ctrl+Alt+Delete, save any work in the other windows. Then exit Windows 95 and start it up again. That DOS program may have sabotaged things on its way out.

Part IV
Been There, Done That: Quick References for Moving to Windows 95

The 5th Wave   By Rich Tennant

Ever the innovator, Larry beta-tests the Personal Belt Buckle Assistant/Wireless Fax

Hold on a second, Stu, I'm getting a fax.

In this part . . .

Moving from Windows 3.1 to Windows 95 is like moving into a new house and trying to find the bathroom in the dark. Until you get used to the floor plan, you'll be bumping into things.

After you learn where things are, that sense of urgency disappears and you can relax. Other people, however, always miss their old place, with its familiar light switches, windows, and plumbing.

This part of the book is for Windows 3.1 owners who've already paid their dues, figuring out the old Program Manager and File Manager. Here, you find ways to make Windows 95 work like the old standby, Windows 3.1. Or if you're looking for the quickest way to get the most done, you can find that here as well.

Chapter 15

Make Windows 95 Work Like My *Old* Windows!

● ●

In This Chapter

▶ Bringing back Program Manager

▶ Resurrecting File Manager

▶ Replacing the Task List

▶ Finding Cardfile and Calendar

▶ Finding Paint

● ●

*F*ile Manager and Program Manager may not have been perfect, but hey, at least their faults were *familiar* to the 60 million Windows 3.1 users out there. This chapter shows how to make Windows 95 act like old, faithful, Windows 3.1.

Where Did My Program Manager Go?

Windows 95 dumped Program Manager in favor of the Start menu, which pops up when you click on the famous Windows 95 Start button. And when you scratch your head (and play with the thing for about 15 minutes), the similarities between the Start menu and Program Manager start to appear.

For example, Program Manager lets you organize your programs in separate Program Group windows. The Windows 95 Start menu organizes programs in separate folders branching out from the menu's <u>P</u>rograms listing.

But if you prefer Windows 3.1's Program Manager for starting programs — or you want to use Program Manager until you grow more accustomed to Windows 95 — here's how to bring the ol' Program Manager back to life:

1. **Click on the Start button and choose <u>R</u>un from the menu.**

   A box pops up, asking you to type the name of a program you'd like to run.

2. Type progman **into the Open box and click on the OK button.**

The box should look like the one in Figure 15-1. When you click on the OK button, Program Manager appears, as shown in Figure 15-2.

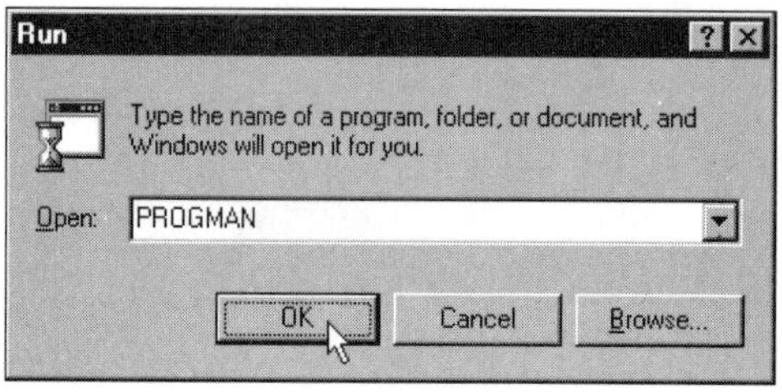

Figure 15-1:
Type
progman
into the
Open box
and click on
OK to start
the Program
Manager.

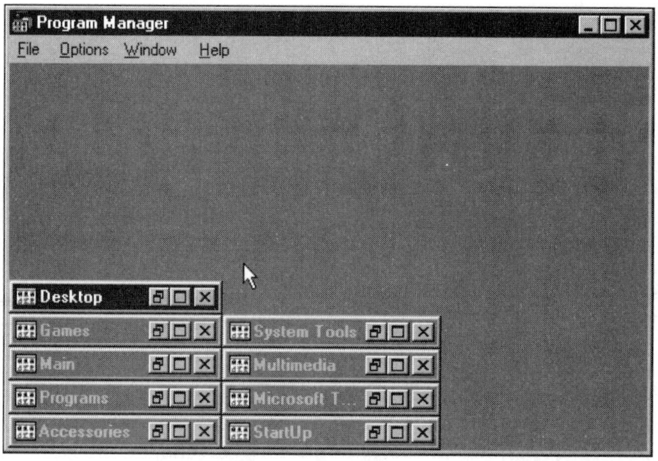

Figure 15-2:
Although
Program
Manager
comes with
Windows 95,
it may not
look or act
quite the
same as
your
Windows 3.1
version.

Be prepared for a few adjustments, however. Program Manager is wearing Windows 95 clothing, as shown in Figure 15-2. Minimized Program Groups stack themselves along the screen's bottom like cigars in a box, and the tiling and cascading features don't work as well as they do in Windows 3.1

Resize the windows, and Program Manager looks a little more familiar, as shown in Figure 15-3.

Figure 15-3:
When the
icons are
turned into
windows,
Program
Manager
looks more
familiar.

✔ Program Manager still has some limitations. For example, some newly installed programs won't install their icons on Program Manager — they put them on the Start menu instead.

✔ To put a program's icon on Program Manager, just drag the icon there from the My Computer or Explorer program. Windows 95 automatically turns the icon into a shortcut for launching the program. (After all, Windows 95's fancy shortcuts are almost the same as the icons in Windows 3.1's Program Manager.)

✔ The new Program Manager makes it much harder to drag and drop icons onto Program Groups that are minimized along the screen's bottom. The minimized group icons are much closer together than they used to be, making it harder to tell where your dropped icon will fall.

✔ Program Manager hails from the older, 16-bit school of programs, so it can't handle long filenames very well. In fact, if you drag a file called Egyptian Stone from My Computer to Program Manager, Program Manager will rename the file Egypti~1. That funny ~ thing, covered more extensively in Chapter 12, is how Windows 95 abbreviates long filenames so that older programs can still recognize them.

✔ Closing Program Manager no longer shuts down Windows 95. To shut down, you need to click on the Start button and choose Shut Down from the menu.

✔ If you _really_ prefer Program Manager over the Start menu, tell Windows 95 to automatically load Program Manager whenever you turn on your computer. The secret is to put the file PROGMAN.EXE in the StartUp folder. (The file's in your Windows folder, and Chapter 11 explains how to add a program to the StartUp folder.)

Where Did File Manager Go?

Nobody really likes the Windows 3.1 File Manager, except perhaps the old-timers who struggled with the Windows 3.0 File Manager.

Although File Manager's replacements — the My Computer and Explorer programs included with Windows 95 — are slightly easier to use, file management will never compete with a hockey game for entertainment.

If you don't want to learn any new tricks, however, feel free to bypass My Computer and Explorer and return to File Manager — it's included with Windows 95. Here's how to bring the File Manager to life:

1. **Click on the Start button and choose <u>R</u>un from the menu.**

   A box pops up, asking you to type the name of a program you'd like to run.

2. **Type** winfile **into the Open box and click on the OK button.**

   When you click on the OK button, the File Manager appears, as shown in Figure 15-4.

File Manager looks pretty much like the one in Windows for Workgroups. The biggest difference is in the minimized windows. Just as with Program Manager, File Manager's minimized windows look like hot dogs dropped to the window's bottom, as shown in Figure 15-5.

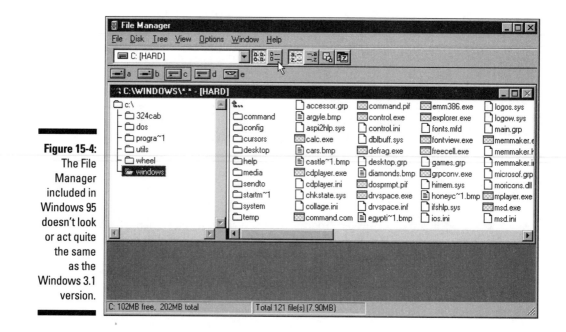

Figure 15-4:
The File Manager included in Windows 95 doesn't look or act quite the same as the Windows 3.1 version.

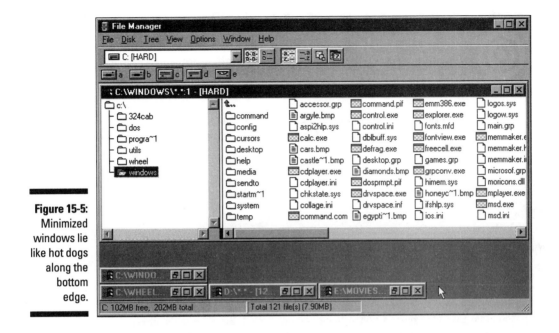

Figure 15-5:
Minimized
windows lie
like hot dogs
along the
bottom
edge.

✔ You can still copy files by dragging them and dropping them into windows inside File Manager. But it's hard to drop a file onto a minimized drive because those minimized drives are now hot-dog thin. And you can't load documents into programs by dragging and dropping them onto the taskbar's list of programs, either; Windows 95 says you can only drag and drop files into open windows.

✔ The Windows 95 version of File Manager, just like its version of Program Manager, still wears an old-school, 16-bit hat. That means it can't recognize the long filenames used by many Windows 95 programs. In fact, when File Manager comes across any filenames longer than 8 characters, it abbreviates them and puts a weird ˜ thing in the name.

✔ File Manager also adds the weird ˜ thing if it comes across any filename with a space in it, like a file named LOST IN or something similar.

✔ When you rest your mouse pointer over an icon in Windows 95, a box usually pops up and explains the icon's purpose for life. You won't find any helpful pop-up boxes in File Manager or Program Manager, however; they're too old to have that trick built in.

✔ In fact, with all its limitations, you probably won't want to spend much time with File Manager. Instead of spending time figuring out File Manager's new limitations, it's probably wiser to spend time figuring out how to use My Computer or Explorer. (They're both covered in Chapter 12.)

Where Did the Task List Go?

The Windows 3.1 Task List — the program that pops up when you double-click on a blank part of your window's wallpaper — is gone for good. Windows 95 has replaced it with the Start menu.

But here's the good news: the Windows 95 Start menu, when combined with the taskbar, can do everything the Task List can do: load programs and switch between them, arrange windows, and quit programs.

Plus, the Windows 95 Start button leaps to life when you press Ctrl+Esc — the same key combination that started the Windows 3.1 Task List.

Bringing the Task List back from the dead

To placate the old-timers, Windows 95 still comes with the Task List program. In fact, the program has been updated a bit to make it more interesting. To load Task List, double-click on Taskman, a program icon in your Windows directory. (Or type **taskman** at the Start menu's Run command line.)

The Task List leaps to the screen.

The Task List doesn't come with a Help file, so you'll have to fiddle with the menus to see what's listed. But it's a fairly powerful program: It lists all the currently running programs and windows so you can choose among them; it can tile or cascade open windows across the screen; and it comes with a command line, like the Start menu's Run area. Plus, it lets you minimize *all* the open windows with one command. It even lets you shut down Windows 95.

The program itself can be customized, allowing for large or small buttons. If you're looking for a handy desktop accessory, check out the Task List before buying a third-party utility.

Where Are Calendar, Cardfile, and Paintbrush?

The Windows 3.1 Calendar and Cardfile are gone for good. Windows 95 doesn't come with them, and Microsoft figured it didn't need to toss in replacements, either.

If you install Windows 95 over Windows 3.1, however, your Calendar and Cardfile programs are still on your computer; they're listed on the Start menu.

A new, "improved" version of Paintbrush comes with Windows 95, and you find it listed in the Start menu's Program area under Accessories. It's now called Paint, and it's described in Chapter 13.

Chapter 16

Just Tell Me the *Easy* Way!

. . . .

In This Chapter

▶ Copying a file to a floppy disk

▶ Finding the Start button and Start menu

▶ Finding a lost file, folder, or program

▶ Adding programs to the Start menu

▶ Arranging open windows

▶ Opening a new compact-disc box

▶ Changing the screen's wallpaper

▶ Installing a new program

. . . .

*T*his is it — quick and easy answers to the Windows 95 questions everybody wants to know. Feel free to put sticky notes next to your favorite answers.

How Do I Copy a File to a Floppy Disk (and Vice Versa)?

Want to copy a file from your hard disk to a floppy disk? Double-click on the My Computer icon and open the folder where your file is currently living. Using the right mouse button, click on the file's icon and stand back: a menu pops out. Point at the Se<u>n</u>d To command, and another menu shoots out. Finally, click on the name of the floppy disk you'd like to send the file to — drive A or drive B, for example.

Oh, and don't forget to put a floppy disk into the drive.

This method doesn't work for copying files from floppies to a hard drive; the hard drive doesn't appear on the Se<u>n</u>d To menu. To move the file there, drag its icon from the floppy drive window to the folder on the hard drive. For more information, head to Chapter 12.

How Do I Make a Copy of a Floppy Disk?

Microsoft made this one a little weird, so please don't blame me for this four-step process.

1. **Put your floppy disk in your disk drive.**

2. **Click on the Start button and click on <u>R</u>un from the menu that pops up.**

3. **Type the following information.**

   If you're copying the disk in drive A, type the following and then press Enter:

   ```
   diskcopy a: a:
   ```

   That's the word DISKCOPY, a space, the letter A followed by a colon, another space, and the letter A followed by a colon.

   If you're copying the disk in drive B, type the following and then press Enter:

   ```
   diskcopy b: b:
   ```

   Everything's the same as before, but you substitute the letter B for the letter A.

4. **Follow the instructions on-screen.**

   A black window pops up on-screen, and gloomy-looking instructions say to make sure that your floppy's in your disk drive and to press any key. The computer begins sucking information off the disk and then tells you to remove the first disk (the program calls it the *source disk*) and insert your second disk (called the *target disk*). After it finishes copying, the helpful program asks whether you'd like to make a second copy or perhaps a copy of a different diskette. Press Y if you want more copies; press N if you'd like to quit and do something else.

   After the disk copying is completed, the black window just sits there rudely. Click on the little X button in the upper-right corner of the black window to make the window vanish.

The Diskcopy command can be handy for making backup copies of your favorite programs.

To simplify the process, Microsoft promises to add a "disk copy" command to the menu of the real version of Windows 95, slated for release later this year.

How Do I Find the Start Button and Start Menu?

Normally, you find the Start button lurking on the end of the taskbar — a long, ribbon-like string that covers an edge of the screen. Can't even find the taskbar? Then press Ctrl+Esc. That almost always brings up the Start menu — the menu that pops up when you click on the Start button.

How Do I Start a Program?

Click on the taskbar's Start button and point your mouse at the word <u>P</u>rograms on the pop-up menu. When you point at the various folders that pop up, the folders open, revealing more options.

Spot the program you're after? Click on its name, and Windows 95 brings the program to life. If you don't spot the program, head for the "How Do I Find a Program?" section coming up next.

More taskbar information lurks in Chapter 11.

 You can also start programs from the My Computer or Explorer programs. Double-click on a folder to open it; double-click on a program to load it. Double-clicking on a file usually loads the program that created the file, as well as opening the file itself.

How Do I Find a File, Folder, or Program?

Click on the Start button, point at the <u>F</u>ind command, and click on the <u>F</u>iles or Folders option. Type the name of your program — just the first few letters will do — and click on the F<u>i</u>nd Now button.

The Find program lists all files, folders, and programs on drive C that begin with the letters you typed. If you spot your program, double-click on it to bring it to life. If you don't spot what you're after, head for Chapter 8 for a more detailed explanation of the Find program.

How Can I Add Programs to the Start Menu?

The congenial Windows 95 allows several ways to add programs, files, and folders to the Start menu, but here's one of the easiest.

Open the My Computer program and find the icon for your program. Point at the program's icon and, while holding down the mouse button, point at the Start button. Then let go of the mouse button. That's all there is to it.

Click on the Start button, and you'll see your newly added program at the top of the menu.

Hit Chapter 11 for more tips.

How Do I Keep My Icons Neatly Arranged?

When first installed, Windows 95 lines up all your icons neatly in their folders. But if you start changing a folder's size or moving icons around, they quickly lose their orderly arrangement and start overlapping.

The solution? Click on a blank part of the folder with your right mouse button and point at Arrange Icons on the menu. Click on Auto Arrange, and Windows 95 automatically keeps your icons arranged in neat rows.

The downside? Lazy Windows 95 makes you repeat this command on *every* window or folder you'd like to keep arranged automatically. Sigh.

How Do I Organize Open Windows So That They're All Visible?

Too many overlapping windows scattered across your screen? Then use one of the tile commands, and Windows 95 will give each window an equal amount of space on your desktop.

1. **Using the right mouse button, click on a blank part of the taskbar.**

   Clicking near the clock usually works well.

2. **Choose Tile Horizontally or Tile Vertically.**

   One command lines up the windows in columns; the other lines them up in rows. Try whichever scheme looks best. Or turn to Chapter 7 for more information.

How Do I Set the Time and Date?

To change the computer's time and date, double-click on the taskbar's clock, usually found at the bottom-right corner of the screen. A calendar and clock pop up, letting you change the date, time, or even the time zone. Hit Chapter 10 for the full scoop.

How Do I Open a New, Plastic-Wrapped Compact Disc Box?

With your teeth, being careful not to scratch your gums. Sometimes a thumbnail works well, or even a letter opener. It's a miracle of technology, but the plastic wrap is often tougher than the plastic case itself.

How Do I Change My Screen's Wallpaper?

Using the right mouse button, click on a blank part of your desktop. Then choose Properties from the pop-up menu. See the list of names in the second column, under the words Wallpaper? Click on one of the names for a quick preview.

More Wallpaper instructions are hanging around in Chapter 10.

How Do I Change the Name of a File or Folder?

Call up My Computer or Explorer and click on the icon of the file or folder you'd like to rename; that highlights the icon, making it change color.

Wait a second or two and then click directly on the file or folder's current name. Start typing the new name, which automatically replaces the old name. Press Enter when you're through.

Windows 95 won't let you change every icon's name, however. For example, you're stuck with the names *Recycle Bin* and *3 1/2 Floppy (A:)*, along with a few others.

How Much Room Do I Have on My Hard Drive?

Open the My Computer program and click on your hard drive's icon with your right mouse button. Choose Properties from the menu that appears, and a box appears, listing your hard drive's size (and showing you a pretty graph, too).

How Do I Install a New Program?

Here's the easy way, if everything works the way it's supposed to:

Double-click on the My Computer program and double-click on the Control Panel living inside it.

When the Control Panel hits the screen, double-click on the Add/Remove Programs icon. When the next window pops up, click on the Install button and follow the instructions (Or flip to Chapter 10 for more detailed instructions; that chapter offers help if the Install button doesn't work, too.)

Part V
Help!

The 5th Wave   By Rich Tennant

"I TELL YA I'M STILL GETTING INTERFERENCE —
— COOKIE, RAGS? RAGS WANNA COOKIE? —
THERE IT GOES AGAIN."

In this part . . .

Windows 95 can do hundreds of tasks in dozens of ways. That means that approximately one million things can fail at any given time.

Some problems are easy to fix. For example, one misplaced double-click in the taskbar makes all your programs disappear. Yet one more click in the right place puts them all back.

Other problems are far more complex, requiring teams of computer surgeons to diagnose, remedy, and bill accordingly.

This part lets you separate the big problems from the little ones. You'll know whether you can fix it yourself with a few clicks and a kick. If your situation's worse, you'll know when it's time to call in the surgeons.

Chapter 17

The Case of the Broken Window

• •

In This Chapter

▶ Realizing you're using a prerelease version of Windows 95

▶ What to do if you're stuck in Menu Land

▶ How to install a new "driver" for a new computer gizmo

▶ How to install other parts of Windows 95

▶ What to do when you click on the wrong button

▶ What to do when your computer freezes

▶ How to deal with DOS programs that don't look right in a window

▶ What to do when your printer is not working correctly

• •

S ometimes you just have a sense that something's wrong. The computer makes quiet grumbling noises, or Windows 95 starts running more slowly than Congress. Other times something's obviously wrong. Pressing any key just gives you a beeping noise, menus keep shooting at you, or Windows 95 greets you with a cheery error message when you first turn it on.

Many of the biggest-looking problems are solved by the smallest-looking solutions. Hopefully, this chapter points you to the right one.

Remember — You Might Be Using the Preview Version

Microsoft's preview version of Windows 95 — released in March, 1995 — isn't the real version of Windows 95. It's a test version, designed to let Microsoft expose Windows 95 to as many different types of computers as possible. That way it could find out the parts that didn't work right and fix them before the *real* version of Windows 95 came out later in the year.

If you bought a version of Windows 95 for about $30, you may be using the preview version — not the real version of Windows 95. That means you shouldn't be surprised if it starts acting funny or doesn't behave like the software described in this book.

Making an Emergency StartUp Disk

Unless you grab a spare floppy right now, this information won't do you any good.

See, Windows 95 can make an emergency StartUp Disk. Then, when Windows 95 refuses to load, you can pop the disk into your computer's mouth, push the reset button, and a "bare bones" version of Windows 95 will come to the screen. That bare bones version might be enough to get you started. At the very least, it will make it easier for a computer guru friend to get your computer started.

So grab a floppy disk that's blank or doesn't have important information on it — this procedure erases the disk's contents.

1. **Double-click on the Control Panel's Add/Remove Programs icon.**

   You can load the Control Panel by clicking on Settings in the Start menu.

2. **Click on the Windows Startup Disk tab.**

   It's the right-most tab of the three along the top.

3. **Click on the Create Disk button.**

   Windows 95 tells you to insert a disk into drive A. Before pushing the disk into the drive, grab a felt pen and write Emergency StartUp Disk on the floppy disk's label.

4. **Insert a blank disk into drive A when told; then click on the OK button.**

   Windows 95 formats the blank disk and copies special files onto it, allowing it to start your computer in the worst of situations. Put the disk in a safe place and hope you never have to use it.

   ✔ In an emergency, put the disk in drive A and push your computer's reset button. The computer will "boot" off the floppy disk; that is, the computer will come to life, even though its hard drive isn't working.

   ✔ When loaded from the floppy disk, Windows 95 comes up in "DOS prompt" mode. It won't look anything like the real Windows 95, but a computer guru might be able use the DOS prompt as a doorway to fix whatever's gone wrong.

My Mouse Doesn't Work Right

Sometimes the mouse doesn't work at all; other times the mouse pointer hops across the screen like a flea. Here are a few things to look for:

- ✔ If there's no mouse arrow on the screen when you start Windows, make sure that the mouse's tail is plugged snugly into the computer's rump. Then exit and restart Windows 95.

- ✔ If the mouse arrow is on-screen but won't move, Windows may be mistaking your brand of mouse for a different brand. You can make sure that Windows 95 recognizes the correct type of mouse by following the Adding New Hardware steps, as described in Chapter 10.

- ✔ If the mouse pointer jumps around, there may be a conflict on its interrupt. You may have to pull out the mouse manual and see how to change its *interrupt setting* to fix this one.

- ✔ A mouse pointer can jump around on-screen if it's dirty. First, turn the mouse upside-down and clean off any visible dirt stuck to the bottom. Then turn the little lever until the mouse ball pops out. Wipe off any crud and blow any dust out of the hole. Pull any stray hairs off the little rollers and stick the ball back inside the mouse. If you wear wool sweaters (or have a cat that sleeps on the mouse pad), you may have to clean the ball every week or so.

- ✔ If the mouse was working fine and now the buttons seem to be reversed, you've probably changed the right- or left-handed button configuration setting in the Control Panel. Double-click on the Control Panel's Mouse icon and make sure that the configuration is set up to match your needs. (That's covered in Chapter 10, by the way.)

I'm Stuck in Menu Land

If your keystrokes don't appear in your work but instead make a bunch of menus shoot out from the top of the window, you're stuck in Menu Land. Somehow you've pressed and released Alt, an innocent-looking key that's easy to hit accidentally.

When you press and release Alt, Windows turns its attention away from your work and toward the menus along the top of the window.

To get back to work, press and release Alt one more time. Alternatively, press Esc. One or the other is your ticket out of Menu Land.

I'm Supposed to Install a New "Driver"

When you buy a new toy for the computer, it should come with a piece of software called a *driver*. A driver is a sort of translator that lets Windows know how to boss around the new toy. If you buy a new keyboard, sound card, compact disc player, printer, mouse, monitor, or almost any other computer toy, you need to install its driver in Windows. Luckily, it's a fairly painless process covered in the "Adding New Hardware" section of Chapter 10.

✔ Companies constantly update their drivers, fixing problems or making the drivers perform better. If the computer device is misbehaving, a newer driver may calm it down. Call the manufacturer and ask for the latest version.

✔ For floppy-disk-insertion etiquette, see Chapter 2.

✔ Not all computer toys work with Windows 95. Check with the store before you buy so that you aren't stuck with something that won't work.

His Version of Windows 95 Has More Programs Than Mine!

Windows 95 installs itself differently on different types of computers. As it copies itself over to a hard drive from floppy disks or a compact disc it brings different files with it. When installed on a laptop, for example, Windows 95 brings along programs that help a laptop transfer files and keep track of its battery life.

Computers with smaller hard drives will probably get the minimum files Windows 95 needs to run. Chapter 3 describes some of the programs and accessories Windows 95 comes with; here's how to copy them to your computer if Windows 95 left them off the first time.

1. **Double-click on the Control Panel's Add/Remove Programs icon.**

   You can load the Control Panel by clicking on <u>S</u>ettings in the Start menu.

2. **Click on the Windows Setup tab.**

   It's the tab in the middle of the three along the top; a box appears that shows the various components of Windows 95, as well as the amount of space they need to nestle onto your computer's hard drive.

3. **Click in the little box by the programs or accessories you'd like to add.**

   A check mark appears in the box of the items you've selected. To select part of a category — a portion of the accessories, for example — click on the category's name and click on the <u>D</u>etails button. Windows 95 lists the items available in that category, so you can only click on the ones you want. If you clicked on the Details button, click on the OK button to continue back at the main categories list.

4. **Click on the OK button and insert your installation disks when asked.**

   Windows 95 copies the necessary files from your installation disks onto your hard drive. You can remove Windows 95 accessories by *removing* the check mark from the box next to their name.

Windows 95 comes with some pretty weird stuff, so don't get carried away and copy *all* of it over — especially until Microsoft gets it all working right.

I Clicked on the Wrong Button (but Haven't Lifted My Finger Yet)

Clicking the mouse takes two steps: a push and a release. If you click on the wrong button on-screen and haven't lifted your finger yet, slowly slide the mouse pointer off the button on-screen. *Then* take your finger off the mouse.

The screen button pops back up, and Windows 95 pretends nothing happened. Thankfully.

My Computer Has Frozen Up Solid

Every once in a while, Windows just drops the ball and wanders off somewhere. You're left looking at a computer that just looks back. Panicked clicks don't do anything. Pressing every key on the keyboard doesn't do anything — or worse yet, the computer starts to beep at every key press.

When nothing on-screen moves except the mouse pointer, the computer has frozen up solid. Try the following approaches, in the following order, to correct the problem:

Approach 1: Press Esc twice.

That action usually doesn't work, but give it a shot anyway.

Approach 2: Press Ctrl, Alt, and Delete all at the same time.

If you're lucky, Windows flashes an error message saying that you've discovered an "unresponsive application" and lists the names of currently running programs — including the one that's not responding. Click on the name of the program that's causing the mess and click on the End Task button. You lose any unsaved work in it, of course, but you should be used to that. (If you somehow stumbled onto the Ctrl+Alt+Delete combination by accident, press Esc at the unresponsive-application message to return to Windows.)

If that still doesn't do the trick, try clicking the Shut down button that's next to the End Task button, or pressing Ctrl+Alt+Delete again.

Approach 3: If the preceding approaches don't work, push the computer's reset button.

The screen is cleared, and the computer acts like you turned it off and on again. When the dust settles, Windows 95 should return to life.

Approach 4: If not even the reset button works, turn the computer off, wait 30 seconds, and then turn it back on again.

Don't ever flip the computer off and on again quickly. Doing so can damage its internal organs.

My DOS Program Looks Weird in a Window

DOS programs are *supposed* to look weird when running in a window. Windows 95 forces the computer to contort into different graphics lifestyles. Most DOS programs look different when displayed in these new graphics modes.

You do have a few alternatives, however:

- ✔ Click on the DOS program window to highlight it and then hold Alt and press Enter. Windows 95 steps to the background, letting the DOS program have the whole screen. *Then* the DOS program looks normal. Press Alt+Enter to put it back in the window. Or hold Alt and press Esc to return to Windows, with the DOS program as an icon listed on the taskbar. (Exit the DOS program normally to automatically return to Windows.)

- ✔ Play with the DOS program's fonts as described in Chapter 14.

- ✔ Buy the Windows or Windows 95 version of the DOS program.

- ✔ Buy a more expensive graphics card that allows for even more graphics modes. Chances are, one of the modes will suit the DOS program a little better.

The Printer Isn't Working Right

If the printer's not working right, start with the simplest solution first: Make sure that it's plugged into the wall and turned on. Surprisingly, this step fixes about half the problems with printers. Next, make sure that the printer cable is snugly nestled in the ports on both the printer and the computer. Then check to make sure that it has enough paper — and that the paper isn't jammed in the mechanism.

Then try printing from different programs, like WordPad and Notepad, to see whether the problem's with the printer, Windows 95, or a particular Windows program. Try printing the document by using different fonts. All these chores help pinpoint the culprit.

The Windows Help program can also pitch in; click on Help from the Start menu, click on the Index tab, and type the words **printer problems** into the box. Press Enter, and Windows 95 will lead you through a program designed to figure out why the printer's goofing off.

You may have to call the printer's manufacturer and ask for a new Windows driver. When the disk comes in the mail, follow the instructions in the "Fiddling with the Printer" section of Chapter 10.

Chapter 18

Error Messages
(What You Did Does Not Compute)

● ●

In This Chapter

▶ A:\ is not accessible. The device is not ready.

▶ Disk drive is full.

▶ The file or folder that this shortcut refers to cannot be found.

▶ This filename is not valid.

▶ There is no viewer capable of reading WordPad document files.

● ●

*M*ost people don't have any trouble understanding error messages. A car's pleasant beeping tone means that you've left your keys in the ignition. A terrible scratching sound from the stereo means that the cat's jumped on the turntable.

Things are different with Windows 95, however. The error messages in Windows could have been written by a Senate subcommittee, if only they weren't so brief. When Windows 95 tosses an error message your way, it's usually just a single sentence. Windows 95 rarely describes what you did to cause the error. And even worse, Windows 95 hardly ever says how to make the error go away for good.

Here are some of the words that you'll find in the most common error messages Windows 95 throws in your face. This chapter explains what Windows 95 is trying to say, why it's saying it, and just what the heck it expects you to do about it.

Not enough memory

Meaning: Windows 95 is running out of the room it needs to operate.

Probable cause: You have too many windows simultaneously open on the screen.

Solutions: A short-term solution is to close some of the windows. DOS windows often take up a lot of memory, so start by shutting them down. Also, make sure that you're not using any large color pictures of peacocks for wallpaper. It takes a lot less memory to tile small pictures across the screen (see Chapter 10 for information about tiling windows). If Windows 95 still acts sluggish, click on the Start button, choose Shut down, and choose the Restart the computer option.

For a long-term solution, make sure that you have plenty of empty space on the hard drive so Windows has room to read and write information. Delete any files or programs you don't use anymore.

Finally, consider buying some more memory. Windows works much better with 8MB of memory than with 4MB of memory. And 12MB or 16MB of memory is better still.

 Whenever you cut or copy a large amount of information to the Clipboard, that information stays there, taking up memory — even after you've pasted it into another application. To clear out the Clipboard after a large paste operation, copy a single word to the Clipboard. Doing so replaces the earlier, memory-hogging chunk, freeing some memory for other programs.

A:\ is not accessible. The device is not ready.

Meaning: Windows can't find a floppy disk in drive A.

Probable cause: There's no floppy disk in there.

Solution: Slide a disk in, push down the little lever if it's a 5 ¼-inch drive, and wish all errors were this easy to fix.

Destination Disk Drive is Full

Meaning: Windows 95 has run out of room on a floppy disk or on the hard drive to store something.

Probable cause: Windows 95 tried saving something to a disk file but ran out of space.

Solution: Clear more room on that disk before saving your work. Delete any junk files on the hard disk. BAK (backup) files and TMP (temporary) files often qualify as junk files that can be deleted, but only if their date shows them to be old and forgotten. Also, delete any programs you don't use anymore. (For example, if you use Word for Windows as your word processor now, you probably don't need to keep the DOS version of Word 4.0 on the disk.)

The file or folder that this shortcut refers to can not be found

Meaning: Windows 95 can't find the program that's supposed to be attached to a Shortcut icon.

Probable cause: One of the programs has moved or deleted a file after a shortcut was attached to it.

Solution: Try using the Windows 95 Find program, described in Chapter 8. If the Find program can't find it, double-click on the Recycle Bin to see if it's in there and can be salvaged.

This filename is not valid

Meaning: Windows 95 refuses to accept your choice of filename.

Probable cause: You've tried to name a file by using one or more of the forbidden characters.

Solution: Turn to the section about renaming a file in Chapter 12 and make sure that you're not naming a file something you shouldn't.

There is no viewer capable of viewing WordPad Document files

Meaning: Windows 95 can't show you what's in that file using Quick View.

Probable cause: You're probably trying to view a word processor file using Quick View, and that file probably ends in the hidden letters DOC. Windows 95, therefore, thinks its about to see a WordPad file and gets confused by another word processor's format.

Solution: Quick View simply can't view this file, unfortunately. To see inside the file, you'll have to load it into its own word processor.

Deleting this file will make it impossible to run this program and may make it impossible for you to edit some documents

Meaning: You're trying to delete a file containing a program.

Probable cause: You're clearing off some hard disk space to make room for incoming programs.

Solution: Just make sure you know what program you're deleting before you delete it. And make sure you have the program sitting on the shelf so you can reinstall it if you decide you needed it after all.

You must type a filename

Meaning: Windows 95 insists that you type a filename into the box.

Probable cause: You've chosen (accidentally or otherwise) the Rename command from a menu or clicked on an icon's title in *just the right* way.

Solution: Type a new filename consisting of mostly numbers and letters, and you'll be fine. Or if you're just trying to get out of the filename box, press Esc, and the Rename box will dissipate.

Chapter 19
Help on the Windows 95 Help System

. . . .

In This Chapter

▶ Finding helpful hints quickly

▶ Using the Windows 95 Help program

▶ Finding help for a particular problem

▶ Moving around in the Help system

▶ Making a master help index

▶ Marking help sections for later reference

. . . .

*J*ust about everybody's written a bizarre computer command (like Alt+F4) on a sticky note and slapped it on the side of the monitor.

Windows 95 comes with its *own* set of sticky notes built right in. You can pop them up on-screen and leave them there for easy access. In a way, they're virtually real sticky notes because they can never escape from inside the computer. Actually, it's probably better that way: You'll never find a "How to Change Wallpaper" sticky note on the bottom of your shoe.

This chapter covers the Windows 95 built-in Help system. When you raise your hand in just the right way, Windows 95 walks over and offers you some help.

Get Me Some Help, and Fast!

Don't bother plowing through this whole chapter if you don't need to: Here are the quickest ways to make Windows 95 dish out helpful information when you're stumped. Each tip is explained more fully later in this chapter.

Press F1

When you're confused in Windows 95, press the F1 key. That key *always* stands for "Help!" Most of the time, Windows 95 checks to see what program you're using and fetches some helpful information about that particular program or your current situation. In fact, pressing F1 usually brings up a huge Help program, described later in this chapter.

Click the right mouse button on the confusing part

Windows 95 tosses a lot of forms in your face. When a particular form, setting, box, or menu item has your creativity stifled, click on it with your right (the opposite of left) mouse button. A What's This? box appears, as shown in Figure 19-1, letting you know that Windows 95 can offer help about that particular area. Click on the What's This? box, and Windows 95 tosses extra information onto the screen, explaining the confusing area you clicked on.

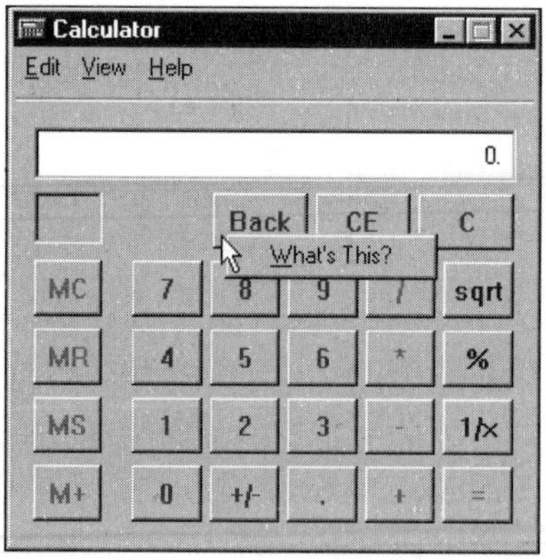

Figure 19-1: Click on confusing areas with your right mouse button; if a What's This? box appears, click on the box to see more information about the confusing area.

Choose Help from the main menu

If pressing F1 doesn't get you anywhere, look for the word Help in the menu along the top of the confusing program. Click on Help, and a menu drops down, usually listing two words: Help Topics and About. Click on Help Topics to make the Windows 95 Help program leap to the screen. (Clicking on About just brings a version number to the screen, which can be dangerously irritating when you're looking for something a little more helpful.)

Click on the "leaping arrows"

Sometimes the Windows 95 Help program scores big: It tells you *exactly* how to solve your particular problem. Unfortunately, however, the Help program occasionally says you need to load a *different* program to solve your problem. Don't get grumpy, though: Look for a little "leaping arrow," like the one shown in Figure 19-2.

Figure 19-2: Click on the little "leaping arrow," and the Windows 95 Help program automatically takes you to the right place.

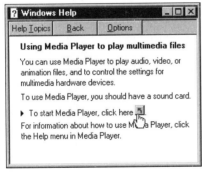

Click on the little leaping arrow, and Windows 95 automatically takes you to that other program you need to use. Yep, it's refreshingly helpful.

Consulting the Windows 95 Built-In Computer Guru

Almost every Windows program has the word Help in its top menu. Click on Help, and the Windows 95 built-in computer guru rushes to your aid. For example, click on Help in Paint, and you see the menu shown in Figure 19-3.

To pick the computer guru's brain, click on Help Topics, and Windows 95 pops up the box shown in Figure 19-4. This box is the table of contents for all the help information Windows 95 can offer on the Paint program.

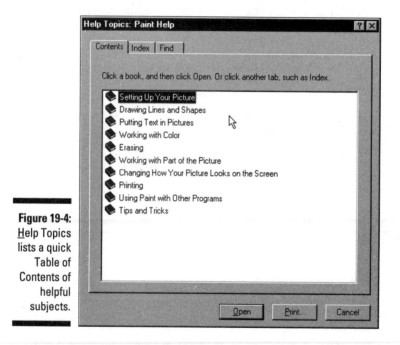

See any subject covering what you're confused about? Then double-click on it. For example, if Erasing has you stumped, double-click on the word *Erasing*; the Help program then shows what additional help it can offer, as shown in Figure 19-5.

Figure 19-5:
Double-click
on a topic to
see more
specific
help areas.

Want to see more information on erasing small areas? Double-click on that
listed subject, and a new window pops up, as shown in Figure 19-6, bringing
even more detailed information to the screen.

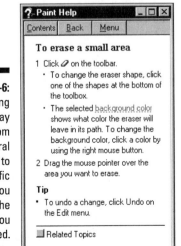

Figure 19-6:
By clicking
your way
from
general
subjects to
specific
areas, you
can find the
help you
need.

Windows 95 can offer help with any underlined topic. As the mouse pointer nears an underlined topic, the pointer turns into a little hand. When the hand points at the phrase that has you stumped, click the mouse button. For example, click on <u>background color</u> in the Paint Help box, and Windows 95 displays more help on what background colors are supposed to mean, as shown in Figure 19-7.

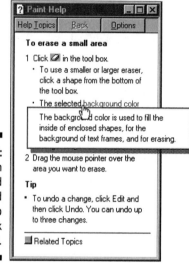

Figure 19-7:
Click on underlined words and phrases to see quick definitions.

The Windows 95 Help system is sometimes a lot of work, forcing you to wade through increasingly detailed menus to find specific information. Still, it can be a lot faster than paging through the chunky Windows 95 manual. And, unlike other computer nerds, it doesn't have any Oreo gunk stuck between its tooth.

✔ The quickest way to find help in any Windows 95 program is to press F1. Windows automatically jumps to the table of contents page for the help information it has for the current program.

✔ Windows 95 packs a lot of information into its Help boxes; some of the words usually scroll off the bottom of the window. To see them, click on the scroll bar (described in Chapter 6) or press PgDn.

✔ Sometimes you click on the wrong topic and Windows 95 brings up something really dumb. Click on the <u>C</u>ontents button at the top of the window, and Windows 95 scoots back to the contents page. From there, click on a different topic to move in a different direction.

✔ Underlined phrases and words appear throughout the Windows 95 Help system. Whenever you click on something that's underlined, Windows 95 brings up a definition or jumps to a spot that has information about that subject. Click on the Help Topics button to return to where you jumped from.

✔ If you're impressed with a particularly helpful page, send it to the printer: Click on Menu and choose Print Topic from the menu that appears. Windows 95 shoots that page to the printer so you can keep it handy until you lose it.

✔ Actually, to keep from losing that helpful page, read about sticking an electronic bookmark on that page, as described later in this chapter.

✔ If you find a particularly helpful reference in the Help system, shrink the window to an icon on the taskbar. Click on the button with the tiny bar near the window's upper-right corner. Then you can just double-click on the taskbar's Help icon to see that page again.

✔ To grab a help message and stick it in your own work, highlight the text with your mouse and choose Copy from the menu. Windows then lets you highlight the helpful words you want to copy to the Clipboard. I dunno why anybody would *want* to do this, but you *can* do it, just the same.

Sticking Electronic Sticky Notes on Help Pages

Windows 95 lets you add your *own* notes to its helpful system of sticky notes. If you make a stunning revelation and want to remember it later, follow these steps to add a paper clip to the current help topic and add your own notes to that help topic:

1. **Click on the word Options at the top of the page.**

   The Options menu appears.

2. **Click on the Annotate option.**

   The Annotate box appears.

3. **Start typing your own notes into the big box.**

   You can type as much as you want. Use the cursor-control keys to move around and the Delete or Backspace key to edit mistakes.

4. **Click on the Save button after you enter your note.**

   Windows paper-clips your words to the current help page; a tiny picture of a paper clip appears to remind you of your additions.

Whenever you see that help page again, click on the paper clip next to the name of the topic, and your words reappear, as shown in Figure 19-8.

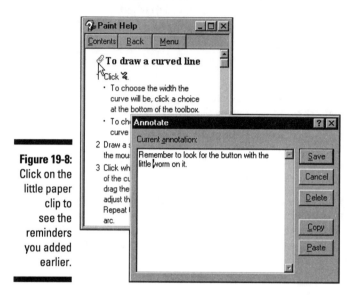

Figure 19-8: Click on the little paper clip to see the reminders you added earlier.

If you ever want to delete your paper-clipped note, click on the paper clip and click on the <u>D</u>elete button. Your note disappears.

Finding Help for Your Problem

If you don't see your problem listed in the particular table of contents page you've accessed, there's another way to find help (although it takes a little more time and effort). Click on the Index tab at the top of any help window; the box shown in Figure 19-9 leaps to the screen. Type a few words describing your problem. When you type them, Windows 95 shows any matches in the box below it.

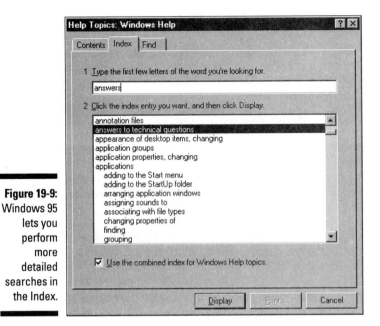

Figure 19-9:
Windows 95
lets you
perform
more
detailed
searches in
the Index.

If Windows matches what you type with an appropriate topic, click on the topic that looks the most pertinent and then click on the button. Windows jumps to the page of information that describes that particular subject the best.

A quicker way to find help is to click on the scroll bar or press PgUp and PgDn to see what subjects Windows is willing to explain. If you see a subject that even remotely resembles what you're confused about, double-click on it. Windows 95 brings up that page of help information.

From there, you can jump around by clicking on underlined words and phrases. Sooner or later, you'll stumble onto the right page of information. When you do, try to give it a *bookmark,* as described in "Trying to Find the Same Page Again," later in this chapter.

✔ Windows searches alphabetically and, unfortunately, isn't very smart. So, if you're looking for help on margins, for example, don't type **adding margins** or **changing margins**. Instead, type **margins** so that Windows jumps to the words beginning with M.

✔ In fact, if you have trouble finding help for your specific problem, use the Find command, described in the next section. Instead of forcing you to type the right words in the right order, the Find command roots through every word in the Help file and brings back every match.

Finding Help on Specific Problems

When you're looking for help on a specific problem, it's sometimes hard to be a casual pointer and clicker. You want help *now!*

For people who want to make sure that they've wrung every ounce of help from the Windows 95 Help system, Microsoft's included a special Find index: You can tell the Help program to make an index of every word it mentions in its help libraries. That way, you can type the word **PCMCIA**, for example, and know you'll see every paragraph in the Help system that contains the word PCMCIA. You won't have that nagging suspicion that Windows 95 didn't give you help because you didn't type **32-bit PCMCIA** or some other sneaky computer gibberish.

Why doesn't Windows 95 come with the Find index already set up and ready to go? Because the Find index can eat up a lot of hard drive space. If you can afford the space, however, create the Find index by following these steps:

1. **From within any program, press F1 to bring up its Help program and then click on the Find tab.**

   The Find tab is along the top of the window, toward the right side.

2. **Choose between** <u>E</u>**xpress or** <u>C</u>**ustom and then click on the Next button.**

   The Express option adds more help files to the index but uses up more space. The Custom option lets you choose which help files to add to the index. The Express option is more foolproof, so go for that one if your computer isn't strapped for hard disk space.

3. **Click on Finish.**

   Twiddle your thumbs for a minute or so while Windows 95 indexes every word, from *a* to *zooming*. You only have to create the index once, thankfully, and then it will be yours for the wringing.

   ✔ After you create an index, clicking on the Find tab brings you straight to the search area. Type the word you're looking for, and, if it's mentioned in the Help system, Windows 95 brings up that nugget of helpful information.

   ✔ You'll have to create an index for each Windows 95 program you use. Although this can be inconvenient, it keeps Windows 95 from grabbing huge chunks of hard drive real estate merely to create indexes of programs you never use.

Trying to Find the Same Page Again

The Windows 95 Help system is better than ever, and finding help for a particular trouble is relatively painless. But how do you return to that page a few minutes — or even a few days — later?

When you find that perfect page, look for the word Bookmark listed along the top. If you spot a button marked Bookmark, you're in luck: Click on Bookmark in the menu bar, select Define from the menu, and click on the OK button.

Now, when you access the Help system days or even years later, you can click on the Bookmark menu item. A menu tumbles down, listing the pages you bookmarked. Click on the name of the page you're after, and Windows hops to that screen. Quick and easy.

The problem? Very few of the Help programs included with Windows 95 come with the Bookmark system. Unfortunately, it seems to be a Windows 3.1 remnant.

Part VI
The Part of Tens

"I'm afraid I don't understand all the reports of our upgrade having a delayed release date. Unless... wait a minute — How many people here DIDN'T KNOW I was speaking in dog-months?"

In this part...

*E*verybody likes to read Top Tens in magazines — especially in the grocery store checkout aisle when you're stuck behind someone who's just pulled a rubber band off a thick stack of double coupons and the checker can't find the right validation stamp.

Unlike the reading material at the grocery store, the chapters in this part of the book don't list ten new aerobic bounces or ten ways to stop your kids from making explosives with kitchen cleansers. Instead, you find lists of ways to make Windows 95 more efficient — or at least not as hostile. You find a few tips, tricks, and explanations of eccentric acronyms like *DLL*.

Some lists have more than ten items; others have fewer. But who's counting, besides the guy wading through all those double coupons?

Chapter 20

Ten New Windows 95 Features Worth Checking Out

• •

In This Chapter

▶ Using the right (not just the left) mouse button

▶ Peeking inside files with Quick View

▶ Using long file names

▶ Using the Recycle Bin

▶ Highlighting icons with a "lasso"

▶ Using the Windows 95 Wizards

▶ Jumping to the right place in Help

• •

*L*ike a new car model, Windows 95 adds several improvements over the old Windows 3.1 version. Some of the changes are cosmetic, like the fancy new lime-green, 3-D mouse pointers. Other changes are more useful, like the way you can peek inside files without having to load a program.

Consider this chapter a pamphlet that explains some of the best new features Windows 95 has to offer.

The Right Mouse Button Now Does Something, Too

Although mice have had at least two buttons for the past decade, Windows has never taken advantage of the right mouse button. The index finger has done all the work, clicking and double-clicking on the left button, while the middle finger rested, unused, on the right mouse button.

Windows 95 puts your middle finger to work by making the right button just as powerful as the left. The buttons don't do the same thing, though, so here's the rundown:

Click *once* on something with your *left* mouse button to select it — to highlight an icon, for example.

Double-click on something with your *left* mouse button to not only select it but to also kick-start it into action — to load a program, for example, or to open a folder.

Click *once* on something with your *right* mouse button to bring up a menu that lists the things you can do with that item — adjust its settings, for example, or copy it to another location.

Figure 20-1 shows the menu that pops up when you use your right mouse button to click on a file in the My Computer window.

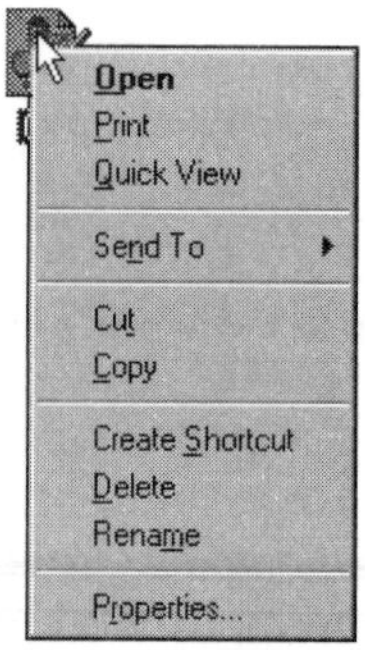

Figure 20-1:
Click on a file's icon with your right mouse button, and a menu appears listing things you can do with the file.

Open
Print
Quick View

Send To ▶

Cut
Copy

Create Shortcut
Delete
Rename

Properties...

When you're unsure of how to work with something on your desktop — a button, icon, or anything weird-looking — click on the confusing entity with your right mouse button. Often, a menu pops up that displays a list of stuff you can do to that confusing thing. By choosing from the options, you can often bluff your way to success.

Peeking into Files without Opening Them

When faced with a plethora of files, how can you tell which one you need? For instance, all the icons for files created by the Paint drawing program look the same. How can you check to see if the file named Sea Food is that lobster picture you've been searching for?

You could load the Sea Food file into Paint, but Quick View provides a faster way. Click on the file with your right mouse button and then click on Quick View from the menu that pops up.

A new window immediately appears, like the one in Figure 20-2, showing you the file's contents.

Figure 20-2:
Click on a file's icon with the right mouse button, choose Quick View, and a window appears, showing the file's contents.

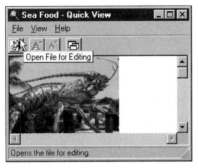

- ✔ Want to open the file for editing? Click on the little Paint icon in the upper-left corner. Windows 95 loads Paint, along with your file. The icon for the program responsible for creating the file is always in the upper-left corner.

- ✔ If the file on the screen isn't the one you're searching for, feel free to drag another file's icon into Quick View's open window. Windows 95 rapidly displays the contents of that file, too.

- ✔ Here's the bad news: The Quick View command only works on certain varieties of files. Only the most popular formats are displayed. You can "quick view" your WordPerfect and Microsoft Word files, for example, but you can't peek inside any files made using WordStar or XyWrite.

- ✔ You can find more information about Quick View in Chapter 8.

Much L-o-n-g-e-r Filenames

Microsoft said it wouldn't happen in our lifetimes, but now people can name their files with descriptions longer than eight characters. Windows 95 even lets you use more than one word to name your files, and you can separate the words by a space!

Figure 20-3 shows a few file names approved by Windows 95; as long as you keep the names under 255 characters, you're pretty much okay. (More detailed details on file names are discussed in Chapter 12.)

Figure 20-3: Windows 95 allows for long file-names containing more than one word.

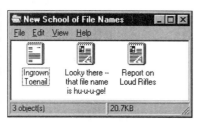

Retrieving Deleted Files from the Recycle Bin

Earlier versions of Windows let you safely retrieve accidentally deleted files, so the concept of the Windows 95 Recycle Bin isn't new. The new part is how much easier the Bin makes it to salvage deleted files.

Whenever you delete a file, the sneaky Windows 95 doesn't *really* delete it. It just hides the file in the Recycle Bin – that green trash can sitting on the desktop. When you get that sinking feeling that you shouldn't have deleted that report on Coelacanth Tailfins, double-click on the Recycle Bin, and you'll find your report inside, undamaged.

The Recycle Bin doesn't hold onto deleted files forever, though. It waits until you've filled up ten percent of your hard drive's storage capacity. For example, if you have a 200MB hard disk, the Recycle Bin always holds onto 20MB of your most recently deleted files. When you fill up that ten percent, Recycle Bin starts shredding the oldest files, and you won't be able to retrieve them.

That ten percent figure is adjustable, and if you want to change it, hit Chapter 11.

Selecting Bunches of Icons with a Lasso

This feature doesn't really seem like much, but you'll probably find yourself using it more than you think.

Windows has always allowed several ways to select files and icons. For instance, hold down the Ctrl key and click on all the icons you want: Windows highlights all the icons you click on.

Or, when selecting items in a list, you can click on the first item, hold down the Shift key, and click on the last item in a list. Whoosh! Windows instantly highlights the first item, the last item, and every item in between.

Windows 95 can still highlight icons those ways, but it's added something new and easier. To select files or folders that are next to each other, you can drag a "lasso" around them. Point just above the first icon you want to grab and, while holding down the mouse button, point just below the last icon you want to grab. Windows 95 draws a rectangle around the icons, as seen in Figure 20-4.

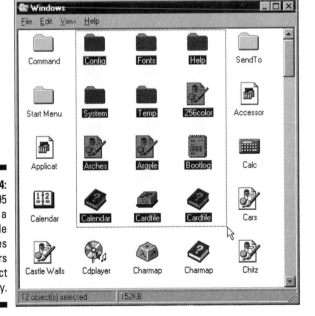

Figure 20-4:
Windows 95 can drag a rectangle around files and folders to select them easily.

The lasso can only be rectangular, so all the files and folders have to be next to each other. But you can always lasso the big chunk and then hold down the Ctrl key to select the stragglers who are away from the main pack.

Working with Windows 95 Wizards

Windows 95 tries hard to be personal, adding human touches whenever it can. Honestly, how many times have you wished for a computer wizard to materialize and automatically make your new modem or sound card work with your computer?

Well, Windows 95 comes with several Wizards, each customized for various bits of magic. For example, the Add New Hardware Wizard, seen in Figure 20-5, searches your computer for any new gadgets you've added. When the Wizard finds these accessories, it introduces them to Windows 95 so they can all start working together.

Figure 20-5: The Windows 95 Wizards can help you install new parts to your computer.

An Add Printer Wizard helps install a new printer; a PC Card Wizard helps install the PCMCIA cards found on many of today's laptops.

The Wizards aren't magic, by any means, but they can often work wonders when you need to set up Windows 95 to work with something new.

Jumping to the Right Place in Help

Windows has always come with a helpful Help program. However, the best Windows could do was tell you what part of Windows you needed to use to solve your problem.

Windows 95 goes one more step: It not only tells you where to go, it takes you there. Need to calibrate your joystick, for example? Type **joystick** into the Help program, and Windows 95 explains that you need to use the joystick calibration program. But the Help program also includes a little button; click on the button, seen in Figure 20-6, and the increasingly polite Windows 95 automatically takes you to the Joystick Calibration program you need.

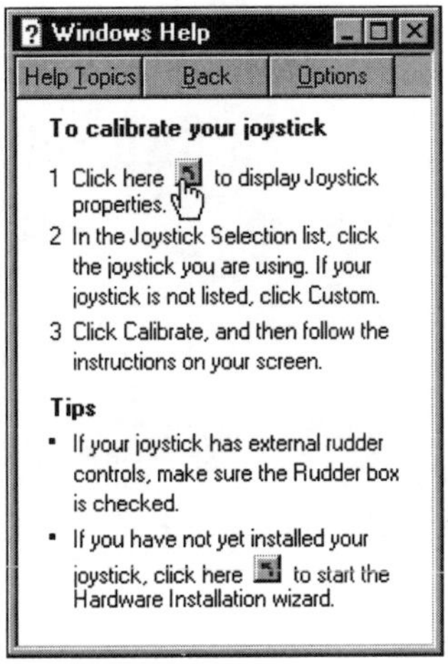

Figure 20-6:
Click on the little buttons in the Help program, and Windows 95 takes you directly to the program that solves your problem.

Windows Help

Help Topics | Back | Options

To calibrate your joystick

1 Click here 🖳 to display Joystick properties.

2 In the Joystick Selection list, click the joystick you are using. If your joystick is not listed, click Custom.

3 Click Calibrate, and then follow the instructions on your screen.

Tips

• If your joystick has external rudder controls, make sure the Rudder box is checked.

• If you have not yet installed your joystick, click here 🖳 to start the Hardware Installation wizard.

Chapter 21

Ten Aggravating Things about Windows 95 (and How to Fix Them)

. . . .

In This Chapter

▶ Bypassing the menus

▶ Keeping track of multiple windows

▶ The taskbar keeps disappearing

▶ Fixing the Print Screen key

▶ It doesn't include the programs listed on the box

▶ Understanding why DOS programs run too slowly

▶ Lining up two windows on the screen

▶ Updating a floppy disk's contents in the Explorer or My Computer program

. . . .

*W*indows 95 would be great if only . . . (insert your pet peeve here). If you find yourself thinking (or saying) this frequently, this chapter is for you. This chapter not only lists the most aggravating things about Windows 95, but it also explains how to fix them.

Those Zillions of Mouse Menus Take Forever

Windows 95 has a zillion menus you can work through with the mouse, but you don't have to use them. If you want, you can use the keyboard to quickly select everything that you can click on in a menu.

Look closely at the words on the menu bar, along the top of each window. Somewhere in almost every word, you can spot a single underlined letter. Press and release the Alt key and then press one of the underlined letters you see in a word. Try pressing the F in File, for example. Presto! The File menu leaps into place. Look for underlined letters on the newly displayed File menu. For example, now press S for Save. Presto again! Windows 95 saves the current file, without a single mouse click.

To save a file in nearly any Windows 95 program, press and release Alt, press F, and then press S. It's that simple (after you memorize the combination, that is).

You find these underlined letters everywhere in Windows 95. In fact, you've been seeing underlined letters in this book as well. They're the keys you can use to avoid rooting through all the menus with a mouse.

Note: A list of the most commonly used key combinations is included in the Cheat Sheet at the front of this book.

When maneuvering through the options listed in the Start menu, you only need to click once: Just click on the Start button to bring the Start menu to life. All the other menus contained in Start menu pop up automatically as the mouse pointer hovers over them. When you spot the program or choice you're after, click on it, and the Start menu loads that program or choice.

✔ To move from box to box while filling out a form, press the Tab key. Each press of the key takes you to a new part of the form to fill out. Ecstasy!

✔ For some keys, you hold Alt while pressing a function key. For example, to close any Windows 95 program, hold down Alt and press F4 (Alt+F4).

✔ If you accidentally press Alt and are stuck in Menu Land, press Alt again. Alternatively, press Esc and bark loudly until it lets you out.

It's Too Hard to Keep Track of All Those Windows

You don't *have* to keep track of all those windows. Windows 95 does it for you with the taskbar. Hold Ctrl and press Esc, and the taskbar rises to the forefront. (If it doesn't, see the very next section.)

The taskbar, covered in Chapter 11, lists every currently open window by name. Double-click on the name of the window you want, and that window hops to the top of the pile.

Even better, shrink all the open windows into icons except for the window you're currently working on. Then click on the taskbar with your right mouse button and click on one of the tile commands to line everything up neatly on the screen.

In Chapter 8, you find more soldiers to enlist in the battle against misplaced windows, files, and programs.

The Taskbar Keeps Disappearing!

The taskbar's a handy Windows 95 program that's always running — if you can just find it. Unfortunately, it sometimes vanishes from the screen. Here are a few ways to bring it back.

First, try holding down the Ctrl key and pressing Esc. Sometimes this makes the Taskbar appear, but sometimes it only brings up the Start menu.

Still no taskbar? Try pointing at the very edge of your screen, stopping for a second or two at each of the four sides. If you point at the correct side, some specially configured taskbars will stop goofing around and come back to the screen.

If you can only see a slim edge of the taskbar — the rest of it hangs off the edge of the screen, for example — point at the edge you *can* see. When the mouse pointer turns into a two-headed arrow, hold down your mouse button and move the mouse toward the screen's center to drag the taskbar back into view.

In Windows 3.1, double-clicking on the desktop brings up the Task List, which lists all the currently running programs. Double-clicking on the desktop in Windows 95 just makes two clicking noises in rapid succession. (The taskbar doesn't appear.)

- ✔ If your taskbar disappears whenever you're not specifically pointing at it, turn off its Auto hide feature: Click on a blank part of the taskbar with your right mouse button and choose Properties from the pop-up menu. When the taskbar Options menu appears, click in the Auto hide box until a little check mark disappears. (Or, to turn on the Auto hide feature, add the check mark.)

- ✔ While you're in the taskbar Options menu, described above, make sure there's a check mark in the Always on top box. That way the taskbar will always ride visibly on the desktop, making it much easier to spot.

My Print Screen Key Doesn't Work

Windows 95 takes over the Print Screen key (labeled PrtSc, PrtScr, or something even more supernatural on some keyboards). Instead of sending the stuff on the screen to the printer, the Print Screen key sends it to the Windows 95 Clipboard, where it can be pasted into other windows.

✔ Some keyboards make you hold Shift while pressing Print Screen.

✔ If you hold Alt while pressing Print Screen, Windows 95 sends the current *window* — not the entire screen — to the Clipboard.

✔ If you *really* want a printout of the screen, hold Shift and press Print Screen to send a picture of the screen to the Clipboard. Paste the contents of the Clipboard into Paint and print from there. (That's explained in Chapter 13.)

It Doesn't Come with All the Programs Listed on the Box

In an attempt to make friends with everybody, Windows 95 comes with gobs of programs — more than anybody would ever want. So, to keep from making enemies with everybody, Windows 95 doesn't fill up everybody's hard drive with every possible program.

For example, Windows 95 comes with sounds that make your computer sound like a robot or squawking bird. But it doesn't automatically install those sounds, nor does it tell you about them. If you want to add those sounds, you'll have to go back and do it by hand.

Start by double-clicking on the Add/Remove Programs icon in the Control Panel and then click on the Windows Setup tab along the top. Windows 95 lists the programs it can install and offers to install them for you — a process described in Chapter 13.

(And if you want the robot sounds, double-click on the word Multimedia from the list and choose Robotz Sound Scheme.)

My DOS Programs Run Too Slowly (or Not at All) under Windows 95

DOS programs almost always run more slowly under Windows 95 than if they had the whole computer to themselves. And they run the slowest when they're in a window. And some DOS programs won't run at all.

Running DOS programs in a full screen speeds them up a little, as does beefing up the computer: adding more memory, upgrading to a faster 486 or Pentium computer, and buying a bigger hard drive.

What's the best solution? Well, Windows 95 is like a camper shell that is put on a pickup truck. Although the truck is more comfortable, it is slower and can't go underneath low bridges. To get back the speed and maneuverability, you simply have to remove the shell (or buy a more powerful engine).

That means don't run DOS programs under Windows 95. Click on the Shut down command from the Start menu and choose the Restart in M̲S-DOS Mode option.

When you're in DOS, type the word **exit** and press Enter to return to Windows 95.

It's Too Hard to Line Up Two Windows on the Screen

With all its cut-and-paste stuff, Windows 95 makes it easy for you to grab information from one program and slap it into another. With its drag-and-drop stuff, you can grab names of files in File Manager and drag them into Program Manager to install them as icons.

The hard part of Windows 95 is lining up two windows on the screen, side by side. That's where you need to call in the taskbar. First, put the two windows anywhere on the screen. Then turn all the other windows into icons by clicking on the button with the little line that lives in the top-right corners of the windows.

Now click on a blank area of the taskbar with your right mouse button and click on one of the two tile commands listed on the menu. The two windows line up on the screen perfectly.

The My Computer and Explorer programs Show the Wrong Stuff on My Floppy Disk

The My Computer and Explorer programs sometimes get confused and don't always list the files currently sitting on a disk drive. To prod the programs into taking a second look, choose the R̲efresh command from the W̲indow menu.

Chapter 22

Ten Expensive Things You Can Do to Make Windows 95 Better

In This Chapter

▶ Buy more memory

▶ Shell out the bucks for a bigger hard drive

▶ Order a fast 486 or Pentium computer

▶ Put a graphics accelerator card on the credit card

▶ Beg for or borrow a bigger monitor

*G*ive a Ford Fairlane to the right teenage boy, and he'll get right to work: boring out the cylinders, putting in a high-lift cam, and adding a double-roller timing chain. And replacing the exhaust system with headers, if his cash holds out.

Computer nerds feel the same way about getting under the hood of their computers. They add a few new parts, flip a few switches, and tweak a few things here and there to make Windows 95 scream.

Even if you're not a computer nerd, you can still soup up Windows 95 a bit. Take the computer back to the store and have the *store's* computer nerd get under the hood.

This chapter talks about what parts to ask for so you don't end up with high-lift cams rather than more memory.

Buy More Memory

If you bought a 386, 486, or Pentium computer, the salesperson probably tried to talk you into buying more memory, or RAM, for the computer. Windows 95 probably talks just as loudly about this issue as the salesperson.

See, Windows 95 can read and write information to RAM very quickly. The phrase *lightning quick* comes to mind. But when Windows 95 runs out of RAM, it starts using the hard drive for storage. Compared with RAM, hard drives are slow, mechanical dinosaurs. If you're short on memory, you can hear the hard drive grinding away as you switch between programs and Windows 95 frantically tries to make room for everything.

Windows 95 runs slowly on a computer with only 4MB of RAM. Twice that amount of RAM speeds things up more than twice as much. With 12MB or 16MB of RAM, Windows 95 can juggle programs even more quickly (and without dropping them as often).

If you're tired of waiting for Windows 95, toss the computer in the back seat, take it back to the computer store, and have the store people put some more RAM inside.

- ✔ After Jeff in the back room puts the memory chips inside the computer, he'll flip some switches on the computer's *motherboard* so that it knows that the new chips are there. People who plug in the chips themselves often don't flip the right switch and then wonder why their new chips don't work. (Some newer computers don't have a switch; they know automatically when they have more memory to play with.)

- ✔ Different computers can hold different amounts of RAM. Some can't handle more than 8MB of RAM; others can be stuffed with 64MB or more. Before buying more memory, check with your dealer to make sure that your computer has room for it.

Shell Out the Bucks for a Bigger Hard Drive

Right on the box, Microsoft recommends that a computer have at least 20MB of free hard drive space in order to run Windows 95. That's *if* you want to run *Windows 95* and *no* other programs.

If you buy Microsoft Word for Windows, however, that program wants more than 20MB of hard drive space, too. Add a few other hoggy Windows programs, and you run out of room quickly.

Plus, you should leave part of the hard drive empty so that Windows 95 has room to move around.

The moral is to shop for the biggest hard drive you can afford. Then borrow some money and buy one that's slightly bigger.

Order a Fast 486 or Pentium Computer

Windows 95 works on a 386 computer, but just barely. It's really designed for a fast 486 or Pentium computer.

As a bare minimum, a 386DX computer can handle Windows 95, but it crawls along pretty slowly.

A 486SX is a little faster, followed by the 486DX. The Pentium is the current speed demon. Balance your need for speed with your checking account balance.

You can find this 386/486/Pentium stuff thrashed out in Chapter 2.

Put a Graphics Accelerator Card on the Credit Card

When tossing boxes and bars around, Windows 95 puts a big strain on the computer's *graphics card,* the gizmo that tells the monitor what information to put on-screen.

Windows 95 also puts a strain on the computer's *microprocessor,* the gizmo that tells the graphics card what to tell the monitor.

A *graphics accelerator card* eases the burden on both parties. Simply put, a graphics accelerator is a hot-rodded graphics card. It replaces the VGA or Super VGA card and contains a special chip that handles the dirty work of filling the monitor with pretty pictures.

The result? Dialog boxes that zip on-screen almost instantly. You no longer have to wait for Windows 95 to repaint the screen when you move windows around. Everything just looks snappier.

- You probably don't need to upgrade the monitor when buying an accelerator card. A Super VGA accelerator card works just as well with a Super VGA monitor as the regular Super VGA card does.

- Upgrading the computer from a 386 to a 486 or Pentium also speeds up the graphics, even if you don't buy an accelerator card.

- Finally, computers with special *VESA local bus* or *PCI* slots can speed up graphics the fastest. These slots can accept the speedy VESA local bus (VLB) video or PCI video cards.

- If you're shopping for a computer, make sure it comes with special slots for either local bus video (VLB) or PCI video cards. Anything else was obsolete a few months ago.

Beg for or Borrow a Bigger Monitor

Part of the problem with the Windows 95 stack-of-windows approach to computing is the size of the screen. The Windows 95 desktop is the size of the monitor: a little larger than one square foot. That's why everything constantly covers up everything else.

To get a bigger desktop, buy a bigger monitor. The 17-inch monitors offer almost twice the elbowroom as the standard 14-inchers. You have more room to put windows side-by-side on the screen, as well as more room to spread icons along the bottom. The new 20-inchers give you an executive-sized desktop but at a mahogany price.

- Before buying, make sure that the new monitor and video card can work together as a team. Not all cards work with all monitors.

- If you have a stack of phone books holding up one side of your desk, buy a new desk when you buy the new monitor. Those big monitors can weigh 50 pounds or more.

Chapter 23

Ten Atrocious Acronyms

In This Chapter

▶ Ten (plus seven) acronyms in alphabetic order

▶ Helpful pronunciation tips so you won't just mumble them quietly

▶ What they mean to computer nerds

Computer geeks have a certain fascination for long, complicated strings of words. They've reduced these syllables into short grunts called *acronyms*.

This chapter lists, in alphabetic order, what the nerds are saying, what their grunts stand for, and what those grunts are supposed to mean.

ASCII

What it stands for: American Standard Code for Information Interchange

Pronunciation: ASK-ee

What they're talking about: A standard for saving information — usually words and numbers — so that most other programs can read it. Windows 95 Notepad, for example, saves text files in ASCII format.

BIOS

What it stands for: Basic Input/Output System

Pronunciation: BUY-ohss

What they're talking about: Information stored inside a computer that tells programs how the computer is designed. For example, if a program wants data to go to the printer, the program politely tells the BIOS, which subsequently sends the data to the printer. Windows 95 sometimes bypasses the BIOS and sends information directly to the computer's parts. This procedure is often faster but can sometimes confuse the rest of the computer.

DDE

What it stands for: Dynamic Data Exchange

Pronunciation: Dee-dee-ee

What they're talking about: A way Windows programs can share information automatically in the background. Today, OLE is much more fashionable and powerful.

DLL

What it stands for: Dynamic Link Library

Pronunciation: Dee-ell-ell

What they're talking about: A file containing information for a program. You can find bunches of files ending with DLL on the hard drive. Don't think that they're trash and delete them, or you'll have some wide-eyed programs wandering around the system, searching for their DLLs.

DRV

What it stands for: Driver

Pronunciation: DRY-ver

What they're talking about: Drivers contain brand-specific information about a computer's parts: printers, mice, monitors, and other goodies. You see files ending in DRV scattered throughout the hard drive. Don't delete them, or Windows 95 won't be capable of talking to your computer's parts.

EMS

What it stands for: Expanded Memory Specification

Pronunciation: Ee-em-ess

What they're talking about: A special part of the computer's memory used by some DOS programs. When filling out a DOS program's settings in its Properties box, you may need to change this option.

GPF

What it stands for: General Protection Fault

Pronunciation: Gee-pea-eff

What they're talking about: Windows 3.1 programs sometimes crash for no apparent reason. Before they zonk themselves into unconsciousness, they say that they have experienced a GPF. Windows 95 doesn't have as many GPF problems. Instead, the errors are labeled with a bunch of other terms, as described in Chapter 18.

IBM

What it stands for: International Business Machines

Pronunciation: Aye-bee-em

What they're talking about: A huge computer company that designed the first PC that's like the ones almost everybody uses today. Now, IBM's playing catch-up because all the other companies copy and improve upon its original design. Windows 95 requires an IBM-compatible computer.

INI

What it stands for: Initialization

Pronunciation: IN-ee (as opposed to an OUT-ee)

What they're talking about: A file containing customized instructions for a program. Many Windows 3.1 programs look for their own INI file to make sure that they're working according to the user's whims. In Windows 3.1, a file called WIN.INI contains information about the way *you* like Windows: its colors, the settings you've made in the Control Panel, and other information.

Don't mess with the INI files unless you have a specific reason to do so. Changing them around can seriously affect how programs run in Windows.

Windows 95 now stores most of its customizing information in a more organized area called a *Registry*.

IRQ

What it stands for: Interrupt Request Line

Pronunciation: Aye-are-cue

What they're talking about: The way parts of a computer can get the attention of the computer's main processor. For example, every time you move the mouse, the mouse sends a signal down its IRQ to the computer's processor, which stops what it's doing and displays the mouse's new position on-screen. Each device needs its own IRQ; if two computer toys try to share one IRQ, both work in a wacky way.

MSN

What it stands for: The Microsoft Network

Pronunciation: Emm-ess-enn

What they're talking about: Microsoft's new *on-line service* — a way to grab information over the phone lines using a modem. The Microsoft Network is still in its infancy, but it's described in Chapter 13.

OLE

What it stands for: Object Linking and Embedding

Pronunciation: Oh-LAY

What they're talking about: A way to merge varieties of data into one file. For example, your boss can stick an icon into a letter file and give the file to your coworker; when your coworker double-clicks on the icon, he'll hear your boss's voice telling him that he's fired. Or you can add a chart icon to a word-processing file; when you double-click on the chart icon, a chart editor pops up, grabs the chart from your hard drive, and lets you change the figures around. When you save the chart and go back to your word-processing file, the OLE technology saves the *original* chart file, too, ready for somebody else to edit.

PCX

What it stands for: Nothing

Pronunciation: Pee-see-ex

What they're talking about: Some guy thought of a way to store graphics in computer files. He picked the letters PCX out of the blue. Today, PCX is one of the most widespread graphics standards. Windows 3.1 Paintbrush can read and write graphics as PCX files; so can most other graphics programs.

Paintbrush's Windows 95 replacement, Paint, can no longer write PCX files. Instead, Paint can only save files in Microsoft's own graphics file format, known as *bitmap* or BMP files.

PIF

What it stands for: Program Information File

Pronunciation: Piff (rhymes with *sniff*)

What they're talking about: A file containing the instructions Windows 95 needs to nurse along troublesome DOS programs. The PIF contains information about that program's memory needs, along with other data that helps DOS programs live pleasantly with Windows 95.

RAM

What it stands for: Random-Access Memory

Pronunciation: Ram (rhymes with *cram*)

What they're talking about: The memory Windows 95 reads and writes to when it makes stuff happen on-screen. When the power's turned off, RAM erases itself.

ROM

What it stands for: Read-Only Memory

Pronunciation: Rahm (rhymes with *bomb*)

What they're talking about: Memory that can't be written to — only read from. For example, a computer's BIOS is stored in ROM. Computerized microwave ovens and other fun consumer electronic goodies sometimes store their instructions on ROM chips as well. The latest technology, called Flash ROM, *can* be written to more than once, but only with special programs.

XMS

What it stands for: Extended Memory Specification

Pronunciation: Ex-em-ess

What they're talking about: The special type of memory that comes with 286, 386, 486, and Pentium computers. Windows 95 comes with a memory manager that can harness XMS memory and dole it out to DOS or Windows programs when they need it. The more memory your computer has, the happier you and your programs will be.

Chapter 24

Ten Windows 95 Icons and What They Do

● ●

*W*indows 95 uses different icons to stand for different types of files. That means it's packed with enough icons to befuddle the most experienced iconographer.

Table 24-1 shows pictures of the most common icons you'll come across in Windows 95 in the Explorer and My Computer programs and what the icons are supposed to represent.

Table 24-1	Icons in Explorer and My Computer Windows
What It Looks Like	*What It Stands For*
	3½-inch floppy drive
	5¼-inch floppy drive
	Hard drive
	CD-ROM drive
	Folder or directory; a computerized storage area for files
	DOS program
	Word processor file, usually created by either WordPad or Microsoft Word
	Batch file; a collection of DOS commands for the computer to run automatically
	Movie (usually stored in Microsoft's Audio Video Interleave — AVI — format)

(continued)

Table 24-1 *(continued)*

What It Looks Like	What It Stands For
	Sound; a recorded sound saved as a wave file
	Music; a MIDI file containing specially formatted instructions that tell synthesizers or sound cards what sounds to create
	System file; technical files for Windows 95 to use
	Old-style fonts that are stored in a certain size
	Newer, TrueType fonts that can be easily shrunk or enlarged
	Help file; contains instructions stored in a special format for the Windows 95 Help system
	Bitmap file; graphics usually created by Paint (in Windows 95) or Paintbrush (in Windows 3.1)
	A text file containing technical information, usually special settings for a program
	Text; usually created by Notepad
	A file Windows 95 doesn't think it recognizes

✔ Unfortunately, Windows 95 judges a book by its cover: It doesn't look *inside* a file to see what information it contains. Instead, Windows 95 merely looks at the file's name, particularly the last three letters of the file's name. If Windows 95 recognizes those three letters, it assumes that it recognizes the file. The result? Sometimes Windows 95 will use a familiar icon to represent a file but will refuse to open the file when you double-click on the icon.

✔ For example, Windows 95 uses the word processor file icon for files containing Word for Windows 2.0 documents. But if you don't have a copy of Word for Windows 2.0 installed when you double-click on the icon, Windows 95 stops, saying that WordPad can't open Word for Windows 2.0 documents.

Glossary

· ·

*W*indows 95 no longer comes with a separate Glossary program; it's built in. If you spot an unfamiliar word in the Help program — and it's underlined — click on the word, and Windows 95 defines it for you. But if Windows 95 refuses to give you a helping hand, here's a list of some of the more common Windows 95 words you'll encounter.

32-bit: Computers push their information through "pipes." The first IBM PC used eight pipes. The next version, the 286, used 16 pipes. A 386 computer can use 32 pipes, but most programs just shoot their stuff through 16 pipes. For extra speed and power, Windows 95 uses all 32 pipes at the same time.

8514/A: One of the more expensive (and esoteric) video cards released by IBM and now copied by other companies.

active window: The last window you clicked on — the one that's currently highlighted — is considered active. Any keys you press affect this window.

Apply: Click on this button, and Windows 95 immediately applies and saves any changes you've made from the current list of options.

AUTOEXEC.BAT: A file that old-school MS-DOS computers read when first turned on. The file contains instructions that affect any subsequently running DOS programs — and older Windows programs, as well. Windows 95 no longer needs an AUTOEXEC.BAT file, but it keeps one around in case older programs might need to use it.

bitmap: A graphic consisting of bunches of little dots on-screen. They're saved as bitmap files, which end with the letters BMP. The Windows 95 program called Paint can create and edit BMP files.

border: The edges of a window; you can move the border in or out to change the window's size.

case-sensitive: A program that knows the difference between upper- and lowercase letters. For example, a case-sensitive program considers *Pickle* and *pickle* to be two different things.

click: To push and release a button on the mouse.

Clipboard: A part of Windows 95 that keeps track of information you've cut or copied from a program or file. It stores that information so you can paste it into other programs.

command prompt: The little symbol that looks like C : \ or [C : \ ] or A : \ or something similar. It's the place where you can type instructions — *commands* — for DOS to carry out.

CONFIG.SYS: A file that your computer reads every time it boots up. The file contains information about how the computer is set up and what it's attached to. Both DOS and Windows programs rely on information contained in the CONFIG.SYS file. Windows 95 no longer needs a CONFIG.SYS file, but it keeps one around in case other programs need one to run.

cursor: The little blinking line that shows where the next letter will appear when you start typing.

default: Choosing the default option enables you to avoid making a decision. The *default option* is the one the computer chooses for you when you give up and just press Enter.

desktop: The area on your screen where you move windows and icons around. Most people cover the desktop with *wallpaper* — a pretty picture.

directory: A separate *folder* on a hard disk for storing files. Storing related files in a directory makes them easier to find. Windows 95 no longer uses the word directory and prefers the word *folder*, instead.

document: A file containing information like text, sound, or graphics. Documents are created or changed from within programs. See *program*.

double-click: Pushing and releasing the left mouse button twice in rapid succession. (Double-clicking the *right* mouse button doesn't do anything special.)

DOS: Short for Disk Operating System, it's an older operating system for running programs. Windows 95 can run programs designed for DOS as well as programs designed for Windows.

drag: A four-step mouse process that moves an object across your desktop. First, point at the object — an icon, a highlighted paragraph, or something similar. Second, press and hold your left mouse button. Third, point at the location to which you'd like to move that object. Fourth, release the mouse button. The object is "dragged" to its new location.

drop: Step four of the *drag* technique, described in the preceding entry. *Dropping* is merely letting go of the mouse button and letting your object fall onto something else, be it a new window, directory, or area on your desktop.

DRV: A file ending in DRV usually lets Windows talk to computer gizmos such as video cards, sound cards, CD-ROM drives, and other stuff. (DRV is short for *driver.)*

file: A collection of information in a format designed for computer use.

folder: An area for storing files to keep them organized (formerly called a directory). Folders can contain other folders for further organization. (See *subdirectory.*)

format: The process of preparing a disk to have files written on it. The disk needs to have "electronic shelves" tacked onto it so that Windows 95 can store information on it. Formatting a disk wipes it clean of all information.

highlighted: A selected item. Different colors usually appear over a highlighted object to show that it's been singled out for further action.

icon: The little picture that represents an object — a program, file, or command — making it easier to figure out that object's function.

INI: Short for *initialization,* INI usually hangs on the end of files that contain special system settings. They're for the computer to mess with, not users.

maximize: The act of making a window fill the entire screen. You can maximize a window by double-clicking on its title bar — that long strip across its very top. Or you can click on its maximize button — that button with the big square inside, located near the window's upper right-corner.

memory: The stuff computers use to store on-the-fly calculations while running.

minimize: The act of shrinking a window down to a tiny icon to temporarily get it out of the way. To minimize a window, click on the minimize button — that button with the little horizontal bar on it, located near the window's upper right corner.

multitasking: Running several different programs simultaneously.

network: Connecting computers with cables so that people can share information without getting up.

operating system: Software that controls how a computer does its most basic stuff: stores files, talks to printers, and performs other gut-level operations. Windows 95 is an operating system.

path: A sentence of computerese that tells a computer the precise name and location of a file.

program: Something that lets you work on the computer. Spreadsheets, word processors, and games are *programs*. See *document*.

RAM: Random-Access Memory. See *memory*.

scrap: When you highlight some text or graphics from a program, drag the chunk to the desktop, and drop it, you've created an official Windows 95 *scrap* — a file containing a copy of that information. The scrap can be saved or dragged into other programs.

Shortcut: A Windows 95 icon that serves as a push button for doing something — loading a file, starting a program, or playing a sound, for example. Shortcuts have little arrows in their bottom corner so you can tell them apart from the icons that *really* stand for files and programs.

shortcut key: As opposed to a Shortcut, described in the preceding entry, a shortcut key is an underlined letter in a program's menu that lets you work with the keyboard instead of the mouse. For example, if you see the word Help in a menu, the underlined H means you can get help by pressing Alt+H.

shortcut button: A button in a Help menu that takes you directly to the area you need to fiddle with.

Shut Down: The process of telling Windows 95 to save all its settings and files so that you can turn off your computer. You must click the Shut Down option, found on the Start menu, before turning off your computer.

Start button: A button in the corner of your screen where you can begin working. Clicking the Start button brings up the Start menu.

Start menu: A menu of options that appears when the Start button is clicked. From the Start menu, you can load programs, load files, change settings, find programs, find help, or shut down your computer so you can turn it off.

subdirectory: A directory within a directory, used to further organize files. For example, a JUNKFOOD directory might contain subdirectories for CHIPS, PEANUTS, and PRETZELS. (A CELERY subdirectory would be empty.) In Windows 95, a subdirectory is a folder that's inside another folder.

taskbar: The bar in Windows 95 that lists all currently running programs and open folders. The Start button lives on one end of the taskbar.

virtual: A trendy word to describe computer simulations. It's commonly used to describe things that *look* real but aren't really there. For example, when Windows 95 uses *virtual memory,* it's using part of the hard disk for memory, not the actual memory chips.

VGA: A popular standard for displaying information on monitors in certain colors and resolutions. It's now being replaced by SVGA — Super VGA — which can display even more colors and even finer resolution.

wallpaper: Graphics spread across the background of your computer screen. The Windows 95 Control Panel lets you choose among different wallpaper files.

window: An on-screen box that contains information for you to look at or work with. Programs run in *windows* on your screen.

Appendix
Removing Windows 95

● ●

*S*ome people immediately find Windows 95 to be a new friend. Others warm up to the program a little more slowly. And some people find that early-release, Windows 95 "Preview" version to be an annoying houseguest who refuses to leave.

If you want to kick Windows 95 off your hard drive and go back to whatever system worked before — perhaps an earlier version of Windows, DOS, or even that OS/2 Warp stuff — you've found the right part of the book.

Uninstalling Windows 95

Windows 95 acting wimpy? Then get rid of it. If you punch the right buttons, Windows 95 automatically removes itself from your computer, putting your old versions of Windows and DOS back in their former places. (Or, if you're enchanted with Windows 95, you can tell it to remove your old versions of Windows and DOS, leaving more room on your computer for games and other programs.)

Here's how to make Windows 95 either remove itself or remove any old versions of Windows lying around your hard drive.

If you've compressed your hard drive after installing Windows 95, this trick won't work.

1. Click on the Start button, point at Settings and click on Control Panel from the menu that pops up.

   The Windows 95 Control Panel will appear, as seen in Figure A-1.

2. Double-click on the Add/Remove Programs icon.

   A special Windows 95 "butler" program will pop up, as shown in Figure A-2, ready to welcome any new Windows 95 programs or purge old programs that simply didn't live up to the fancy words on their packaging.

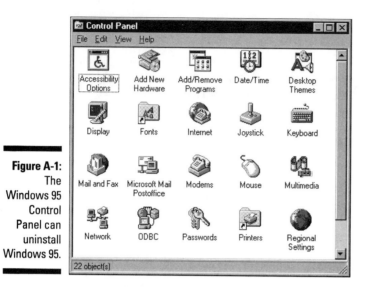

Figure A-1:
The
Windows 95
Control
Panel can
uninstall
Windows 95.

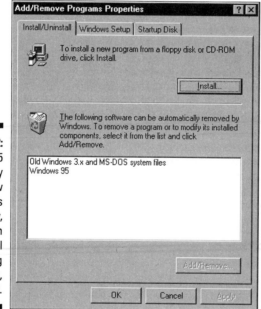

Figure A-2:
Windows 95
can not only
install new
programs
automatically,
but it can
uninstall
disappointing
programs,
as well.

3. Click on the words "Windows 95" listed in the bottom box, and click the Add/Remove button.

Or, if you want to remove your old version of DOS and Windows — freeing up 6MB of hard disk space in the process — click on the words "Old Windows 3.x and MS-DOS system files" instead.

Windows 95 will take offense at the idea that you're trying to get rid of it or its old versions. So, it sends out a last-ditch, fervent message, shown in Figure A-3, asking if you're *sure* you want it to uninstall itself.

4. When Windows 95 asks if you're sure, click the Yes button.

Windows 95 will remove itself from your hard drive, leaving your computer with your old version of Windows and DOS.

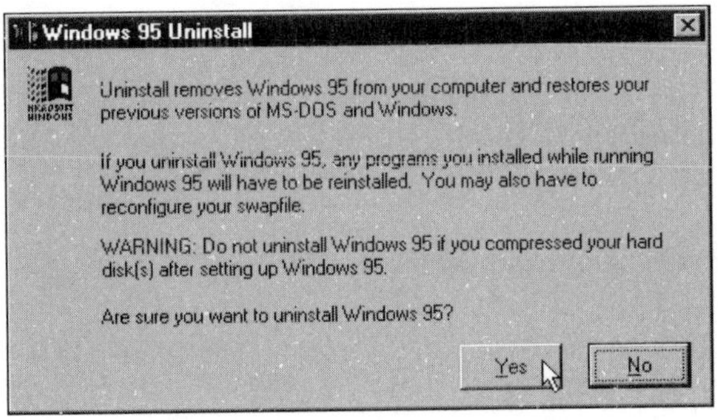

Figure A-3:
If you're
sure you
want
Windows 95
to peel itself
off your
hard drive
and re-
install your
old version
of Windows,
click the Yes
button.

5. When Windows 95 says it will check your hard disk for errors and remove all long filenames, click the Yes button.

Older versions of Windows can't handle filenames longer than eight characters, so Windows 95 will have to snip any long names. Also, prepare yourself for some thumb-twiddling while it checks your hard disk for any errors.

6. Click OK to continue.

After Windows 95 has fixed any disk errors and shortened the filenames, it asks for a final click of the OK button. Give it a click, and Windows 95 will start wiping itself off your hard drive, restoring your old version of Windows in the process.

7. When instructed, remove any floppy disks from drive A and press Enter.

Windows 95 will restart, hopefully coming back to life with your old faithful version of Windows in tow.

✔ Didn't work? Well, Windows 95 can only reinstall your old version Windows if you left it on your hard drive. Think back to when you installed Windows 95. When the incoming Windows 95 asked if you wanted to leave your old version installed as a backup, did you answer "Yes"? If you didn't, you'll have to reinstall your old version from scratch.

✔ The programs you installed while running Windows 95 won't be waiting for you when Windows 95 deletes itself. You'll have to reinstall them so they'll run under your old version of Windows.

✔ You'll need to reconfigure your old Windows swapfile, too; the one that Windows 95 used probably won't be compatible with your older version of Windows.

Removing the Windows 95 Preview Version

Unlike the *real* version of Windows 95, the $30 preview holds on to your computer tightly.

Plus, once you've removed it, you'll have to reinstall your older version of Windows and probably reinstall a good portion of your favorite Windows programs. Since this adds up to a lot of extra work, don't try extricating your Windows 95 Preview on a Friday afternoon when you have a Monday morning deadline, or you probably won't be able to go fishing over the weekend.

To remove Windows 95, you need a bootable floppy disk from your previous version of MS-DOS. Plus, that disk needs to contain a copy of your previous DOS version's copy of the SYS.COM program. If you've been using MS-DOS 6.2 or MS-DOS 6.0, you're safe: Disk 1 from either of those versions works fine. If you were using DOS 5.0 or an earlier version, you'll need to dig up a bootable floppy you'd made yourself, and make sure it contains a copy of SYS.COM.

The steps outlined here not only remove the Windows 95 Preview from your hard drive, but remove *all* the files, programs, and subdirectories stored in the Windows 95 directory. If you have any important data stored there, be sure to copy it to a floppy disk, back it up to a tape-backup program, or move it to another part of your hard disk.

At the end of this 19-step process, you need to reinstall your old versions of DOS and Windows. If you'd prefer a one-step process, consider reformatting your hard drive as explained later in this Appendix: One command wipes the entire hard drive completely clean, and lets you start reinstalling all of your programs. If you've backed up all your data, reformatting your hard drive might be the quickest way to get your computer back to normal.

Later versions of the Windows 95 Preview come with an uninstall feature built in. Before going through the agonizing process described below, see if your version of the Windows 95 Preview lets you take the easy way out: Click on the Control Panel's Add/Remove Programs icon and see if Windows 95 is listed in the box. If so, you can simply click on its name, click on the Add/Remove button beneath it, and kiss the Windows 95 Preview goodbye.

1. **Click on the Windows 95 Start button and click on Sh<u>u</u>t down... when the little menu pops up.**

   Another menu will appear in the center of the screen.

2. **Click on the <u>S</u>hut down the computer? option and then click on the <u>Y</u>es button.**

   Your computer makes shutting down noises, and then the screen turns dark and Windows says, "You can now safely turn off your computer. If you want to restart your computer press CTRL+ALT+DEL."

3. **Hold down the Control, Alt, and Delete keys simultaneously.**

   Your computer reboots itself. Keep a careful eye on the screen, however, because Step 4 comes up quickly.

4. **As soon as you see the words "Starting Windows 95," press the F8 key.**

   Your computer stops what it's doing and a little text menu appears on the screen.

5. **Choose Command prompt only from the menu.**

   Choosing the Command prompt only option tells Windows 95 to bring a C:\> prompt to the screen.

6. **At the C:\> prompt, type the following two commands, pressing Enter after each one:**

```
C:\> COPY \WINDOWS\COMMAND\DELTREE.EXE C:\
C:\> COPY \WINDOWS\COMMAND\SCANDISK.* C:\
```

Copying the DELTREE.EXE file to the boot drive makes it easier to delete files, directories, and, more important, subdirectories strewn throughout Windows 95. The SCANDISK program helps you weed out any files that earlier versions of Windows and DOS can't recognize — long filenames, for example.

7. At the C:\> prompt, type the following command and press Enter:

```
C:\> EDIT SCANDISK.INI
```

A quick and dirty word processor will display a weird-looking file.

8. Change the following two lines in the file from Off to On:

```
LabelCheck = On
SpaceCheck = On
```

This one's kind of tricky, but bear with me. About midway through the file, you'll see a section that looks like this:

```
[ENVIRONMENT]
    Display     = Auto     ; Auto, Mono, Color, Off
    Mouse       = On       ; On, Off
    ScanTimeOut = Off      ; On, Off
    NumPasses   = 1        ; 1 through 65,535 (anything over
           10 is slow)
    LabelCheck  = Off      ; On, Off
    LfnCheck    = On       ; On, Off
    SpaceCheck  = Off      ; On, Off
    Mount       = Prompt ; Prompt, Always, Never
```

See the lines that read LabelCheck = Off ;On, Off and SpaceCheck = Off ;On, Off? Change those two lines from = Off to = On (the On, Off stuff listed *after* the semicolon really doesn't matter).

9. Save the file by pressing Alt, F, X, and Y, in that order.

The program asks if you want to save the file; pressing the Y key says "Yes, please."

10. Type the following command at the C:\> prompt and press Enter:

```
C:\> SCANDISK C:
```

The Scandisk program ferrets out anything your earlier version of DOS might not recognize. If it finds something weird, it usually corrects it automatically. Or, if it asks for your permission before fixing something, answer Yes.

11. Type the following command at the `C:\>` **prompt and press Enter:**

```
C:\> DELTREE WINDOWS
```

Deltree politely asks you to confirm that you want to delete the WINDOWS directory and all its subdirectories. If you're sure, press the Y key and press Enter — but not before reading the warning below.

This command not only wipes out the Windows 95 directory, but every file, program, and subdirectory in the Windows 95 directory. Make sure you've backed up anything you want to save, or you'll lose it.

12. Type the following four commands at the `C:\>` **prompt, pressing Enter after each one:**

```
C:\> DELTREE CONFIG.SYS
C:\> DELTREE AUTOEXEC.BAT
C:\> DELTREE RECYCLED
C:\> DELTREE PROGRA~1
```

Again, press Y and the Enter key after typing each command.

You'll find that funky ~ thing in the top, left corner of your keyboard above the key that looks like the apostrophe key.

13. Type the following commands at the `C:\>` **prompt, pressing Enter after each one:**

```
C:\> DELTREE WINBOOT.*
C:\> DELTREE SUHDLOG.DAT
C:\> DELTREE SYSTEM.1ST
C:\> DELTREE *.W40
C:\> DELTREE SETUPLOG.*
C:\> DELTREE BOOTLOG.*
C:\> DELTREE IO.SYS
C:\> DELTREE MSDOS.SYS
```

Again, to let the Deltree program know you really want to delete the files, you'll have to press Y and Enter after typing in each command. (Some of these files might be invisible, so they won't show up with your normal DIR command.)

If you used Windows 95 disk compression utilities, you might find some of these files on the root directory of the host drive, not the C: drive.

14. **Type these two commands at the** C:\> **prompt, pressing Enter after each one:**

```
C:\> DELTREE DETLOG.*
C:\> DELTREE D??SPACE.BIN
```

Using Stacker version 3.1? Then either skip this step or back up the STAC DBLSPACE.BIN file before deleting the files. Also, if you're using a compression program, these programs might be on the host drive, not the C: drive.

15. **Type the following command at the** C:\> **prompt (or, if the drive is compressed, from the** C:\> **prompt and the root of the host drive).**

```
C:\> DELTREE COMMAND.COM
```

16. **Put your bootable floppy disk with your earlier version of DOS into drive A, and press the Control, Alt, and Delete keys simultaneously.**

Your computer reboots from the floppy disk, running from that disk's operating system. If the computer asks for the current time and date, just press Enter.

If you're booting from Disk 1 of your DOS 6.0 or 6.2 disks, DOS will think you want to install it. Make it hold its horses by pressing F3 twice.

17. **Type the following command at the** A:\> **prompt:**

```
A:\> SYS C:
```

That command copies the operating system from the floppy disk to the hard disk.

18. **Type the following commands at the** C:\> **prompt, pressing Enter after each one:**

```
C:\> DEL SCANDISK.*
C:\> DEL DELTREE.*
```

Using disk compression? Then copy DBLSPACE.BIN to the root directory of the boot drive to finish the process.

19. **Reinstall your previous versions of MS-DOS and Windows.**

Windows 95 messed up some of those files when it was first installed. Plus, deleting your Windows directory also deleted many of your Windows programs and their important files.

✔ If you're using MS-DOS version 6.0 and are using hard drive compression, copy DBLSPACE.BIN from the DOS directory to the root directory of your boot drive. Also, for all versions of MS-DOS, if you have a shell= statement referencing COMMAND.COM from a different directory, copy COMMAND.COM to the root directory. Then remove the floppy disk, and restart the computer from the hard disk.

✔ If everything's still messed up, for some reason, you can always go the drastic route: Reformat your entire hard drive, as described below, and start from scratch. Hopefully, you've backed up all your important files, and the only thing you'll be losing will be time.

Simply Starting Over from Scratch . . .

Windows 95 takes a strangle hold over your computer, and peeling it off the hard drive can take some considerable time and effort. If you've already backed up your data files, you might want to simply reformat your hard drive. After all, you still need to reinstall DOS, Windows, and all your Windows programs at the end of the 17-Step process described above.

Reformatting your hard disk wipes out *everything* on it: files and programs. Make sure you've saved all your important files before reformatting it.

If you're using DOS 6.0 or later, use Disk 1 that comes with the DOS software. If you're using DOS 5.0 or earlier, you need a boot disk with the Format command on it.

Type the following command at the A:\> prompt:

```
A:\> FORMAT /S C:
```

Press Enter, and DOS wipes your hard drive clean, purging it of Windows 95 in the process. Reinstall Windows, DOS, and all your programs, and you'll be back to normal.

Hopefully you'll like Windows 96 a little better.

Index

(continued)

(continued)

(continued)